AQA

Scie A

Revision Guide

Pauline Anning
Niva Miles
John Scottow

Series Editor
Lawrie Ryan

Nelson Thornes

Published in 2011 by:
Nelson Thornes Ltd
Delta Place
27 Bath Road
CHELTENHAM
GL53 7TH
United Kingdom

13 14 15 / 10 9 8 7 6 5 4

A catalogue record for this book is available from the British Library

ISBN 978 1 4085 0823 7

Cover photograph: Suzanne Laird/Getty Images (girls); Andrew Butterton/Alamy (background)

Page make-up by Wearset Ltd, Boldon, Tyne and Wear

Printed in China by 1010 Printing International Ltd

Photo acknowledgements
Page 1 Martyn F. Chillmaid; B1.1.4 iStockphoto; B1.1.6 Science Photo Library; B1.1.7 Crown Copyright/Health & Safety Laboratory/Science Photo Library; B1.1.8 Dr Kari Lounatmaa/Science Photo Library; B1.2.5 Mel Yates/Getty Images; B1.3.6 AFP/Getty Images; B1.4.3 De Agostini/Getty Images; B1.4.4 Ron Austing/FLPA; B1.5.3 iStockphoto; B1.6.2 Linn Currie/Shutterstock; B1.7.1 National Geographic Society/Corbis; B1.7.3 Gerard Lacz/FLPA; C1.2.3 iStockphoto; C1.2.4 AKP Photos/Alamy; C1.3.1 Fotolia; C1.3.2 Fotolia; C1.3.3 iStockphoto; C1.3.4 Chris R Sharp/Science Photo Library; C1.3.5 iStockphoto; C1.3.6 (left) Eco Images/Universal Images Group/Getty Images; C1.3.6 (right) iStockphoto; C1.4.1 iStockphoto; C1.4.4 Photolibrary; C1.4.5 Fotolia; C1.5.1 Paul Rapson/Science Photo Library; C1.5.2 Fotolia; C1.5.3a iStockphoto; C1.5.3b CC Studio/Science Photo Library; C1.6.3 iStockphoto; C1.6.4 Fotolia; C1.7.3 Stocktrek RF/Getty Images; P1.1.7 iStockphoto; P1.1.8 Olsberg; P1.3.2 ChinaFotoPress/Getty Images; P1.3.3 (top) iStockphoto; P1.3.3 (bottom) Martyn F. Chillmaid/Science Photo Library; P1.4.2 (top) Skyscan/Science Photo Library; P1.4.2 (bottom) Canada Press/PA Photos; P1.5.4 Photolibrary/Peter Arnold Images; P1.6.5 Mark Garlick/Science Photo Library.

Science A Contents

Welcome to AQA GCSE Science!

Key points

At the start of each topic are the important points that you must remember.

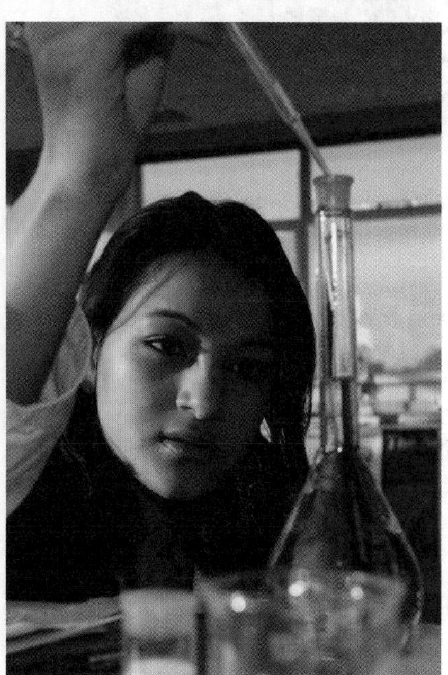

This book has been written for you by very experienced teachers and subject experts. It covers everything you need to revise for your exams and is packed full of features to help you achieve the very best that you can.

Key words are highlighted in the text and are shown **like this**. You can look them up in the glossary at the back of the book if you're not sure what they mean.

Where you see this icon, you will know that this topic involves How Science Works – a really important part of your GCSE.

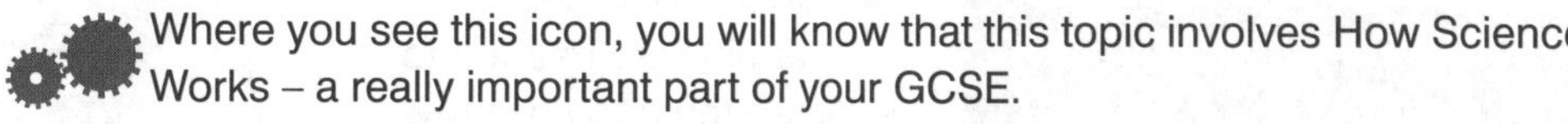

These questions check that you understand what you're learning as you go along. The answers are all at the back of the book.

Many diagrams are as important for you to learn as the text, so make sure you revise them carefully.

Higher

Anything in the Higher boxes must be learned by those sitting the Higher Tier exam. If you're sitting the Foundation Tier, these boxes can be missed out.

The same is true for any other places that are marked [**H**].

Study tip

Study tips are hints giving you important advice on things to remember and what to watch out for.

Bump up your grade

How you can improve your grade – this feature shows you where additional marks can be gained.

Maths skills

This feature highlights the maths skills that you will need for your Science exams with short, visual explanations.

At the end of each chapter you will find:

End of chapter questions

These questions will test you on what you have learned throughout the whole chapter, helping you to work out what you have understood and where you need to go back and revise.

And at the end of each unit you will find:

Examination-style questions

These questions are examples of the types of questions you will answer in your actual GCSE, so you can get lots of practice during your course.

You can find answers to the End of chapter and Examination-style questions at the back of the book.

Student Book pages 24–25 **B1**

1.1 Diet and exercise

Key points

- A balanced diet includes everything needed to keep the body healthy.
- Different people need different amounts of energy because the metabolic rate varies from person to person.
- If the energy (food) taken in is less than the energy used the person will lose mass. The more exercise you take, the more food you need.

Study tip

The term 'metabolic rate' is often used in exams – remember it refers to the chemical reactions in cells.

- A healthy diet has the right balance of food types. Carbohydrate, fat and protein are used by the body to release energy and to build cells.
- Mineral ions and vitamins are needed to keep the body healthy. If the diet is unbalanced a person can become **malnourished**.

Use the eatwell plate to learn about proportion in balanced diets. The proportion of fruit and vegetables is $\frac{1}{3}$ of a balanced diet.

1 *What happens to your body if you take in too much energy or too few vitamins?*

- If you exercise, more energy is used by the body. Exercise increases the **metabolic rate**, which means that the chemical reactions in cells work faster.
- The proportion of muscle to fat in your body and your **inherited** factors can also affect your metabolic rate.

Key words: malnourished, metabolic rate, inherited

Student Book pages 26–27 **B1**

1.2 Weight problems

Key points

- If you eat more food (take in more energy) than you need your mass will increase.
- People who are very fat are said to be 'obese'.
- Obesity can lead to health problems such as Type 2 diabetes.
- It is also unhealthy to be seriously underweight.
- Exercise helps to keep the body healthy.

- It is important for good health to get the energy balance correct.
- If the energy you take in equals the energy you use then your **mass** will stay the same. Eating too much food can lead to becoming **overweight** and **obese**.
- Long-term obesity can lead to severe health problems including Type 2 diabetes (high blood sugar).
- These problems can be reduced by eating less carbohydrate and increasing the amount of exercise.

1 *Why do people become obese?*

- Some people are unhealthy because they have too little food (starvation). They find it difficult to walk about and may suffer from deficiency diseases due to lack of vitamins or minerals.

2 *Why do starving people find it difficult to walk about?*

Key words: mass, overweight, obese

Student Book pages 28–29 **B1**

1.3 Inheritance, exercise and health

Key points

- Inherited factors affect our health. These include metabolic rate and cholesterol levels.
- People who exercise regularly are usually healthier than those who take little exercise.

- Your metabolic rate can be affected by the genes you inherit from your parents.
- There are two types of cholesterol. You need 'good' cholesterol for your cell membranes and to make vital substances.
- Small numbers of the population inherit high levels of 'bad' cholesterol, which can lead to heart disease.
- Foods rich in saturated fat can also increase blood cholesterol levels.
- By exercising regularly a person can increase their metabolic rate and lower high cholesterol levels.

1 ***How can people change their lifestyle to help lower their blood cholesterol levels?***

Bump up your grade

You will 'bump' up your grade if, when you are asked to **explain** something, your answer contains more than a description. For example, to explain why eating too much makes you put on weight (mass) – you need to say:

'The food contains energy, and any excess energy is stored in the body as fat.'

Student Book pages 30–31 **B1**

1.4 Pathogens and disease

Key points

- Pathogens are microorganisms that cause infectious disease.
- Most pathogens are either bacteria or viruses.
- Pathogens reproduce rapidly inside the body and may produce toxins.
- Viruses reproduce inside cells and damage them.
- Washing hands removes pathogens from them. Semmelweiss was the first doctor to realise this.

- **Pathogens** cause **infectious diseases**.
- Pathogens are tiny **microorganisms** – usually **bacteria** or **viruses**.
- When bacteria or viruses enter the body they reproduce rapidly. They can make you feel ill by producing toxins (poisons).
- Viruses are much smaller than bacteria and reproduce inside cells. The damage to the cells also makes you ill.

1 ***How do pathogens make you feel ill?***

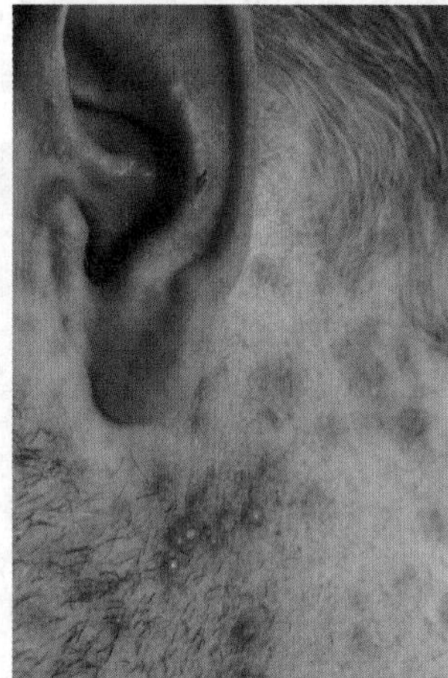

Bacteria and viruses can make you ill

- Before bacteria and viruses had been discovered, a doctor called Semmelweiss realised that infection could be transferred from person to person in a hospital.
- Semmelweiss told his staff to wash their hands between treating patients. However, other doctors did not take him seriously. We now know that he was right!

2 ***Why did it take a long time for others to accept the ideas of Semmelweiss?***

Study tip

Remember that viruses damage cells when they reproduce inside them.

Key words: pathogen, infectious disease, microorganism, bacteria, virus

Student Book pages 32–33 **B1**

1.5 Defence mechanisms

Key points

- The body prevents most pathogens getting in.
- Pathogens which enter the body can be destroyed by white blood cells.

- The skin prevents pathogens getting into the body.
- Pathogens are also trapped by mucus and killed by stomach acid.

1 *How are many pathogens prevented from entering the body?*

White blood cells are part of the **immune system**. They do three things to defend the body:

- They can ingest pathogens. This means they digest and destroy them.
- They produce antibodies to help destroy particular pathogens.
- They produce antitoxins to counteract the toxins (poisons) that pathogens produce.

2 *How do white blood cells defend the body?*

Bump up your grade

To get maximum marks in the exam, remember the three ways in which white blood cells defend the body.

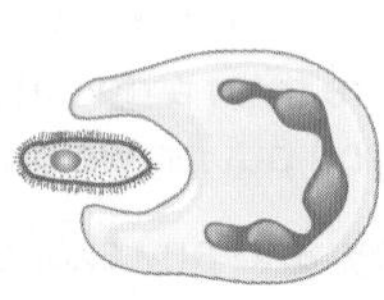

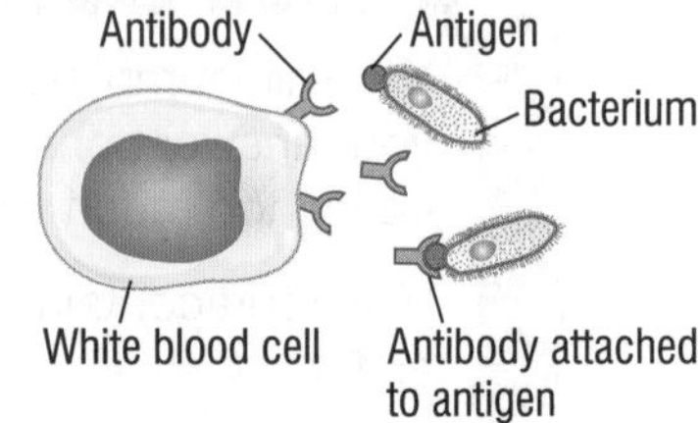

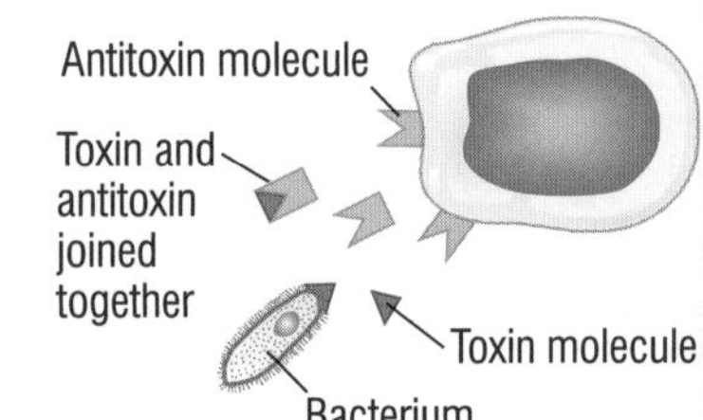

White blood cells ingest bacteria, make antibodies and make antitoxins

Key words: white blood cell, immune system

Student Book pages 34–35 **B1**

1.6 Using drugs to treat disease

Key points

- Some medicines may relieve the symptoms of disease but not kill the pathogens that cause it.
- Antibiotics cure bacterial diseases by killing the bacteria inside your body.
- Antibiotics cannot destroy viruses.
- Viruses are difficult to destroy because they reproduce inside body cells.

- **Antibiotics** kill infective bacteria in the body.
- Penicillin is an antibiotic, but there are many others. It was first discovered by Alexander Fleming in 1928.
- Viruses are difficult to kill because they reproduce inside the body cells, so any treatment could also damage the body cells.
- Painkillers and other drugs relieve the symptoms of a disease but do not kill the pathogen.
- Your immune system will usually overcome the viral pathogens.

Penicillin was discovered by Alexander Fleming and developed into a drug by Florey and Chain. Hundreds of lives were saved by this antibiotic during the Second World War.

1 *Why are antibiotics only able to kill bacteria?*

Study tip

Remember that antibiotics kill bacteria but have no effect on viruses.

Key word: antibiotic

Student Book pages 36–37 **B1**

1.7 Growing and investigating bacteria

Key points

- Bacteria can be grown on agar jelly.
- All the materials and equipment must be sterilised. This ensures that unwanted microorganisms do not infect the culture.
- Uncontaminated cultures can be used to investigate the effect of antibiotics and disinfectants on the bacteria.

Study tip

Remember that the air contains microorganisms. To keep a bacterial culture pure, the microorganisms from the air must be killed or prevented from entering the culture.

- Pure cultures of non-pathogenic (safe) bacteria can be used for laboratory investigations.
- A culture of microorganisms can be used to find the effect of antibiotics on bacteria.
- Investigations need uncontaminated cultures of microorganisms. Strict health and safety procedures are used to protect yourself and others.
- Contamination might come from your skin, the air, the soil or the water around you.
- If the culture is contaminated other bacteria could grow, including pathogens.

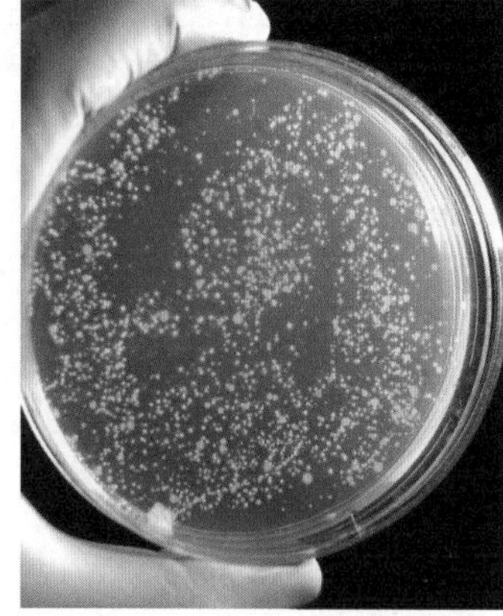

Bacteria can be grown on agar jelly in a Petri dish

Growing cultures

To culture (grow) microorganisms in a laboratory you must:

- Give them a liquid or gel containing nutrients – a **culture medium**. It contains carbohydrate as an energy source, various minerals and sometimes other chemicals. A culture medium called **agar** jelly is used.
- Provide warmth and oxygen.
- Keep them incubated at 25 °C in school laboratories and at 35 °C in industry.

1 ***Why do industrial laboratories use 35 °C instead of 25 °C as in schools?***

To keep the culture pure you must:

- Kill all the bacteria on the equipment – pass metal loops through a flame; boil solutions and agar.
- Prevent microorganisms from the air getting into the equipment.

2 ***How do you make sure that unwanted microorganisms do not contaminate a pure culture of bacteria?***

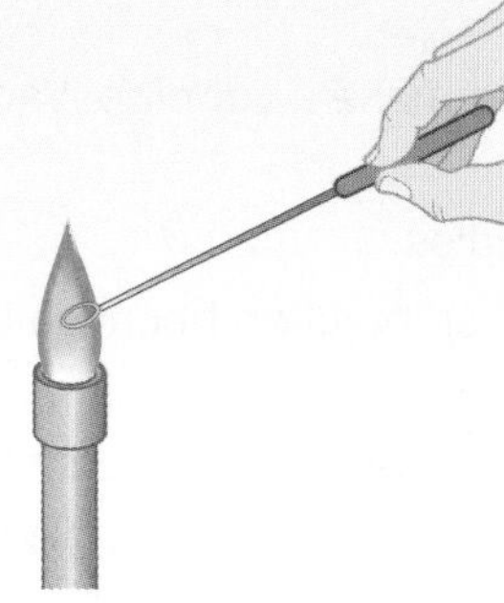

Sterilise the inoculating loop used to transfer microorganisms to the agar by heating it until it is red hot in the flame of a Bunsen and then letting it cool. Do not put the loop down or blow on it as it cools.

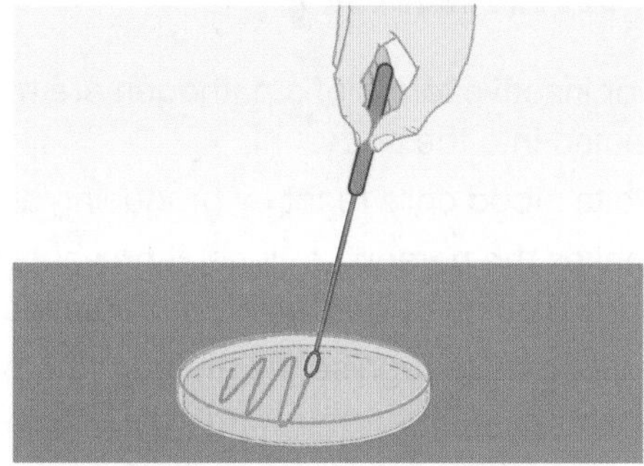

Dip the sterilised loop in a suspension of the bacteria you want to grow and use it to make zigzag streaks across the surface of the agar. Replace the lid on the dish as quickly as possible to avoid contamination.

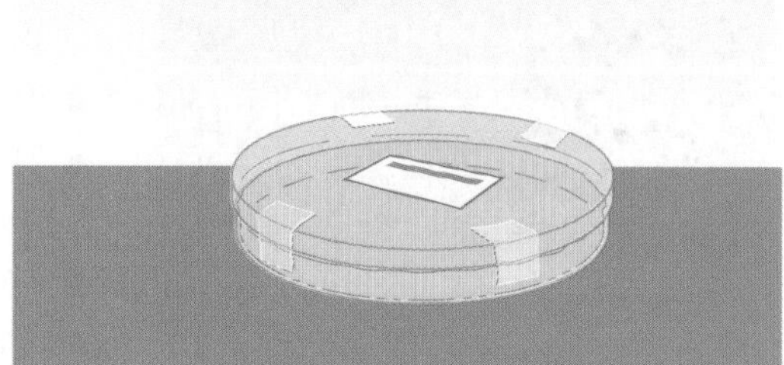

Seal the lid of the Petri dish with adhesive tape to prevent microorganisms from the air contaminating the culture – or microbes from the culture escaping. Do not seal all the way around the edge so oxygen can get into the dish and harmful anaerobic bacteria do not grow.

Culturing microorganisms safely in the laboratory

Key words: culture medium, agar

Student Book
pages 38–39 **B1**

1.8 Changing pathogens

Key points

- If a pathogen changes by mutation the new strain may spread rapidly.
- Some new strains can cause epidemics and pandemics.
- Some bacteria have developed resistance to antibiotics by natural selection. [H]

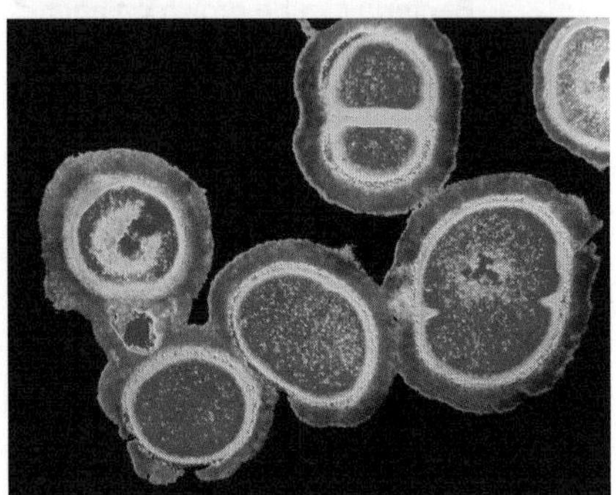

MRSA bacteria (the bacterium Methicillin-resistant *Staphylococcus aureus*) magnified 9560 times by a scanning electron micrograph

- Some pathogens, particularly viruses, can mutate (change) resulting in a new form called a mutation.
- Very few people are immune to these changed pathogens so disease can spread quickly.
- Diseases that spread within a country result in an **epidemic**. Those that spread across countries result in a **pandemic**.

1 *Why do some pathogens spread rapidly?*

Antibiotic-resistant bacteria

The **MRSA** 'super bug' is a bacterium that has evolved through **natural selection**. MRSA and other bacteria have become resistant to the common antibiotics.

Mutations of pathogens produce new strains, some are resistant to antibiotics.

Antibiotics kill individual pathogens of the non-resistant strain.

The resistant bacteria survive and reproduce and a whole population of a resistant strain develops. This is natural selection.

Antibiotics should not be used for mild infections in order to slow down the rate of development of resistant strains.

2 *How does natural selection cause resistant populations of bacteria to develop?* [H]

Key words: epidemic, pandemic, MRSA, natural selection

Student Book
pages 40–41 **B1**

1.9 Immunity

Key points

- A wide range of vaccines are given to immunise people against disease.
- Vaccines contain dead or inactive pathogens.
- Vaccines can protect against both bacterial and viral pathogens.
- Vaccines encourage your white blood cells to produce antibodies that destroy the pathogens.

- Dead or inactive forms of a pathogen are used to make a **vaccine**. Vaccines can be injected into the body.
- The white blood cells react by producing antibodies.
- This makes the person immune. It prevents further infection because the body responds quickly by producing more antibodies.
- The antibodies recognise the antigen (the protein shape) on the pathogen.
- The MMR **vaccination** (**immunisation**) is one of several vaccines. MMR is given to prevent measles, mumps and rubella.

1 *What is meant by vaccination?*

Study tip

Remember that diseases caused by a virus are difficult to treat. It is better to prevent them by vaccination.

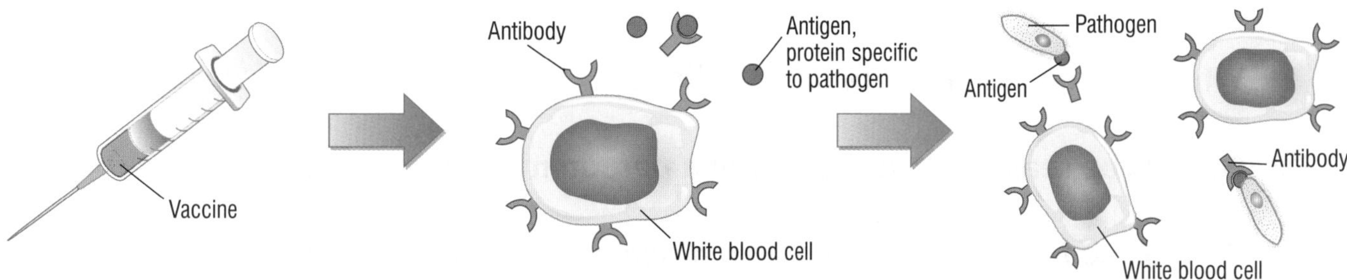

Small amounts of dead or inactive pathogen are put into your body, often by injection.

The antigens in the vaccine stimulate your white blood cells into making antibodies. The antibodies destroy the antigens without any risk of you getting the disease.

You are immune to future infections by the pathogen. That's because your body can respond rapidly and make the correct antibody as if you had already had the disease.

This is how vaccines protect you against dangerous infectious diseases

Key words: vaccine, vaccination, immunisation

Student Book pages 42–43 **B1**

1.10 How do we deal with disease? 

Key points

- Vaccination protects individuals and society from the effects of disease.
- The treatment of disease has changed as our understanding of antibiotics and immunity has increased.

Bump up your grade

When you are asked to 'evaluate', you will get more marks if you make sure you give advantages, disadvantages and a conclusion. Use the quick headings 'pros', 'cons' and 'conclusion' in your answer to remind you when writing the answer.

- Most people in a population need to be vaccinated to protect society from very serious diseases.
- Diseases such as measles can lead to long term damage to the body, such as deafness and occasionally death.
- Some vaccines cause side effects which may be mild or serious. So there are advantages and disadvantages of vaccination (immunisation).

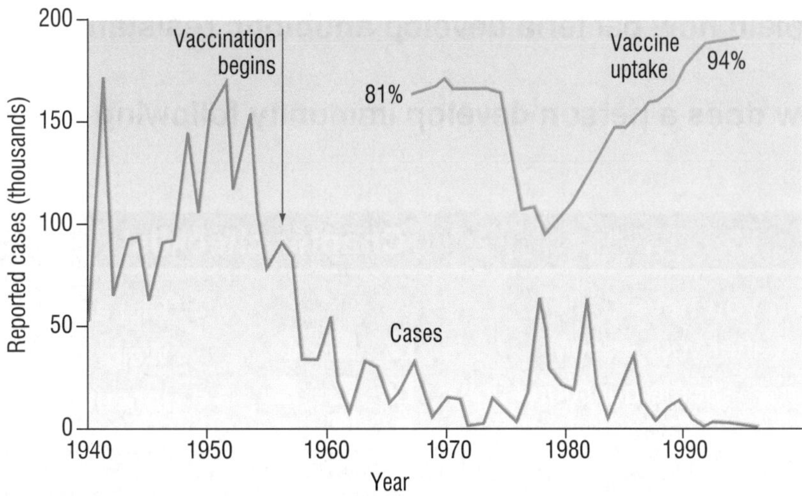

Graph showing the effect of the whooping cough scare on both uptake of the vaccine and the number of cases of the disease (Source: Open University)

1 *What are the advantages and disadvantages of vaccination?*

- Overuse of antibiotics can lead to the development of new strains of bacteria.
- Doctors do not prescribe antibiotics for mild infections such as minor sore throats.
- Scientists are always trying to find new ways of treating disease.

2 *Why is it necessary to develop new medicines?*

1 What do we mean by a 'balanced diet'?

2 Give three reasons to explain why a person may be malnourished.

3 Give three factors that affect how much energy a person needs.

4 What is meant by 'metabolic rate' and what factors affect the rate?

5 a What is a 'pathogen'?
  b What is an 'antibiotic'?

6 Why is it difficult to produce medicines to destroy viruses?

7 How are the ideas of Semmelweiss used in modern hospitals?

8 What is meant by a 'mutation' of a pathogen?

9 How is a pandemic different from an epidemic?

10 Why don't doctors give antibiotics for mild throat infections?

11 Explain how bacteria develop antibiotic resistance. [H]

12 How does a person develop immunity following vaccination?

Chapter checklist

Tick when you have:
reviewed it after your lesson ✓ ☐ ☐
revised once – some questions right ✓ ✓ ☐
revised twice – all questions right ✓ ✓ ✓

Move on to another topic when you have all three ticks

	✓	✓	✓
Diet and exercise	☐	☐	☐
Weight problems	☐	☐	☐
Inheritance, exercise and health	☐	☐	☐
Pathogens and disease	☐	☐	☐
Defence mechanisms	☐	☐	☐
Using drugs to treat disease	☐	☐	☐
Growing and investigating bacteria	☐	☐	☐
Changing pathogens	☐	☐	☐
Immunity	☐	☐	☐
How do we deal with a disease?	☐	☐	☐

Student Book pages 46–47 **B1**

2.1 Responding to change

Key points

- The nervous system allows humans to react to their surroundings and coordinates behaviour.
- Receptors detect external stimuli.
- Electrical impulses pass to the brain along neurons.
- The brain coordinates responses.

Study tip

Remember that neurons are nerve cells which are found in nerves. They carry electrical impulses.

- The **nervous system** has **receptors** to detect **stimuli**.
- The receptors are found in **sense organs**, the eye, ear, nose, tongue and skin.
- Light stimulates receptors in the eye and electrical **impulses** then pass to the brain along **neurons** (nerve cells). Other stimuli include sound, chemicals, temperature changes, touch and pain.
- The brain coordinates responses to many stimuli.

1 ***What stimuli are detected by the sense organs?***

- The brain and spinal cord form the **central nervous system (CNS)**.
- **Nerves** contain neurons. **Sensory neurons** carry impulses from receptors to the CNS.
- **Motor neurons** carry impulses from the CNS to **effector organs** which may be muscles or glands. The muscles respond by contracting. The glands respond by **secreting** (releasing) chemicals.

2 ***How do impulses pass from the receptor to the CNS?***

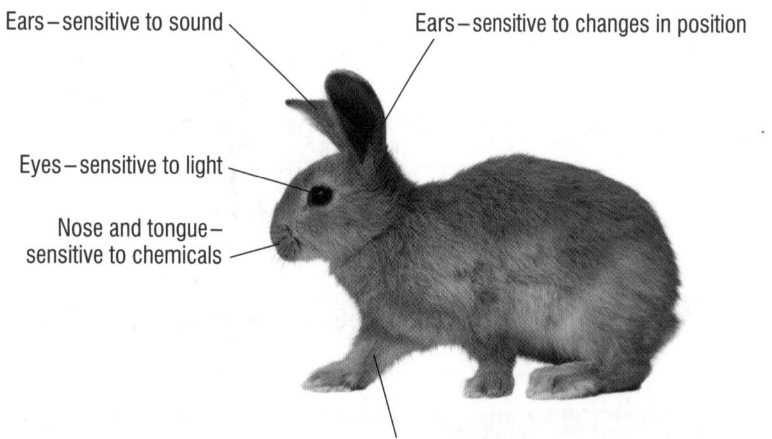

Being able to detect changes in the environment is important

Key words: nervous system, receptor, stimuli, sense organ, impulse, neuron, central nervous system (CNS), nerve, sensory neuron, motor neuron, effector organ, secreting

Student Book pages 48–49 **B1**

2.2 Reflex actions

Key points

- Reflex actions are rapid, automatic responses to a stimulus.
- Reflexes protect us from damage.

Bump up your grade

To improve your grade learn the sequence of a reflex action. Whatever the example, the sequence of events is always the same. Don't panic if the situation is new to you, identify the stimulus and response and the rest is what you know.

The main steps involved in reflex actions (**reflexes**) are:

- A receptor detects a stimulus (e.g. a sharp pain).
- A sensory neuron transmits the impulse to the CNS.
- A relay neuron passes the impulse on.
- A motor neuron is stimulated.
- The impulse passes to an effector (muscle or gland).
- Action is taken (the response).

At the junction between two neurons is a **synapse**. Chemicals transmit the impulse across the gap.

The sequence from receptor to effector is a **reflex arc**.

1 *What is the function of a relay neuron?*

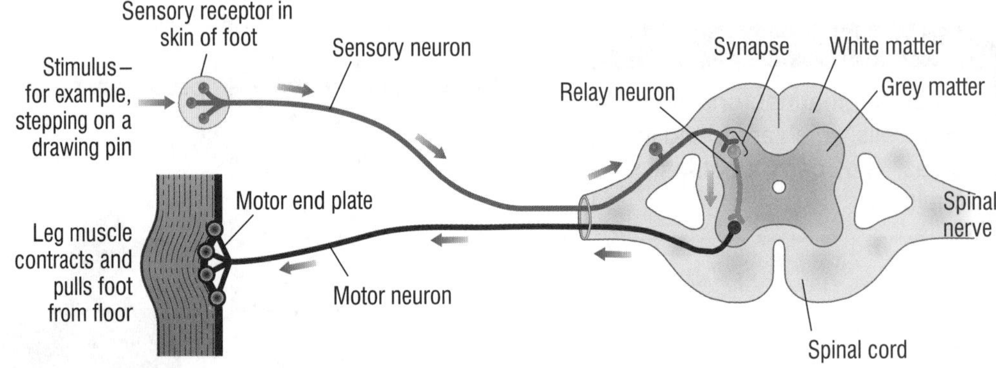

The reflex action which moves your foot away from a sharp object can save you from a nasty injury

Key words: reflex, synapse, reflex arc

Student Book pages 50–51 **B1**

2.3 Hormones and the menstrual cycle

Key points

- The **menstrual cycle** takes 28 days, with ovulation about 14 days into the cycle.
- The cycle is controlled by three hormones.

Study tip

Make a list of the hormones involved in the menstrual cycle and note:

- what they do
- how they affect other hormones.

- Follicle stimulating hormone (**FSH**) is made by the **pituitary gland** and causes the egg to mature and oestrogen to be produced.
- **Oestrogen** is produced by the **ovaries** and inhibits (stops) the further production of FSH. It stimulates the production of LH and also stimulates the womb lining to develop to receive the fertilised egg.
- Luteinising hormone (LH) is made by the pituitary gland and stimulates the mature egg to be released from the ovary (**ovulation**).

1 *Which hormones are made in the pituitary gland?*

Key words: menstrual cycle, FSH, pituitary gland, oestrogen, ovary, ovulation

Student Book pages 52–53 **B1**

2.4 The artificial control of fertility

Key points

- Contraceptive pills contain oestrogen and/or progesterone to inhibit FSH.
- FSH can be given to a woman to help her to produce eggs.

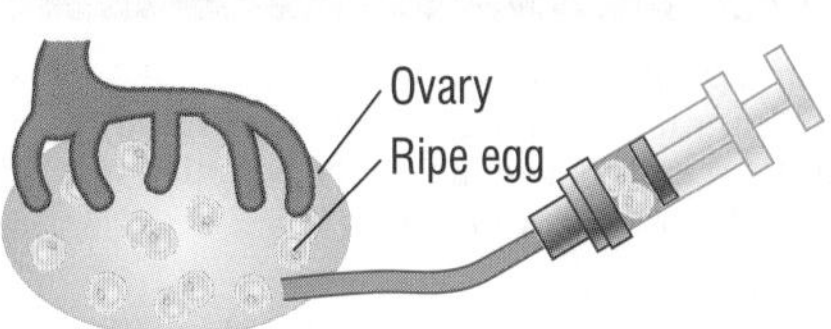

1 Fertility drugs are used to make lots of eggs mature at the same time for collection

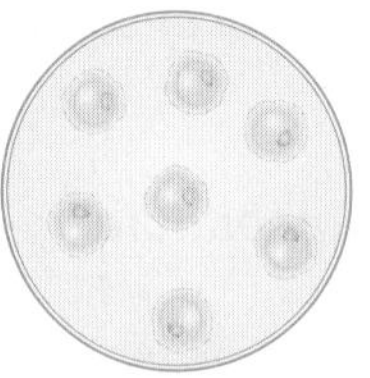

2 The eggs are collected and placed in a special solution in a Petri dish

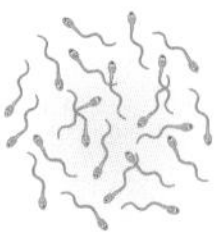

3 A sample of semen is collected

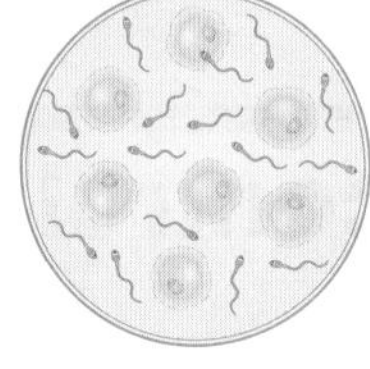

4 The eggs and sperm are mixed in the Petri dish

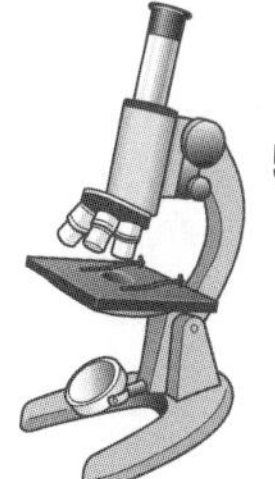

5 The eggs are checked to make sure they have been fertilised and the early embryos are developing properly

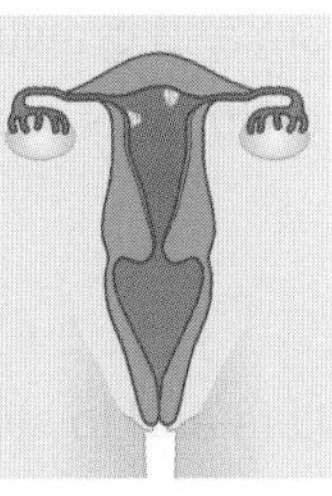

6 When the fertilised eggs have formed tiny balls of cells, 1 or 2 of the tiny embryos are placed in the uterus of the mother. Then, if all goes well, at least one baby will grow and develop successfully.

Fertility treatment

- The **contraceptive pill** (**oral contraceptive**) may contain oestrogen and **progesterone**. Some pills are progesterone-only pills and have fewer side effects.
- The contraceptive pill prevents the production of FSH so no eggs mature.
- If a woman cannot produce mature eggs then FSH and LH can be given. This is known as 'fertility treatment'.
- The FSH causes eggs to mature. The luteinising hormone (LH) stimulates ovulation.

1 ***Which hormone is inhibited by the contraceptive pill but is given in fertility treatment?***

How Science Works

Here are some of the issues involved in fertility treatment:

Advantages	Disadvantages
Contraceptive pills have helped to reduce family size which has reduced poverty in some areas. It allows women to plan their pregnancies.	The contraceptive pill can cause side effects. Some people object to its use for ethical or religious reasons.
Fertility drugs can help infertile couples who are having IVF. IVF helps couples to have a baby.	IVF is an expensive process. Some people think it is unethical when older women have babies by IVF. Extra embryos produced may be stored or destroyed.

Study tip

Think about the issues involved in contraception and fertility treatment. Make sure you can write a balanced argument about their use.

Key words: contraceptive pill, oral contraceptive, progesterone

Student Book pages 54–56 **B1**

Key points

- It is very important that the internal conditions of the body are kept within certain limits. The nervous system and hormones help to do this.
- Water and ion content, as well as temperature and blood sugar level, are all carefully controlled.

Bump up your grade

To improve your grade make sure you understand why internal conditions should be kept within very small limits. Link the condition to the reason why it must be kept constant.

2.5 Controlling conditions

The body carefully controls its **internal environment**. Internal conditions that are controlled include:

- water content
- ion content
- temperature
- blood sugar level.

Some people who work in a hot environment, such as chefs, may need to replace salt as well as water because it is likely they will sweat a lot

Water is leaving the body all the time as we breathe out and sweat. We lose any excess water in the urine (produced by the **kidneys**). We also lose ions in our sweat and in the **urine**.

We must keep our temperature constant, otherwise the **enzymes** in the body will not work properly (or may not work at all).

Sugar in the blood is the energy source for cells. The level of sugar in our blood is controlled by the **pancreas**.

1 *Why is it important to control our body temperature?*

Key words: internal environment, kidney, urine, enzyme, pancreas

Student Book pages 56–57 **B1**

Key points

- Plants respond to light, gravity and moisture.
- Shoots grow towards light and away from gravity.
- Roots grow towards gravity and water.
- Hormones such as auxin cause these changes.
- Plant hormones have uses in agriculture and horticulture.

Study tip

Light, gravity and water are stimuli which cause the shoot and roots to respond. This is controlled by auxin, a plant hormone.

2.6 Hormones and the control of plant growth

Plants are sensitive to light, gravity and moisture.

- Plant shoots grow towards light. This response is **phototropism**.
- Roots grow down towards gravity. This response is **gravitropism**.
- Roots also grow towards water.
- **Auxin** is the hormone which controls phototropism and gravitropism.
- Unequal distribution of auxin causes unequal growth. This results in bending of the shoot or root.

1 *Why do shoots bend towards light?*

- Plant growth hormones can be used as weed killers and to stimulate root growth.

Bump up your grade

You will bump up your grade if you are clear about coordination in the body. Learn the sequence in reflex actions and the functions of both human and plant hormones.

1 A normal young bean plant is laid on its side in the dark. Auxin is equally spread through the tissues.

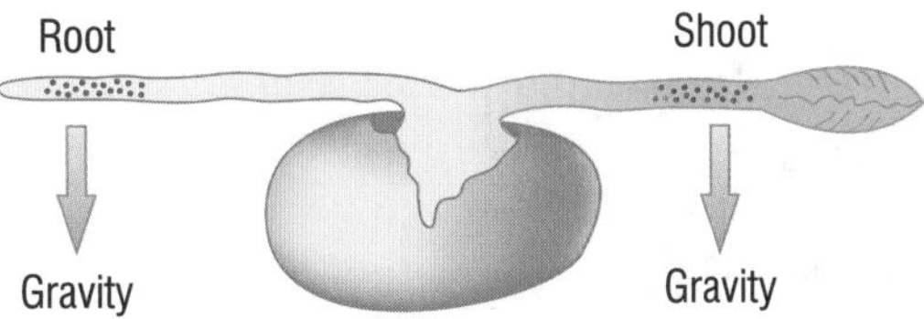

2 In the root, more auxin gathers on the lower side.

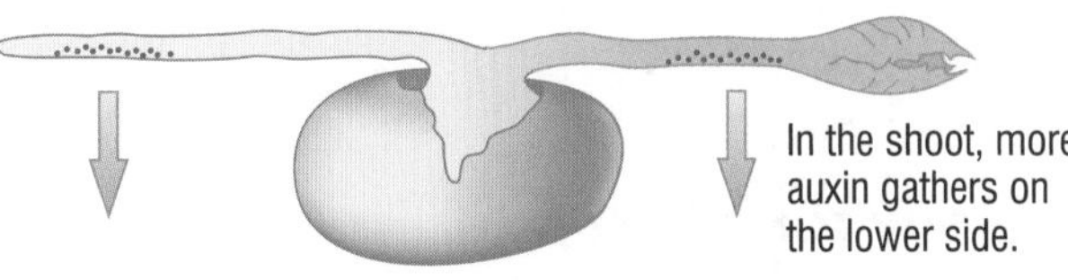

3 The root grows *more* on the side with *least* auxin, making it bend and grow down towards the force of gravity. When it has grown down, the auxin becomes evenly spread again.

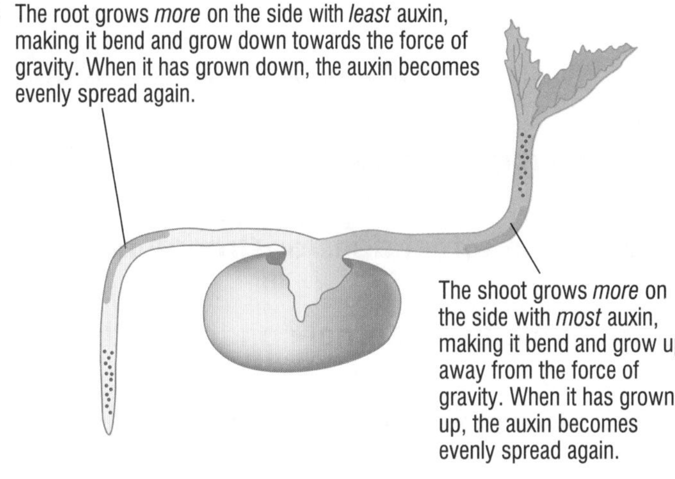

Gravitropism (or geotropism) in shoots and roots. The uneven distribution of the hormone auxin causes unequal growth rates so the roots grow down and the shoots grow up.

Key words: phototropism, gravitropism, auxin

Student Book **pages 58–59** **B1**

2.7 Using hormones

Key points

- It is important to evaluate the advantages and disadvantages of using hormones to control fertility.
- The incorrect use of plant hormones can damage the environment.

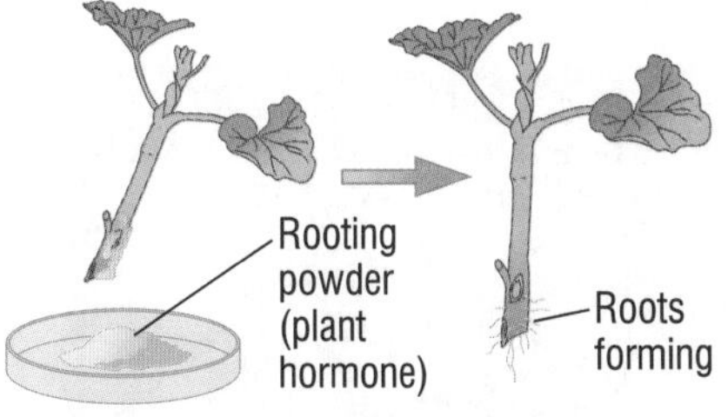

Plant growth hormones are used as rooting powder to stimulate growth

In women

- Many women use the contraceptive pill to prevent unwanted pregnancies. It helps them to plan when they have a baby.
- Other women use hormones to help them become pregnant.
- Sometimes hormone treatment is used to help older women to have babies. This may involve using an egg donor who is given hormones to produce extra eggs.

1 ***What are the benefits to women of taking hormones?***

- Taking hormones for a long time can lead to side effects in some women.

2 ***What are the ethical concerns about using fertility drugs?***

In plants

- Plant hormones can be used by farmers and gardeners.
- Weedkillers are used to kill unwanted plants on lawns.
- When cuttings are taken from plants, hormones are used to encourage roots to grow before the cutting is planted.
- Some hormones are used to encourage fruit to ripen.
- If plant hormones are used incorrectly they can cause damage to the environment, e.g. weedkillers may harm other more useful plants.

3 ***Why is it important to use plant hormones correctly in agriculture?***

1 Name the two main types of effector in the human body.

2 Name three stimuli which affect humans.

3 What effect does oestrogen have on FSH production?

4 State two internal conditions that need to be controlled.

5 How are impulses transmitted across a synapse?

6 What type of cell detects a change in the environment?

7 Name a plant hormone.

8 What is gravitropism?

9 Why do plant shoots bend towards light?

10 How does the contraceptive pill work?

11 Why are FSH and LH given in fertility treatment?

12 Describe the sequence of events in a reflex action.

Chapter checklist

Tick when you have:

reviewed it after your lesson	✓	☐	☐
revised once – some questions right	✓	✓	☐
revised twice – all questions right	✓	✓	✓

Move on to another topic when you have all three ticks

	✓	✓	✓
Responding to change	☐	☐	☐
Reflex actions	☐	☐	☐
Hormones and the menstrual cycle	☐	☐	☐
The artificial control of fertility	☐	☐	☐
Controlling conditions	☐	☐	☐
Hormones and the control of plant growth	☐	☐	☐
Using hormones	☐	☐	☐

Student Book pages 62–63 **B1**

3.1 Developing new medicines

Key points

- New drugs have to be thoroughly tested before they are sold as medicines.
- Drugs are tested to see if they work, to find out if they are toxic and to see if they cause side effects.
- Thalidomide was developed as a sleeping drug but not tested for preventing morning sickness, so some babies had birth defects.

Study tip

Make sure you understand what is meant by a double-blind trial.

- Large numbers of substances are tested to see if they might cure a disease or relieve symptoms.
- The first tests are in scientific laboratories on cells and tissues or organs. If the drug seems to work it is then tested on animals, healthy human volunteers and finally on patients.
- Healthy people are given very low doses of the drug to find out if it is safe.
- In some trials, with patients, **placebos** are used. Placebos do not contain a drug. Half the patients have the drug, the other half are given the placebo. This is to check that the drug being tested really does have an effect on the patient.
- In a **double-blind trial**, neither the doctor nor patient knows who is given a drug.
- People taking part in a drug trial are asked to report any side effects.

1 *Why is it important to test new drugs?*

- **Thalidomide** was developed as a sleeping pill, but doctors realised it could control morning sickness in pregnant women. Unfortunately it had not been tested for use in pregnancy.
- Some babies were born with limb abnormalities as a result of their mothers taking thalidomide.
- The drug was banned and the rules for drug testing were improved.
- More recently thalidomide has been used to treat other conditions, including leprosy, but it is never given to pregnant women.

Key words: placebo, double-blind trial, thalidomide

Student Book pages 64–65 **B1**

3.2 How effective are medicines? 

Key points

- Statins are drugs which lower blood cholesterol levels. Their use has lowered cardiovascular disease in the population by over 40%.
- Double-blind trials should be used to check if both non-prescribed and prescribed drugs actually work.

- **Statins** are drugs which lower the amount of 'bad' cholesterol carried in the blood.
- They are given to older people and are taken daily.
- Trials using very large numbers of people have shown that the incidence of heart disease and strokes has gone down by over 40%.

1 *Why do doctors prescribe statins?*

- Some people prefer to take drugs which are not prescribed by doctors. Herbs are often used instead of prescribed medicines.
- A herb called St John's Wort is sometimes taken to treat **depression** instead of anti-depressants such as Prozac.
- The only way to be sure that the herb works as well as or better than Prozac is to conduct a double-blind trial.

2 *Why should herbal remedies be tested in a double-blind trial?*

Key words: statin, depression

Student Book pages 66–67 **B1**

3.3 Drugs

Key points

- Drugs are chemicals which alter the body's chemistry. You can become addicted to some drugs.
- Both illegal drugs and legal ones, such as alcohol and tobacco, may harm your body.
- Chemicals in cannabis may cause mental health problems.
- Heroin and cocaine are very addictive.

- Useful **drugs**, made from natural substances, have been used by indigenous people for a very long time.
- When we develop new drugs to help people, we have to test them over a long time to make sure that there are no serious side effects.
- Recreational drugs are used by people for pleasure.
- Heroin and cocaine are recreational drugs. They are very addictive and illegal.
- Cannabis is a recreational drug. It is also illegal. Some argue that using cannabis can lead to using 'harder' drugs.
- If you try to stop taking addictive drugs you will suffer **withdrawal symptoms**.

1 *Why are some drugs addictive?*

Bump up your grade

You may get a question in an examination asking whether taking cannabis leads to taking harder drugs. You must try to make both sides of the argument, as there is no 'right' answer. If you *only* make an argument for or against, you will lose up to half of the marks.

Key words: drugs, withdrawal symptom

Student Book pages 68–69 **B1**

3.4 Legal and illegal drugs

Key points

- Many recreational drugs cause changes in the brain and nervous system. Some are very harmful.
- Recreational drugs may be legal or illegal.
- More people use legal drugs, so their impact on health is greater than that of illegal drugs.

Study tip

Drugs may be:

- legal or illegal
- addictive or non-addictive.

Learn examples of all of these.

- Medicinal drugs are developed over many years and are used to control disease or help people that are suffering. Many medicinal drugs are only available on prescription from a doctor.
- Recreational drugs are used only for pleasure and affect the brain and the nervous system. They may also have adverse affects on the heart and circulatory system.
- Recreational drugs include cannabis and heroin, which are both illegal.
- As recreational drugs affect the nervous system it is very easy to become addicted to them.
- Nicotine and caffeine (in coffee and coke) are legal drugs which are used recreationally. Alcohol is also legal for people over the age of 18 in this country.
- There are many health problems associated with legal recreational drugs, e.g. alcoholic poisoning, addiction to nicotine leading to lung cancer from cigarette smoke.
- Some drugs used for medicinal purposes can be used illegally, e.g. stimulants used by sports people.

1 *Why is it easy to become addicted to recreational drugs?*

Student Book pages 70–71 **B1**

Key points

- Cannabis is an illegal drug which must be bought from drug dealers. This can put the user in contact with hard drugs.
- The chemicals in cannabis smoke may cause mental illness in some people, particularly teenagers.

3.5 Does cannabis lead to hard drugs? 

- There is evidence that cannabis can cause mental illness in some people.
- Teenagers who smoke cannabis increase their risk of getting depression.
- Cannabis is an illegal drug which must be bought from dealers.
- This brings cannabis users in contact with hard drugs such as heroin.
- Not all cannabis users go on to use hard drugs.
- Nearly all heroin users previously smoked cannabis.

1 *Why do some cannabis users go on to use heroin?*

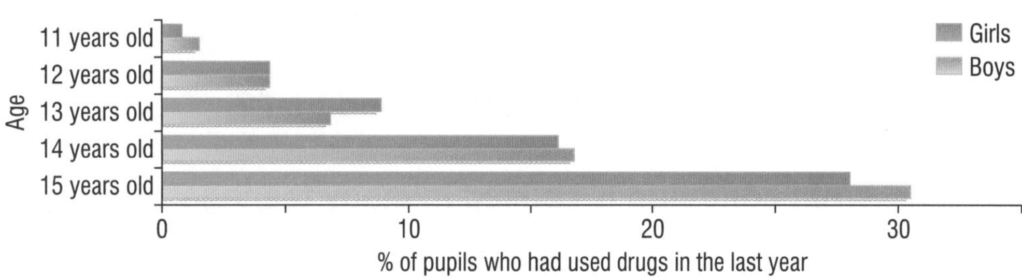

Most of the young people who have used drugs have smoked cannabis. The number of 15-year-old students who have tried drugs is causing a lot of concern.

Student Book pages 72–73 **B1**

Key points

- Some athletes use drugs to make them perform better.
- Steroids are one type of performance-enhancing drug.
- The use of performance-enhancing drugs is considered unethical by most people.

Some athletes work very hard to build their muscles so they get stronger. It is not fair if other athletes cheat by taking steroids.

3.6 Drugs in sport

Some athletes are tempted to use drugs to improve their performance.

- **Steroids** are drugs which are used to build up muscle mass. Other drugs may be used to increase stamina.
- Strong pain killers are banned because the athlete might ignore an injury and suffer further damage.
- Many performance-enhancing drugs are very expensive. This gives an unfair advantage to those who can afford them.
- Using performance-enhancing drugs can damage the body permanently and even lead to death.
- Most people think it is unethical to take drugs to enhance performance.

1 *Why do some athletes take drugs to improve their performance?*

Study tip

Write a list of the reasons why athletes risk taking drugs. Then write reasons why drug taking by athletes is unethical.

Key word: steroid

1. What does 'illegal' mean?
2. a Why was thalidomide given to pregnant women years ago?
   b Why is thalidomide never given to pregnant women nowadays?
3. Name two very addictive drugs.
4. What is meant by the term 'recreational drugs'?
5. Why do some athletes take steroids?
6. What is meant by a 'double-blind trial'?
7. What condition is caused in many teenagers who smoke cannabis?
8. What causes people to become addicted to drugs?
9. Which parts of the body are affected by recreational drugs?
10. Why does the use of legal drugs in the UK produce more health problems than the use of illegal drugs?
11. What stages must a new drug pass through before it is sold as a medicine?
12. Why do some people progress from smoking cannabis to using heroin?

Chapter checklist

Tick when you have:

reviewed it after your lesson	✓	☐	☐
revised once – some questions right	✓	✓	☐
revised twice – all questions right	✓	✓	✓

Move on to another topic when you have all three ticks

	✓	✓	✓
Developing new medicines	☐	☐	☐
How effective are medicines?	☐	☐	☐
Drugs	☐	☐	☐
Legal and illegal drugs	☐	☐	☐
Does cannabis lead to hard drugs?	☐	☐	☐
Drugs in sport	☐	☐	☐

Student Book pages 76–77 **B1**

4.1 Adapt and survive

Key points

- All organisms need a supply of materials to survive and reproduce. They get these from their surroundings and from other living organisms.
- Organisms are adapted to survive in the conditions in which they normally live.
- Microorganisms have a wide range of adaptations which enable some of them to live in extreme conditions.

- To survive and reproduce, organisms require materials from their surroundings and from the other organisms living there.
- Plants need light, carbon dioxide, water, oxygen and nutrients, such as mineral ions from the soil.
- Animals need food from other organisms, water and oxygen.
- Different microorganisms need different materials. Some microorganisms are like plants, others are like animals, and some do not need oxygen or light to survive.
- Special features of organisms are called **adaptations**.
- Adaptations allow organisms to survive in a particular habitat, even when the conditions are extreme, e.g. extremely hot, very salty or at high pressure.

1 *What is meant by an 'adaptation'?*

- Plants are adapted to obtain light and other materials efficiently in order to make food by photosynthesis.
- Animals may be plant eating (**herbivores**) or eat other animals (**carnivores**). Their mouthparts are adapted to their diet.
- Most organisms live in temperatures below 40 °C so their enzymes can work.
- **Extremophiles** are microorganisms which are adapted to live in conditions where enzymes won't usually work because they would **denature.**

Study tip

Make sure you understand what is meant by the terms 'adaptation' and 'extremophile'.

Key words: adaptation, herbivore, carnivore, extremophile, denature

Student Book pages 78–79 **B1**

4.2 Adaptation in animals

Key points

- Animal adaptations help them to survive in the conditions where they normally live.
- Animals in cold areas are usually large with a small surface area : volume ratio.
- Animals in hot dry areas may have a large surface area : volume ratio.
- Coat colour may change in different seasons giving year-round camouflage.

- If animals were not adapted to survive in the areas they live in, they would die.
- Animals in cold climates (e.g. in the Arctic) have thick fur and fat under the skin (blubber) to keep them warm.
- Some animals in the Arctic (e.g. Arctic fox, Arctic hare) are white in the winter and brown in the summer. This means that they are camouflaged so they are not easily seen.
- Bigger animals have smaller surface areas compared to their volume. This means that they can conserve energy more easily but it is also more difficult to cool down.
- In hot dry conditions (desert) animals are adapted to conserve water and to stop them getting too hot. Animals in the desert may hunt or feed at night so that they remain cool during the day.

1 *Why do large animals find it difficult to cool down?*

Study tip

Adaptations are not just to do with what the animal looks like; some adaptations are about the animal's behaviour.

Maths skills

It is important to understand that larger organisms have a smaller surface area : volume (SA : V) ratio. The SA : V of a cube with sides 1 cm long is 6 : 1.

- calculate the SA : V ratio of a cube with sides of 2 cm long.

Student Book pages 80–81 **B1**

4.3 Adaptation in plants

Key points

- Plants lose water vapour from the leaf surface.
- To survive in dry conditions plants have adaptations to reduce the surface area of leaves, and to have tissues which store water and extensive root systems.

Cacti are well adapted to conserve water and to stop animals eating them

- Plants need light, water, space and nutrients to survive.
- Plants need to collect and conserve water. They can lose water as water vapour through holes in the leaves called **stomata**.
- Water can be collected if the plant has an extensive root system.
- Water can be conserved if the plant has very small or waxy leaves. A plant might have a swollen stem to store the water.
- In dry conditions, e.g. in deserts, plants (such as cacti) have become very well adapted to conserve water. Others (such as the mesquite tree) have adapted to collect water using extensive root systems.
- Plants are eaten by animals. Some plants have developed thorns, poisonous chemicals and warning colours to put animals off.

1 *Give three ways a plant can conserve water.*

Study tip

There are many ways plants conserve water in dry environments. These include extensive roots, waxy leaves, small leaves and water storage in stems. Don't limit yourself to one idea in an exam!

Key word: stomata

Student Book pages 82–83 **B1**

4.4 Competition in animals

Key points

- Animals often compete with each other for food, mates and territory.
- Well-adapted animals are good competitors.

Some predators are adapted for speed and may be camouflaged by long grass

- Animals are in **competition** with each other for water, food, space, mates and breeding sites.
- An animal's **territory** will be large enough to find water, food and have space for breeding.
- Predators compete with their prey, as they want to eat them.
- Predators and prey may be camouflaged, so that they are less easy to see.
- Prey animals compete with each other to escape from the predators and to find food for themselves.
- Some animals, e.g. caterpillars, may be poisonous and have warning colours so that they are not eaten.

1 *Why do animals need a territory?*

Study tip

Make a list of all the possible ways animals might be adapted to compete and survive. Start with warning colours, camouflage, speed, horns. Explain why they are good adaptations.

Key words: competition, territory

Student Book **pages 84–85** **B1**

4.5 Competition in plants

Key points

- Plants compete with each other for light, water and mineral ions from the soil.
- Well-adapted plants are good competitors.

- All plants compete for water, nutrients and light. For example, in woodland some smaller plants (e.g. snowdrops) flower before the trees are in leaf. This ensures they get enough light, water and nutrients.
- Plants which grow deep roots can reach underground water better than those with shallow roots.
- Some plants spread their seeds over a wide area so that they do not compete with themselves.
  - Some of these plants use animals to spread their fruits and seeds.
  - Some plants use the wind (e.g. sycamore) or mini-explosions to spread their seeds (e.g. broom)

Bump up your grade

To improve your grade, read all the information given about adaptations and relate these to where the animal or plant lives. Fur colour may aid camouflage, but fur can also prevent energy loss. Make sure your answer is in the correct context.

1 *Why do plants try to spread their seeds as far as possible?*

Study tip

Plants do have structures to enable them to compete, e.g. extensive root systems. However, it is also important to mention their successful growing habits. For example, they grow quickly so that they gain as much light as possible, or they grow at a time when other plants are dormant, e.g. snowdrops in a wood.

Student Book **pages 86–87** **B1**

4.6 How do you survive?

Key points

- Organisms have adaptations which enable them to survive in the conditions in which they normally live.
- Plants often compete with each other for light, water and nutrients from the soil.
- Animals often compete with each other for food, mates and territory.

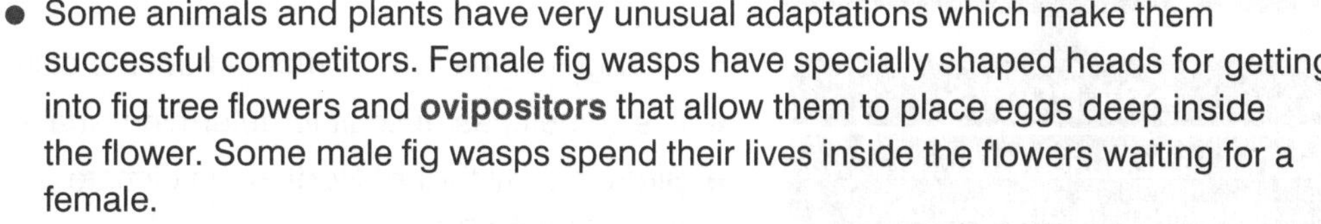

- Some animals and plants have very unusual adaptations which make them successful competitors. Female fig wasps have specially shaped heads for getting into fig tree flowers and **ovipositors** that allow them to place eggs deep inside the flower. Some male fig wasps spend their lives inside the flowers waiting for a female.

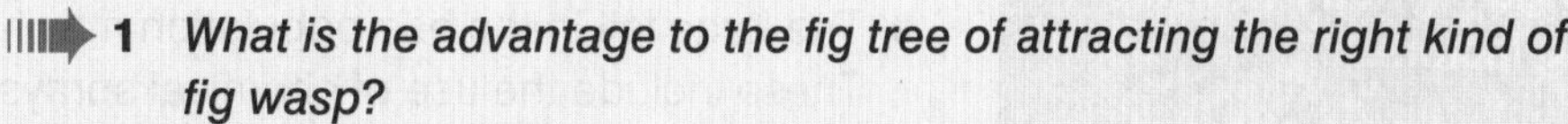

1 *What is the advantage to the fig tree of attracting the right kind of fig wasp?*

- The star-nosed mole lives underground and is almost blind, but is very sensitive to touch and smell.
- Venus fly traps are insect eating plants. They have sweet, sticky nectar and are bright red inside.

2 *How are the star-nosed mole and Venus fly trap adapted for survival?*

Look at the difference in this resurrection plant after 24 hours and a supply of water. What is the advantage to the plant?

Study tip

Do not be put off if you are given facts about an unusual animal or plant. Read the information carefully before answering the questions.

Key word: ovipositor

Student Book pages 88–89 **B1**

4.7 Measuring environmental change

Key points

- Changes in the environment affect the distribution of living organisms.
- These changes can be caused by living or non-living factors.
- Environmental changes can be measured using non-living indicators.
- Living organisms can be used as pollution indicators.

Study tip

Make sure you know which are the environmental factors, e.g. oxygen levels, and which organisms are the living pollution indicators, e.g. invertebrates.

Animals and plants are affected by their environment. If the environment changes the organisms may not be able to live there anymore.

- Non-living factors which might change include: temperature, rainfall, light and oxygen levels.
- Living factors which might change include: arrival of a new predator or disease, or the introduction of new plants which might provide new food or habitats.

1 *Name three non-living environmental factors.*

Pollution indicators and monitoring

- Lichens indicate the level of air pollution, particularly sulfur dioxide. The more species of lichen growing, the cleaner the air. They are an example of an **indicator species**, which indicate changes in environmental pollution levels.
- Freshwater invertebrates indicate the level of water pollution in the same way, in particular the concentration of dissolved oxygen in the water. The wider the range of these invertebrates the cleaner the water in the streams, river or pond. Some freshwater invertebrates will only live in polluted water.
- Equipment such as rain gauges, thermometers, pH and oxygen sensors and data loggers can be used to monitor non-living changes in the environment.

Key word: indicator species

Student Book pages 90–91 **B1**

4.8 The impact of change

Key points

- The distribution of living organisms is affected by changes in non-living and living factors.
- The data on the effect of environmental change is not always easy to interpret.

Bump up your grade

You can gain extra marks by using data from any graphs or diagrams, as well as the written information in questions, when describing environmental changes.

- Changes in the environment affect the distribution of living organisms.
- It is sometimes difficult to determine what is affecting the organism.
- Birds may fly further North if the climate gets warmer. Other birds may then have new competitors.
- The large fall in the bee population may have been caused by several factors. These include the use of chemical sprays by farmers, a viral disease or possibly changes in flowering patterns in plants due in turn to climate change.

1 *Why do some birds fly further North to find nesting sites?*

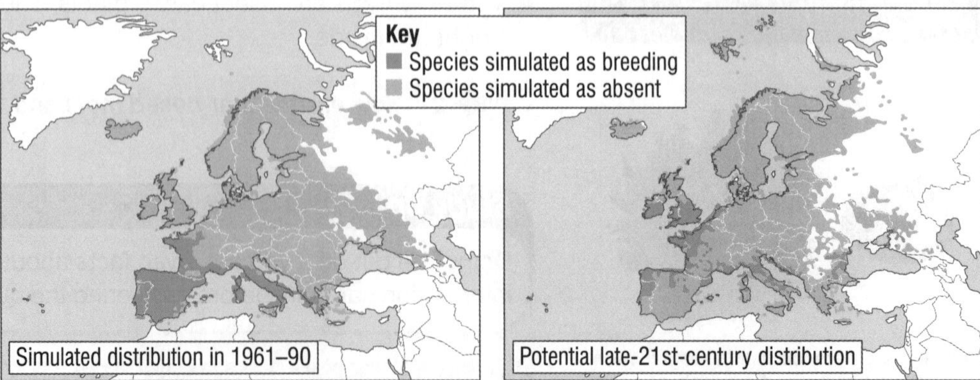

What are the predicted changes in distribution of the Dartford warbler as shown by these maps?

1. State three things that plants compete for.
2. Why are Arctic foxes white in the winter?
3. State three possible ways a plant might conserve water.
4. Why do warning colours prevent some animals being eaten?
5. Why do some animals move North during the summertime and return South in the winter?
6. Why do some woodland plants grow and flower early in the year?
7. Name an instrument which can record environmental change over a few weeks.
8. What is the advantage for some predators to be camouflaged?
9. An elephant has a small surface area to volume ratio. How will this affect the elephant in hot climates?
10. A farmer plants some seeds in rows 10 cm apart. The plants grow well. He wonders if he should plant them closer next year. Explain why this might not produce a better yield.
11. Suggest why some animals in a desert spend all day in a burrow and come out at night.
12. Why is it difficult to interpret data about changes in the distribution of animals and plants?

Chapter checklist

Tick when you have:	✓	✓	✓
reviewed it after your lesson	☑	☐	☐
revised once – some questions right	☑	☑	☐
revised twice – all questions right	☑	☑	☑

Move on to another topic when you have all three ticks

Topic	✓	✓	✓
Adapt and survive	☐	☐	☐
Adaptation in animals	☐	☐	☐
Adaptation in plants	☐	☐	☐
Competition in animals	☐	☐	☐
Competition in plants	☐	☐	☐
How do you survive?	☐	☐	☐
Measuring environmental change	☐	☐	☐
The impact of change	☐	☐	☐

Student Book pages 94–95 **B1**

5.1 Pyramids of biomass

Key points

- Radiation from the Sun is the main source of energy for living organisms.
- Green plants and algae capture light energy during photosynthesis.
- Biomass is the dry mass of living material in an organism.
- The biomass at each stage in a food chain is less than at the previous stage.

- **Biomass** is the mass of living material in plants and animals.
- A **pyramid of biomass** represents the mass of the organisms at each stage in a food chain. It may be more accurate than a pyramid of numbers. For example, one bush may have many insects feeding on it but the mass of the bush is far greater than the mass of the insects.
- Green plants transfer **solar (light) energy** to chemical energy which is then passed through the food chain.

1 *Why are plants always at the base of the pyramid of biomass?*

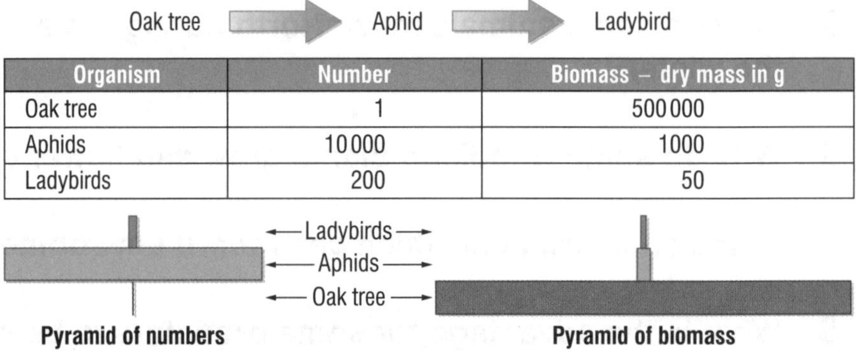

Organism	Number	Biomass – dry mass in g
Oak tree	1	500 000
Aphids	10 000	1000
Ladybirds	200	50

Using a pyramid of biomass shows us the amount of biological material involved at each level of this food chain much more effectively than using a pyramid of numbers

Biomass of tertiary consumer (carnivore)
Biomass of secondary consumer (carnivore)
Biomass of primary consumer (herbivore)
Biomass of plants (producers)

Any food chain can be turned into a pyramid of biomass

Bump up your grade

Examiners always try to present information in new ways. To gain maximum marks from data, which may be given as tables, graphs, charts, unusual diagrams as well as in writing, read the stem of the question carefully, check you know what information is given on all the illustrations. If you have not used the data in your answer you may have missed the point of the question.

Key words: biomass, pyramid of biomass, solar (light) energy

Student Book pages 96–97 **B1**

5.2 Energy transfers

Key points

- There is less biomass and energy available at each successive stage in a food chain.
- Materials are used at each stage and energy may be transferred to the surroundings.

- There is energy wastage between each stage of a food chain. This means that not all of the energy taken in by an organism results in the growth of that organism.
- Not all of the food eaten can be digested, so energy is stored in faeces or as **urea** in urine (waste materials).
- Some of the biomass (food) is used for respiration, which releases energy for living processes. This includes movement, so the more something moves the more energy it uses and the less is available for growth.
- In animals that need to keep a constant temperature, energy from the previous stage of the food chain is used simply to keep the animal at its normal body temperature.
- Much of the energy released in respiration is eventually transferred to the surroundings.

1 *Which process in cells releases energy from food material?*

Study tip

Sankey diagrams are a type of graph that are used to show energy intake and energy use or transfer in an animal. Practise calculations on Sankey diagrams.

Bump up your grade

To improve your grade, check that you understand what is happening to the biomass through a food chain. Energy is never 'lost', it is transferred. Not all the energy which is transferred to the next stage is converted into growth. The energy may heat the surroundings or be stored in faeces.

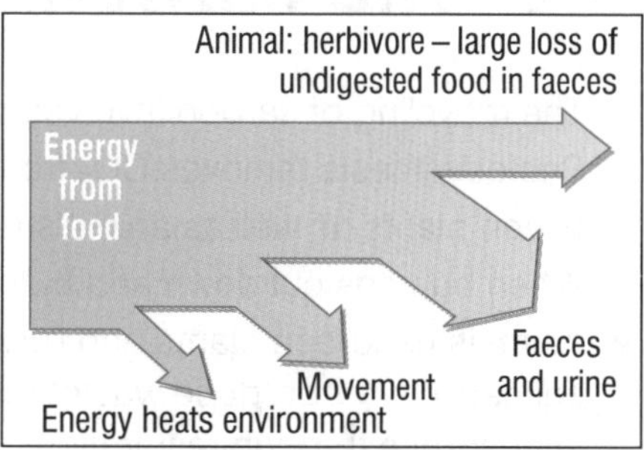

Animal: carnivore – little loss of undigested food in faeces

Energy from food

Faeces and urine

Movement

Energy heats environment

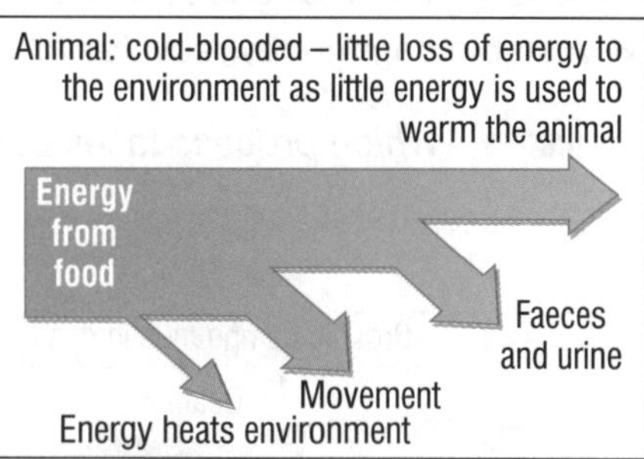

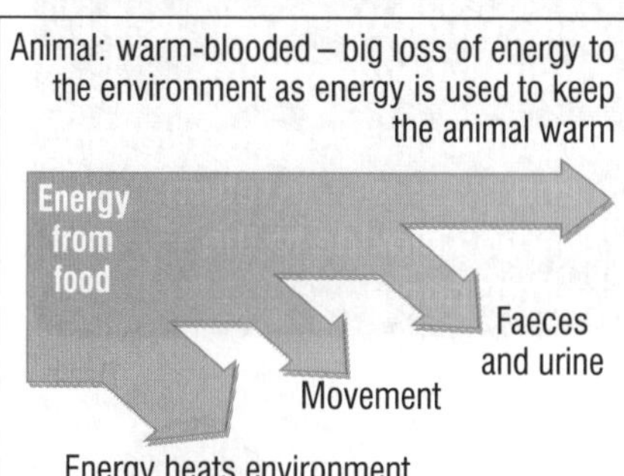

Sankey diagrams show how energy is transferred in a system. We can use them to look at the energy which goes in to and out of an animal and predict whether it eats plants or is a carnivore.

Key word: urea

Student Book pages 98–99 **B1**

5.3 Decay processes

Key points

- Living organisms remove materials from the environment which are returned when the organism dies.
- Microorganisms decay waste and dead plants and animals.
- Decay is quicker in warm, moist, aerobic conditions.
- Processes which use materials must be balanced by those which release them.

This tomato is slowly being broken down by the action of decomposers. You can see the fungi clearly but the bacteria are too small to be seen.

- All organisms take up nutrients. If they didn't eventually release them, the nutrients would run out.
- **Detritus feeders** (such as some types of worm) may start the process of decay by eating dead animals or plants and producing waste materials. Decay organisms then break down the waste or dead plants and animals.

1 *Give an example of a detritus feeder.*

- Decay organisms are microorganisms (bacteria and fungi). They are called **decomposers**. Decay is faster if it is warm and wet. Many decomposers also need oxygen.
- All of the materials from the waste and dead organisms are recycled, returning nutrients to the soil.
- Humans can recycle waste in **sewage treatment plants** and **compost heaps**.

2 *What is meant by a decomposer?*

Study tip

Make sure you understand why materials need to be recycled in nature.

Key words: detritus feeder, decomposer, sewage treatment plant, compost heap

Student Book pages 100–101 **B1**

5.4 The carbon cycle

Key points

- The constant cycling of carbon in nature is known as the **carbon cycle**.
- During photosynthesis carbon dioxide is removed from the atmosphere.
- The processes of respiration and **combustion** return carbon dioxide to the atmosphere.

- The recycling of carbon involves both photosynthesis and respiration.
- Photosynthesis removes CO_2 from the atmosphere.
- Green plants as well as animals respire. This returns CO_2 to the atmosphere.
- When humans cut down and burn trees, CO_2 is released into the atmosphere.
- Animals eat green plants and build the carbon into their bodies. When plants or animals die (or produce waste) microorganisms release the CO_2 back into the atmosphere through respiration.
- A stable community recycles all of the nutrients it takes up.

1 ***Which process takes carbon dioxide out of the atmosphere?***

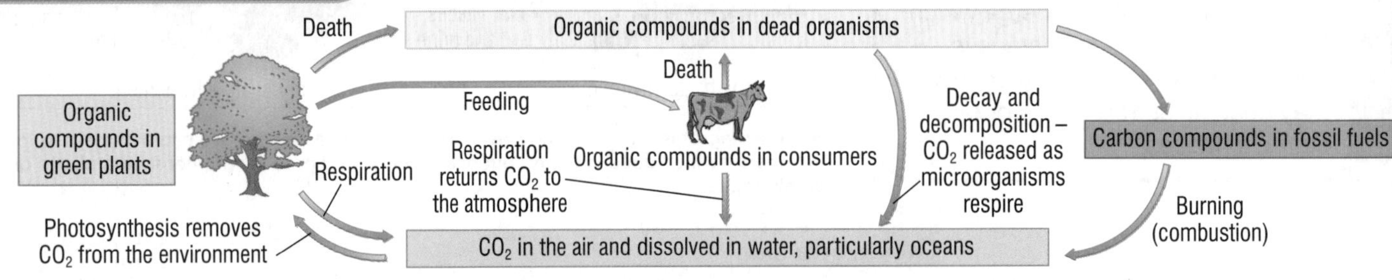

The carbon cycle in nature. Organic compounds include carbohydrates, fats and proteins which all contain carbon.

Key words: carbon cycle, combustion

Student Book pages 102–103 **B1**

5.5 Recycling organic waste 

Key points

- Recycling organic kitchen and garden waste is necessary to: reduce landfill, reduce methane production, recycle minerals and nutrients in the waste.
- There are various methods of recycling organic waste.

- Waste vegetables and peelings from the kitchen, or grass cuttings and clippings from trees in the garden, contain **organic waste**. This can be recycled.
- Organic waste can be composted in several ways.
- The most efficient methods of composting allow the waste to be mixed with oxygen and moisture. They also allow energy to escape by heating the surroundings.
- Gardeners may add worms and layers of garden soil to composters to speed up the process.

1 ***Why do gardeners add worms to compost?***

- Councils also collect garden waste and use shredders and large bins to compost the material.

2 ***Suggest why councils shred garden waste before putting it into big bins.***

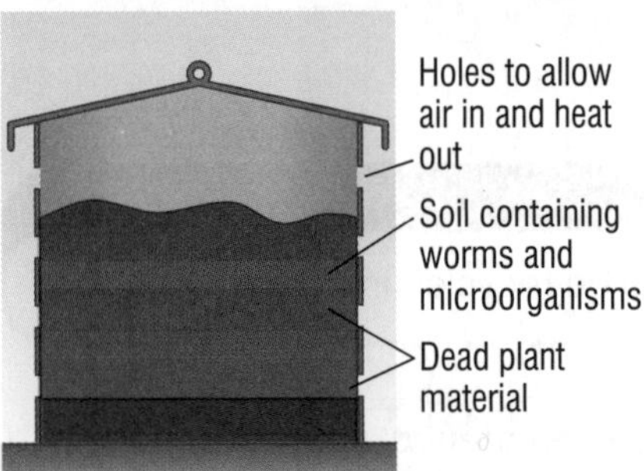

A well-designed compost heap allows air (containing oxygen) in, heat out and has room for soil between the organic waste

Study tip

Find out how people in your area deal with organic waste. Is there a good recycling scheme? Look for methods of dealing with organic waste on the internet.

Key word: organic waste

1. What does the word 'biomass' mean?
2. What is meant by 'organic waste'?
3. Which processes return carbon dioxide into the atmosphere?
4. How can energy wastage be reduced in a food chain?
5. Give an example of a detritus feeder.
6. What is a Sankey diagram?
7. Why does a compost heap get hot?
8. Why do we normally eat herbivores rather than carnivores?
9. What do we mean by a stable community in terms of recycling of nutrients?
10. When a calf eats grass, only about 30% of the material is turned into new growth of the calf. What happens to the other 70%?

Chapter checklist

Tick when you have:

reviewed it after your lesson	✓	☐	☐
revised once – some questions right	✓	✓	☐
revised twice – all questions right	✓	✓	✓

Move on to another topic when you have all three ticks

	✓	✓	✓
Pyramids of biomass	☐	☐	☐
Energy transfers	☐	☐	☐
Decay processes	☐	☐	☐
The carbon cycle	☐	☐	☐
Recycling organic waste	☐	☐	☐

Student Book pages 106–107 **B1**

6.1 Inheritance

Key points

- Organisms have similar characteristics to their parents.
- Genes are passed in sex cells from parents to offspring.
- Genes control the characteristics of your body.

- The nucleus of a cell contains thread-like structures called **chromosomes**.
- The chromosome threads carry the **genes**.
- In the nuclei of sex cells (**gametes**) there is only a single set of chromosomes.
- Therefore nuclei of male and female sex cells contain one set of genes.

1 *Where are genes found?*

- The genetic information from the parents is passed on to the offspring during reproduction. So the offspring cells contain two sets of genes, inherited from both parents.
- Different genes control the development of different characteristics of the offspring.
- In most body cells the chromosomes are in pairs. One set came from the female gamete (from the mother) and one set from the male gamete (from the father).

2 *What do genes control?*

Study tip

Remember it is the individual genes that control the characteristics of the offspring. Chromosomes are simply *made up* of genes.

Key words: chromosome, gene, gamete

Student Book pages 108–109 **B1**

6.2 Types of reproduction

Key points

- In asexual reproduction there is no joining of gametes.
- Clones are produced by asexual reproduction.
- Clones are identical copies of one parent.
- Sexual reproduction involves two parents and leads to variety in the offspring.

- **Asexual reproduction** does not involve the fusion of gametes (sex cells). All of the genetic information comes from one parent. All of the offspring are genetically identical to the parent, so there is little variety.
- Identical copies produced by asexual reproduction are called **clones**.
- **Sexual reproduction** involves the fusion of sex cells (gametes). There is a mixing of genetic information, so the offspring show variation.
- In animals, the sex cells are eggs and sperm.
- Offspring produced by sexual reproduction are similar to both parents, but cannot be identical. That is because they have a combination of two sets of genes.

1 *Explain which type of reproduction produces genetically identical offspring?*

- Random mixing of genes leads to variation in the offspring. This is important in survival. Some characteristics may give offspring a better chance of surviving difficult conditions.

2 *Explain which type of reproduction leads to variation in the offspring?*

This litter of puppies have the same parents. The puppies have many similarities but mixing of their parents' genes has led to variations in their appearance. Can you guess what the parents may have looked like?

Study tip

Learn why one type of reproduction results in variation and the other doesn't. It is simply that in sexual reproduction genes are inherited from two parents. However, in asexual (no sex) reproduction there is only one parent, so variation is impossible!

Key words: asexual reproduction, clone, sexual reproduction

Student Book pages 110–111 **B1**

Key points

- Differences in individuals of the same kind can be due to their genes, the environment or both.
- Clones may have some differences due to environmental causes.

6.3 Genetic and environmental differences

- Differences in the characteristics of individuals of the same kind (same species) may be due to:
  - differences in the genes they have inherited,
  - the conditions in which they have developed,
  - a combination of both these genetic and environmental causes.
- Genes are the most important factor in controlling the appearance of an individual.
- Plants may be affected by lack of light, nutrients or space to grow. The weaker plants may have the same genes as the healthier plants but cannot grow well if deprived of nutrients.
- Human development may be affected during pregnancy. If the mother smokes or drinks a lot of alcohol, the baby may have a small birth weight.
- Once animals are born, too much or too little food can alter their characteristics. For example, genes may determine if someone has the potential to be a good athlete. However, training to develop muscles and eating the correct diet will also alter the athlete's body.

1 ***What are the two factors which control some of our characteristics?***

Student Book pages 112–113 **B1**

Key points

- Plant clones can be made quickly by taking cuttings from mature plants.
- Tissue culture is a newer method of cloning.
- Animals can be cloned by transplanting cloned embryos.

Bump up your grade

To improve your grade, make sure you know why clones are identical to their parents *and* how the different types of cloning work. If you only know the names of the different types of cloning, then this is only C/D grade knowledge.

6.4 Cloning

- Individuals which are genetically identical to their parents are known as 'clones'.
- It is much more difficult to clone animals than it is to clone plants.
- Cloning is used to produce new individuals that are useful in farming and agriculture.
- In plants, the process of cloning can be cheap and effective. Plants can be cloned by taking cuttings and growing them.
- Taking small groups of cells from part of a plant and growing them under special conditions (**tissue culture**) is more expensive. Tissue culture can be used to reproduce large numbers of a rare or top quality plant.

1 ***Name a quick, cheap way of cloning plants.***

- Embryo transplants are used to clone animals. In this process an embryo with unspecialised cells is split into smaller groups of cells. Each group of genetically identical cells is transplanted and allowed to develop in a host animal.
- Sometimes animals or plants are **genetically modified** to produce useful substances before they are cloned.

2 ***Why is it more difficult to successfully clone animals than plants?***

Study tip

Remember that clones are formed by asexual reproduction. Taking cuttings, tissue culture and embryo transplantation are artificial forms of asexual reproduction.

Key words: tissue culture, genetically modified

Student Book pages 114–115 **B1**

6.5 Adult cell cloning

Key points

- Scientists have used adult cells to clone animals such as Dolly the sheep.
- The nucleus of an adult cell is transplanted into an 'empty' egg cell. When the animal develops it has the genetic material of the original adult cell.

Study tip

Remember that the nucleus of the adult cell contains the genes. This means that the new embryo is genetically identical to the original adult from which the cell was taken.

- In **adult cell cloning** the nucleus of an adult cell, e.g. a skin cell, replaces the nucleus of an egg cell.
- First the nucleus is removed from an unfertilised egg cell. The nucleus is removed from the skin cell and placed inside the 'empty' egg cell.
- The new cell is given an electric shock which causes it to start to divide. The ball of cells is called an embryo.
- The embryo is genetically identical to the adult skin cell.
- Once the embryo has developed into a ball of cells it is inserted into the womb of a host mother.
- Dolly the sheep was produced by adult cell cloning in 1997.

How Science Works

There are benefits, but also disadvantages, of adult cell cloning:

Benefits:

Development of cloned animals which have been genetically engineered to produce valuable proteins in their milk. These have uses in medicine.

Cloning can save animals from extinction.

Disadvantages:

Concerns about the ethics of cloning.

Cloning limits the variation in a population (limits the gene pool). This can be a problem for natural selection if the environment changes.

Concerns about using the technique to clone humans in the future.

1 *Name the two cells needed in adult cell cloning.*

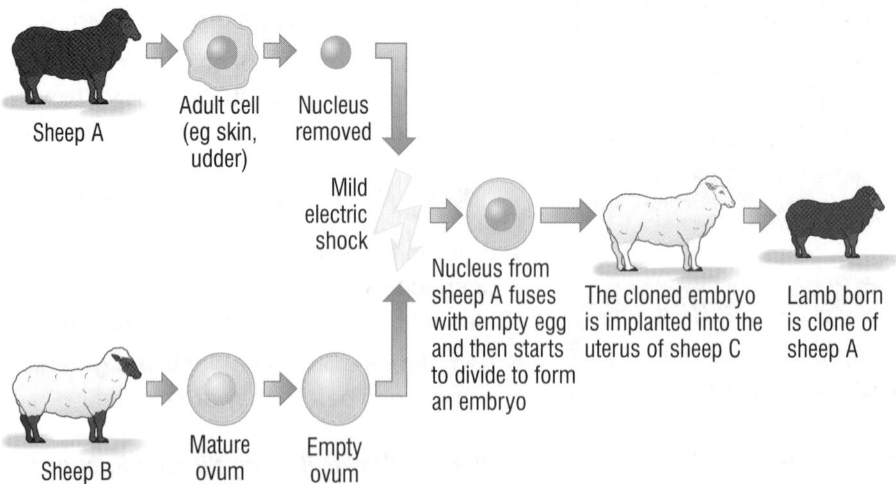

Adult cell cloning is still a very difficult technique – but scientists hope it may bring benefits in the future

Key words: adult cell cloning

Student Book
pages 116–117 **B1**

6.6 Genetic engineering

Key points

- Genetic engineering is used to transfer a gene from one organism to another.
- Enzymes are used to 'cut out' a gene from a human chromosome and then insert it into a bacterial cell.
- Genes can be transferred to the cells of animals and plants at an early stage in their development.

Study tip

Remember that one gene controls one characteristic.

- **Genetic engineering** involves changing the genetic make-up of an organism.
- Genes can be transferred to the cells of animals, plants or microorganisms at an early stage in their development.
- A gene is 'cut out' of the chromosome of an organism using an enzyme. The gene is then placed in the chromosome of another organism.
- The genes may be placed in an organism of the same species to give it a 'desired' characteristic.
- Sometimes genes are placed in a different species, such as a bacterium. For example, the gene to produce insulin in humans can be placed in bacteria. Then the bacteria can produce large quantities of insulin to treat diabetes.

1 *What is used to cut genes out of chromosomes?*

- New genes can be transferred to crop plants.
- Crops with changed genes are called genetically modified (GM) crop plants.
- GM crops may be insect- or herbicide-resistant and usually have increased yields.

Key words: genetic engineering

Student Book
pages 118–119 **B1**

6.7 Making choices about technology

Key points

- There are advantages and disadvantages in the use of cloning and genetic engineering.
- The issues can be economic, social or ethical.

Bump up your grade

If you are hoping to improve your grade, you should always look for the advantages and disadvantages of cloning or genetic engineering and then write a conclusion based on your knowledge and the evidence given in the question.

There are many advantages, but also disadvantages, in using cloning and genetic engineering.

Advantages

- Cloning cattle can produce herds of cattle with useful characteristics.
- Adult cell cloning may be used to make copies of the best animals, e.g. race horses.
- If a person has a faulty gene they may have a genetic disorder. If the correct gene can be transferred to the person they could be cured.
- Several medical drugs have been produced by genetic engineering, such as insulin and antibodies.
- GM crops include ones which are resistant to herbicides or to insects.

Disadvantages

- GM crops have a bigger yield, but farmers have to buy new GM seed every year because the crops are infertile.
- Some people are concerned about accidentally introducing genes into wild flower populations.
- Insects which are not pests may be affected by GM crops.
- Many people worry about the effect of eating GM crops on human health.
- Many people argue about whether or not cloning and genetic engineering are ethical. What will be the long-term effects? Will we create new organisms that we know nothing about? Are these processes ethically correct?

1 *Why do farmers grow GM crops?*

1 How is genetic information passed from parents to offspring?

2 Suggest which humans could be described as 'natural clones'.

3 Plant clones are genetically identical. Why do some clones look different?

4 What is meant by a 'host' animal?

5 What is done to the fused cell to start off the process of cell division in adult cell cloning?

6 Why are you similar to both your parents, but not identical to either of them?

7 In what way are embryo transplants similar to what happens when identical twins form?

8 How are calf embryos cloned?

9 Why is embryo cloning sometimes used by cattle breeders rather than letting the cattle breed naturally?

10 Outline the process of genetic engineering.

11 Give two advantages of genetic engineering.

12 How are crops genetically modified?

Chapter checklist

Tick when you have:

reviewed it after your lesson	✓	☐	☐
revised once – some questions right	✓	✓	☐
revised twice – all questions right	✓	✓	✓

Move on to another topic when you have all three ticks

	✓	✓	✓
Inheritance	☐	☐	☐
Types of reproduction	☐	☐	☐
Genetic and environmental differences	☐	☐	☐
Cloning	☐	☐	☐
Adult cell cloning	☐	☐	☐
Genetic engineering	☐	☐	☐
Making choices about technology	☐	☐	☐

Student Book pages 122–123 **B1**

7.1 Theories of evolution

Key points

- All species of living things have evolved from simple life forms. These simple forms developed more than 3 billion years ago.
- Darwin's theory states that evolution takes place by a process of natural selection.

Study tip

Learn the sequence:
best adapted → survive → breed → pass on genes.

- Scientists have estimated that life began on Earth about 3 billion years ago.
- Before the 18th century there were few scientific ideas about how **evolution** works.
- **Jean-Baptiste Lamarck** suggested a theory called 'the **inheritance of acquired characteristics**'. Lamarck's theory stated that characteristics which develop during an organism's lifetime can be passed on to the next generation. People found this difficult to believe. For example, if two parents were to build up their muscles in the gym, Lamarck's theory would predict that this characteristic would be passed on to their offspring.
- **Charles Darwin** suggested the theory of 'natural selection' after he had made a journey to the Galapagos Islands. He recorded many observations about life on the islands.
- Darwin's theory stated that small changes in organisms took place over a very long time. All organisms in a species vary and therefore some are more likely to survive (natural selection). Those that are best adapted breed and pass on their characteristics.
- Darwin did not know about genes. We can now say that the best adapted organisms survive to breed. They are the ones that pass on their genes to the next generation.

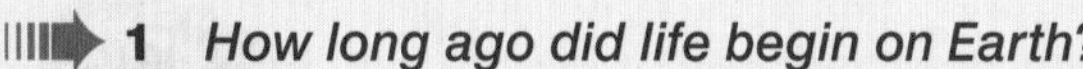

1 *How long ago did life begin on Earth?*

Darwin read about the ideas of other scientists and recorded a great deal of evidence before suggesting his theory of evolution by natural selection

Key words: evolution, Jean-Baptiste Lamarck, inheritance of acquired characteristics, Charles Darwin

Student Book pages 124–125 **B1**

7.2 Accepting Darwin's ideas

Key points

- Darwin's theory of evolution was only gradually accepted.

Study tip

Make sure you understand why modern scientists agree with Darwin's theory of natural selection, but those in his lifetime did not accept it.

Darwin's theory of evolution by natural selection was only gradually accepted for several reasons:

- The theory of natural selection challenged the idea that God made all the animals and plants that live on Earth.
- Many scientists were not convinced because they still did not think there was sufficient evidence for the theory.

1 *What name is given to Darwin's theory of evolution?*

- Darwin could not explain why there was variety in organisms, or how inheritance worked. Scientists did not know about genes and genetics until about 50 years later.
- Darwin had tried to show that birds, such as finches on the Galapagos Islands, could change over time if they lived under different environmental conditions. During his lifetime he could not explain, in terms of genes, why the offspring inherited the useful adaptations.

2 *Which birds did Darwin observe to find evidence for evolution?*

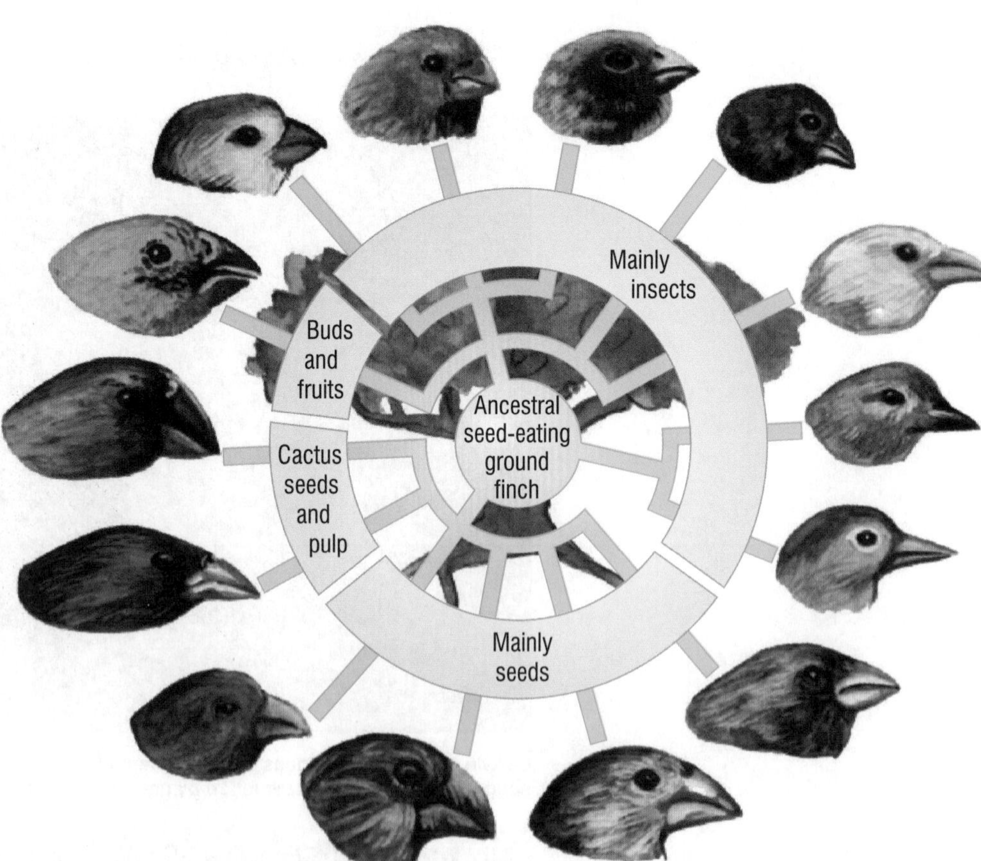

The finches found on the different Galapagos islands look very different, but all evolved from the same original type of finch by natural selection

Student Book pages 126–127 **B1**

7.3 Natural selection

Key points

- Natural selection works because the fittest organisms survive to breed.
- If a gene changes, the new characteristic may enable the organism to survive better.

Bump up your grade

To gain more marks when answering evolution questions, use the following terms accurately and in the best sequence:
mutation → variation → best adapted → survival → breed → genes passed on to offspring.

- Most organisms produce large numbers of offspring. For example, a pair of rabbits may have 800 children, grandchildren and great grandchildren in one 9-month breeding season!
- Individual organisms will show a wide range of variation because of differences in their genes.
- All the organisms in the population will compete for food, shelter from predators, and mates.
- The organisms with the characteristics most suited to the environment will survive. For example, the best camouflage, the best eyesight to find food, the strongest to build a burrow, the quickest to run from a predator, the best suited to the climate. The 'fittest' organisms survive.

1 *Why do organisms show a wide range of variation?*

- The organisms which survive are more likely to breed successfully.
- The genes that have enabled these organisms to survive are then passed on to their offspring.
- Sometimes a gene accidentally changes and becomes a new form of the gene. These changes are called **mutations**. If the mutated gene controls a characteristic which makes the organism better adapted to the environment then it will be passed on to the offspring.
- Mutations may be particularly important in natural selection if the environment changes. For example, when the rabbit disease myxomatosis killed most of the rabbits in the UK, a few rabbits had a mutated gene which gave them immunity. The rabbits with the mutated gene survived to breed.

2 *Why are mutated genes sometimes an advantage?*

Only the rabbits that can escape from a predator will survive to breed

Key word: mutation

Student Book pages 128–129 **B1**

7.4 Classification and evolution

Key points

- We can classify organisms into groups by comparing their similarities and differences.
- Classification helps us to understand evolutionary and ecological relationships.

Study tip

Make sure you understand the term 'natural classification system' and why biologists classify organisms into groups.

- There are millions of different types of living organisms. By putting organisms into groups we can make more sense of how closely they are related. Grouping organisms is called classification.
- Biologists study the similarities and differences between organisms in order to classify them. The system used is called the **natural classification system**.
- The easiest system to understand is one which starts with large groups and splits these up gradually into smaller ones. The largest groups are called **kingdoms**.
- The main kingdoms are:
  - the plant kingdom
  - the animal kingdom
  - the kingdoms which contain the microorganisms.
- The smallest group in the classification system is the **species**.
- Members of a species are very similar and can breed together to produce fertile offspring.

1 *What are the main kingdoms of living organisms?*

- **Evolutionary trees** are models that can be drawn to show the relationships between different groups of organisms.
- When new evidence is found, biologists may modify these **evolutionary relationships**.
- Ecological relationships tell us how species have evolved together in an environment.

2 *Why is it useful to draw evolutionary trees?*

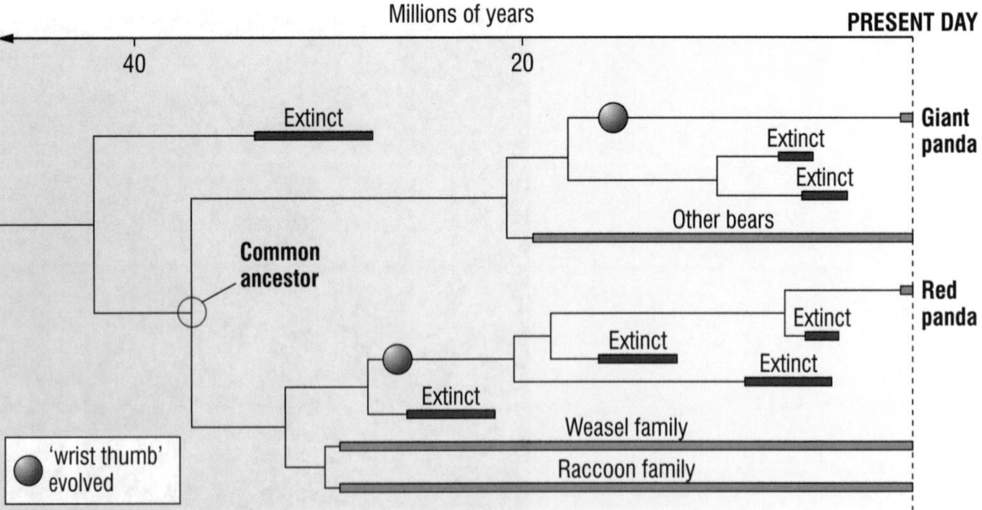

Evolutionary trees like this show us the best model of the evolutionary relationships between organisms

Key words: natural classification system, kingdom, species, evolutionary tree, evolutionary relationship

1. **What is meant by 'evolution'?**
2. **What is the main difference between Lamarck's theory of evolution and Darwin's theory?**
3. **Why did it take so long for Darwin's theory to be accepted?**
4. **Why is it that only some members of a population survive to breed?**
5. **Why is there variation between members of the same species?**
6. **What is meant by the term 'survival of the fittest'?**
7. **What is meant by 'natural selection'?**
8. **What is meant by the term 'species'?**
9. **Suggest three factors that could change in a habitat area, causing problems for the organisms living there.**
10. **Why do biologists draw evolutionary trees?**

Chapter checklist

Tick when you have:

reviewed it after your lesson	✓	☐	☐
revised once – some questions right	✓	✓	☐
revised twice – all questions right	✓	✓	✓

Move on to another topic when you have all three ticks

	✓	✓	✓
Theories of evolution	☐	☐	☐
Accepting Darwin's ideas	☐	☐	☐
Natural selection	☐	☐	☐
Classification and evolution	☐	☐	☐

1 Organisms must be adapted to the conditions in the environment where they live. Some animals live in very cold sea water.

Scientists are concerned that cold water animals will not survive if sea temperatures rise. The scientists collected some organisms from cold water and placed them in water which was a few degrees warmer. The smallest organisms were able to survive better than the bigger ones.

Explain why. *(3 marks)*

2 The diagram shows a method of cloning called 'therapeutic cloning', which could be used to cure diseased organs.

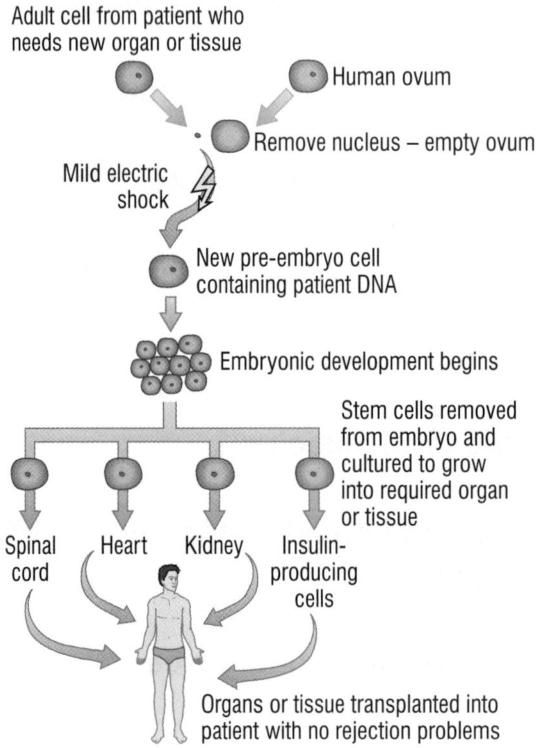

a In what way is this technique different from adult cell cloning? Choose one sentence as the answer.

A human egg has the nucleus removed.

A nucleus is removed from an adult cell.

Stem cells are removed from the embryo. *(1 mark)*

b Which of the following is **not** true about this technique?

The tissues produced will genetically match the patient.

It involves sexual reproduction.

It involves nuclear transfer. *(1 mark)*

c Some people object to this technique. Which is an ethical reason for objecting?

It costs a lot of money.

An embryo is formed.

Only the patient can use the cells. *(1 mark)*

3 Conditions inside the body must be controlled.

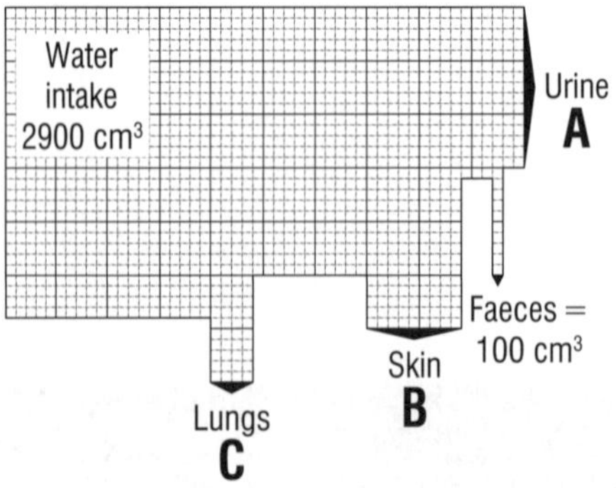

a The diagram shows the amount of water lost by an adult in one day. The width of the arrows shows how much water is lost in each way.

Calculate the amounts of water lost from the urine, lungs and skin.

Write the correct letter, A, B or C, for each of these:

i $400\,cm^3$ *(1 mark)*

ii $900\,cm^3$ *(1 mark)*

iii $1500\,cm^3$ *(1 mark)*

b What proportion of the water intake is lost in the faeces? *(1 mark)*

c The internal body temperature of a human must also be controlled. Explain why. *(2 marks)*

4 *In this question you will be assessed on using good English, organising information clearly and using specialist terms where appropriate.*

A student accidentally touches a drawing pin. Her hand is automatically moved away from the pin. The drawing shows the parts involved in this action.

Describe what happens from the time the pin sticks in the skin until the hand is automatically moved away. *(6 marks)*

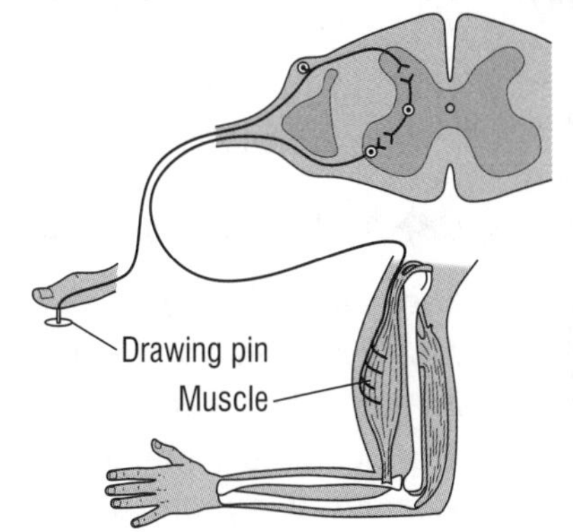

5 Copper compounds are found in water that has drained through ash from power stations. Invertebrate animals are used to monitor the concentration of copper compounds in water. First, scientists must find out which invertebrate animals can survive in a range of concentrations of copper compounds.

This is how the procedure is carried out:

- Solutions of different concentrations of a copper compound are prepared.
- Batches of 50 of each of five different invertebrate species, **A**, **B**, **C**, **D** and **E**, are placed in separate containers of each solution.

After a while, the number of each type of invertebrate which survive at each concentration is counted.

a Give **two** variables that should be controlled in this investigation so that the results are valid. *(2 marks)*

b The graph opposite shows the results for species **B**.

Use the graph to find the concentration of copper compounds (in parts per million) in which 50% of species **B** survived. To obtain full marks you must show clearly on a copy of the graph how you obtained your answer. *(2 marks)*

Number of species **B** that survived: 0, 5, 10, 15, 20, 25, 30, 35, 40, 45, 50

Concentration of copper compound in parts per million: 0, 100, 200, 300, 400, 500, 600

c The graph opposite shows the results of the tests on the other four invertebrate species.

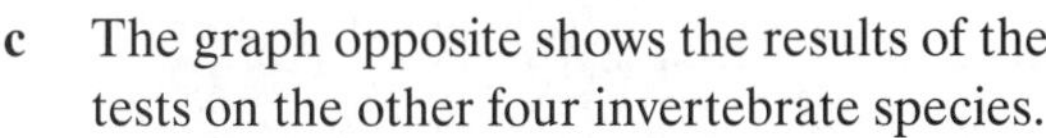

i Which species, **A**, **C**, **D** or **E**, is most sensitive to the concentration of copper in the water? Give the reason for your answer. *(1 mark)*

ii It is often more convenient to use invertebrates rather than a chemical test to monitor water for copper. Suggest **two** explanations for this. *(2 marks)*

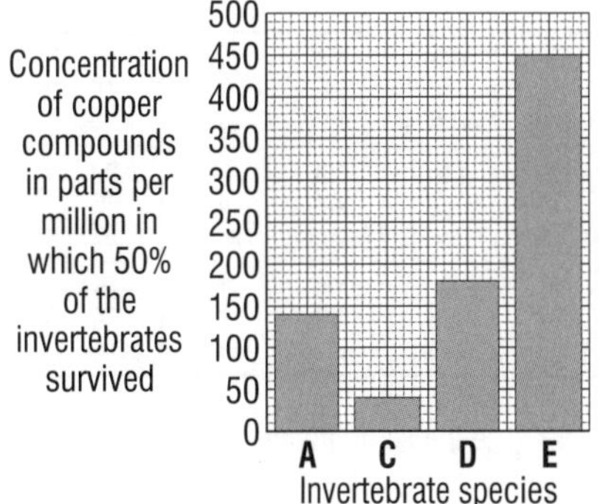

AQA, 2008

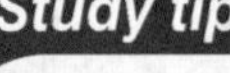

Study tip

Q4 expects a longer written answer. You should write clearly and in a logical sequence to gain full marks.

Plan before you write. Jot down the key scientific words and then number them before putting the ideas into sentences. For a 6-mark answer there will be at least five or six scientific points to include.

Study tip

In Q5, remember that a chemical test analyses one sample of water at a given moment. Invertebrates indicate longer term effects of changes in the water.

Student Book pages 134–135 **C1**

1.1 Atoms, elements and compounds

Key points

- All substances are made of atoms.
- Elements are made of only one type of atom.
- Chemical symbols are used to represent atoms.
- Compounds contain more than one element.

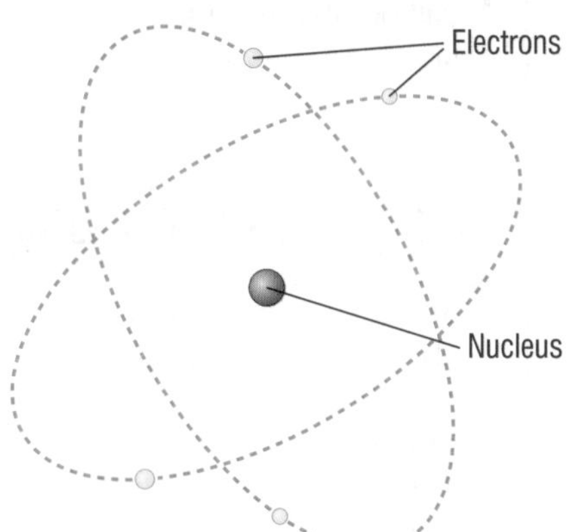

Atoms consist of a small nucleus surrounded by electrons

- There are about 100 different **elements** from which all substances are made. The periodic table is a list of the elements.

1 ***What substances are shown in the periodic table?***

- Each element is made of one type of **atom**.
- Atoms are represented by chemical symbols, e.g. Na for an atom of sodium, O for an atom of oxygen.
- The elements in the periodic table are arranged in columns, called **groups**. The elements in a group usually have similar properties.

2 ***What atom does H represent?***

- Atoms have a tiny **nucleus** surrounded by **electrons**.
- When elements react, their atoms join with atoms of other elements. **Compounds** are formed when two or more elements combine together.

3 ***What type of substance is sodium chloride, NaCl?***

Study tip

Remember that a symbol represents one atom of an element.

Key words: element, atom, group, nucleus, electron, compound

Group numbers

1	2											3	4	5	6	7	0
				H 1 Hydrogen													He 2 Helium
Li 3 Lithium	Be 4 Beryllium											B 5 Boron	C 6 Carbon	N 7 Nitrogen	O 8 Oxygen	F 9 Fluorine	Ne 10 Neon
Na 11 Sodium	Mg 12 Magnesium											Al 13 Aluminium	Si 14 Silicon	P 15 Phosphorus	S 16 Sulfur	Cl 17 Chlorine	Ar 18 Argon
K 19 Potassium	Ca 20 Calcium	Sc 21 Scandium	Ti 22 Titanium	V 23 Vanadium	Cr 24 Chromium	Mn 25 Manganese	Fe 26 Iron	Co 27 Cobalt	Ni 28 Nickel	Cu 29 Copper	Zn 30 Zinc	Ga 31 Gallium	Ge 32 Germanium	As 33 Arsenic	Se 34 Selenium	Br 35 Bromine	Kr 36 Krypton
Rb 37 Rubidium	Sr 38 Strontium	Y 39 Yttrium	Zr 40 Zirconium	Nb 41 Niobium	Mo 42 Molybdenum	Tc 43 Technetium	Ru 44 Ruthenium	Rh 45 Rhodium	Pd 46 Palladium	Ag 47 Silver	Cd 48 Cadmium	In 49 Indium	Sn 50 Tin	Sb 51 Antimony	Te 52 Tellurium	I 53 Iodine	Xe 54 Xenon
Cs 55 Caesium	Ba 56 Barium	Lanthanum see below	Hf 72 Hafnium	Ta 73 Tantalum	W 74 Tungsten	Re 75 Rhenium	Os 76 Osmium	Ir 77 Iridium	Pt 78 Platinum	Au 79 Gold	Hg 80 Mercury	Tl 81 Thallium	Pb 82 Lead	Bi 83 Bismuth	Po 84 Polonium	At 85 Astatine	Rn 86 Radon
Fr 87 Francium	Ra 88 Radium	Actinium see below															

The alkali metals (group 1) — The alkaline earth metals (group 2) — The transition metals — The halogens (group 7) — The noble gases (group 0)

Lanthanides	La 57 Lanthanum	Ce 58 Cerium	Pr 59 Praseodymium	Nd 60 Neodymium	Pm 61 Promethium	Sm 62 Samarium	Eu 63 Europium	Gd 64 Gadolinium	Tb 65 Terbium	Dy 66 Dysprosium	Ho 67 Holmium	Er 68 Erbium	Tm 69 Thulium	Yb 70 Ytterbium	Lu 71 Lutetium
Actinides	Ac 89 Actinium	Th 90 Thorium	Pa 91 Protactinium	U 92 Uranium	Np 93 Neptunium	Pu 94 Plutonium	Am 95 Americium	Cm 96 Curium	Bk 97 Berkelium	Cf 98 Californium	Es 99 Einsteinium	Fm 100 Fermium	Md 101 Mendelevium	No 102 Nobelium	Lr 103 Lawrencium

The periodic table shows the symbols for the elements

Student Book pages 136–137 **C1**

1.2 Atomic structure

Key points

- The nucleus of an atom is made of protons and neutrons.
- Protons have a positive charge, electrons a negative charge and neutrons are not charged.
- The atomic number (or proton number) of an element is equal to the number of protons in the nucleus of its atoms.
- Elements are arranged in order of their atomic numbers in the periodic table.
- The mass number is the sum of the protons and neutrons in the nucleus of an atom.

- The nucleus at the centre of an atom contains two types of particle, called **protons** and **neutrons**. Protons have a positive charge and neutrons have no charge.
- Electrons are tiny negatively charged particles that move around the nucleus. An atom has no overall charge. That is because the number of protons is equal to the number of electrons and their charges are equal and opposite (proton +1 and electron –1).

1 *Why are atoms neutral?*

- All atoms of an element contain the same number of protons. This number is called the **atomic number** (or proton number) of the element. Elements are arranged in order of their atomic numbers in the periodic table. The atomic number is also the number of electrons in an atom of the element.
- The **mass number** is the total number of particles in the nucleus of an atom, so it is the number of protons plus the number of neutrons.

2 ***How many protons, neutrons and electrons are there in an atom of aluminium (atomic number 13, mass number 27)?***

Maths skills

Work out the number of each type of particle in an atom of fluorine from its atomic number of 9 and its mass number of 19.

Number of protons = atomic number = 9

Number of electrons = number of protons = 9

Number of neutrons = mass number – atomic number = 19 – 9 = 10

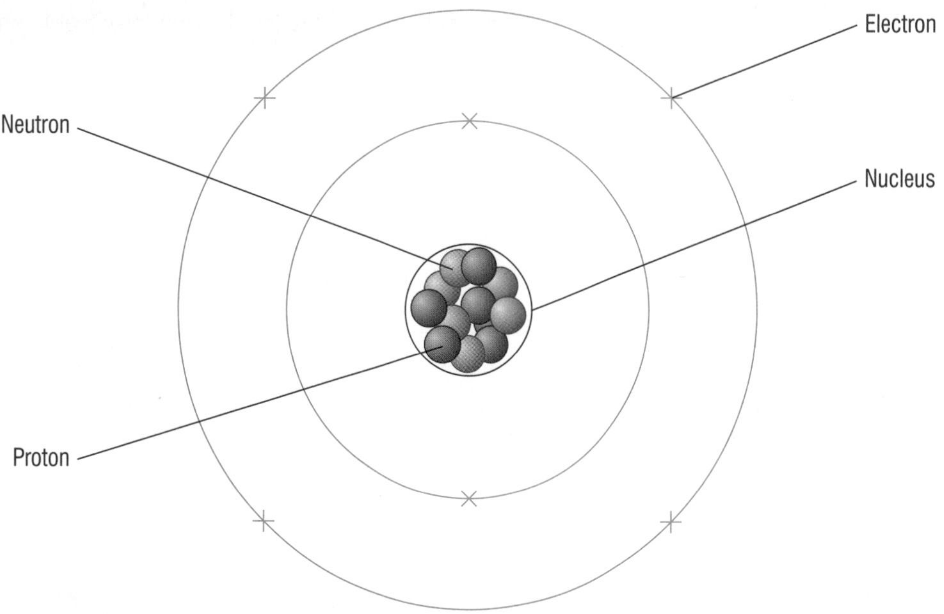

Understanding the structure of an atom gives us important clues to the way substances react together

Key words: proton, neutron, atomic number, mass number

Student Book pages 138–139 **C1**

Key points

- The atoms of the unreactive noble gases (in Group 0) all have very stable arrangements of electrons.
- Electrons in atoms are in energy levels that can be represented by shells.
- Electrons in the lowest energy level are in the shell closest to the nucleus.
- Electrons occupy the lowest energy levels first.
- All the elements in the same group of the periodic table have the same number of electrons in their highest energy level (outer shell).

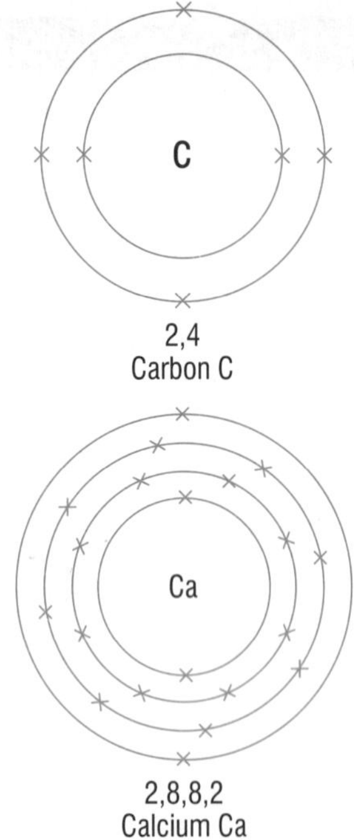

We can draw shells as circles on a diagram, with electrons represented by dots or crosses

1.3 The arrangement of electrons in atoms

- Each electron in an atom is in an **energy level**. Energy levels can be represented as **shells**, with electrons in the lowest energy level closest to the nucleus.
- The lowest energy level or first shell can hold two electrons, and the second energy level can hold eight. Electrons occupy the lowest possible energy levels. The **electronic structure** of neon with 10 electrons is 2,8. Sodium with 11 electrons has the electronic structure 2,8,1.

1 *Draw a diagram to show the electronic structure of an atom of aluminium (atomic number 13).*

- Elements in the same group of the periodic table have the same number of electrons in their highest energy level, e.g Group 1 elements have one electron in their highest energy level.

2 *Explain why nitrogen and phosphorus are both in Group 5 in the periodic table.*

- Group 1 elements include lithium, sodium and potassium. These elements react quickly with water and with oxygen.
- The atoms of the unreactive noble gases (in Group 0) all have very stable arrangements of electrons.

Bump up your grade

You should be able to work out the numbers of protons, neutrons and electrons for any atom from its atomic number and mass number.

Key words: energy level, shell, electronic structure

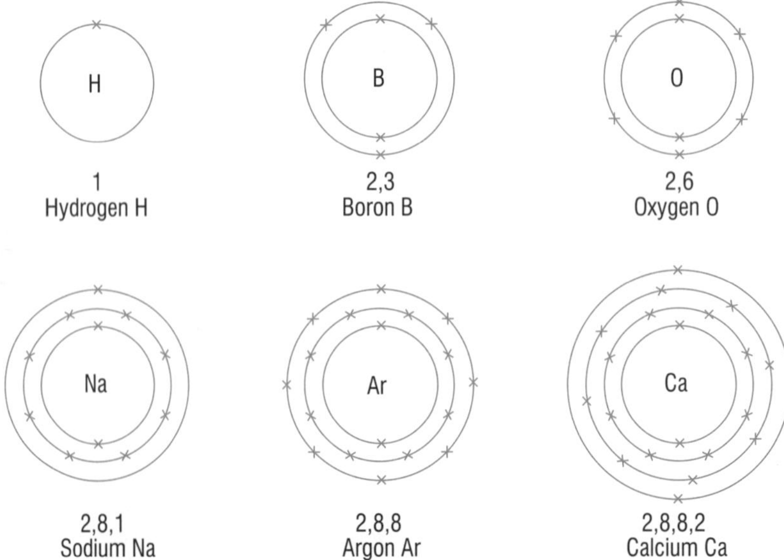

Once you know the pattern, you should be able to draw the energy levels of the electrons in any of the first 20 atoms (given their atomic number)

Student Book pages 140–141 **C1**

1.4 Forming bonds

Key points

- Compounds of metals bonded to non-metals have ionic bonds.
- The formula of an ionic compound shows the simplest ratio of ions.
- Compounds of non-metals have covalent bonds.
- The formula of a molecule shows the number of atoms in the molecule.

Study tip

The formula for ionic compounds and metallic elements is the simplest possible ratio, such as $MgCl_2$ or NaCl.

Study tip

For substances made of molecules the formula shows the number of atoms in the molecule, such as O_2 or C_2H_6.

- When different elements combine they form compounds.
- When a metal reacts with a non-metal, ions are formed. Metal atoms lose one or more electrons to form positively charged ions. Non-metal atoms gain electrons to form negatively charged ions. The oppositely charged ions attract each other strongly and the compound has **ionic bonds**.

1 *Name an example of a compound with ionic bonds.*

- The chemical formula of an ionic compound tells us the simplest ratio of ions in the compound. For example, NaCl shows that sodium chloride is made from equal numbers of sodium ions and chloride ions.

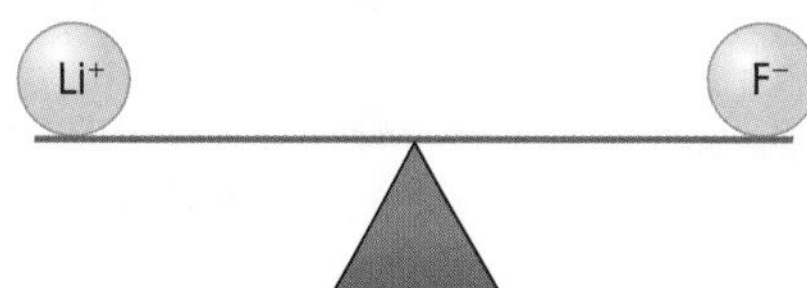

The positive and negative charge on the ions in a compound balance each other, making the total charge zero

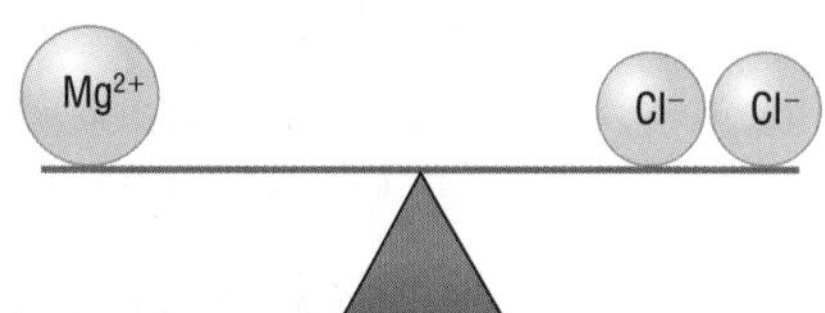

The 2+ positive charge on the magnesium ion balances the two 1– negative charges on the chloride ions in magnesium chloride ($MgCl_2$)

2 *Calcium chloride has the formula $CaCl_2$. What does this tell you about the compound?*

- When non-metals combine, their atoms share electrons to form **covalent bonds** and molecules are formed.
- The chemical formula of a molecule tells us the number of atoms that have bonded together in the molecule. For example, H_2O shows that a water molecule contains two hydrogen atoms and one oxygen atom. Covalent bonds can be shown as lines between the atoms that are bonded together.

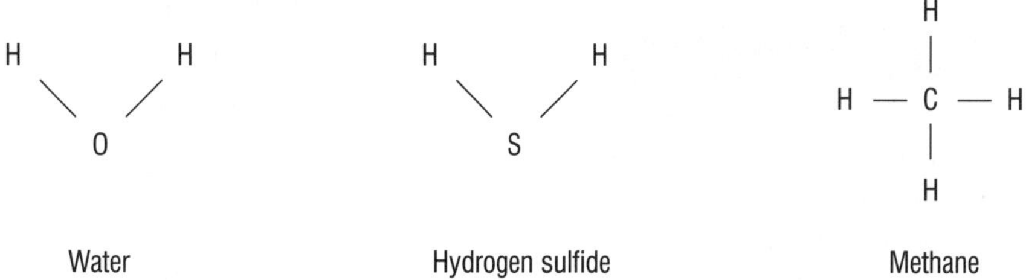

There are strong covalent bonds between the atoms in each of these molecules. These are shown as lines between the symbols of the atoms in the molecule.

3 *The formula of propane is C_3H_8. What does this tell you about propane?*

Key words: ionic bond, covalent bond

Student Book pages 142–143 **C1**

1.5 Chemical equations

Key points

- Atoms get re-arranged in chemical reactions.
- The mass of the products is equal to the mass of reactants.
- Symbol equations should always be balanced.

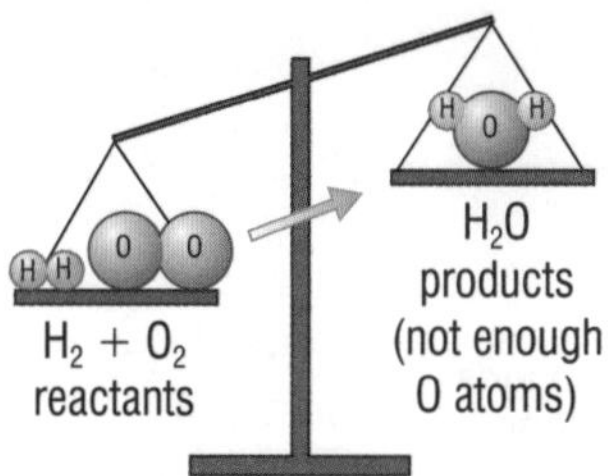

Not balanced

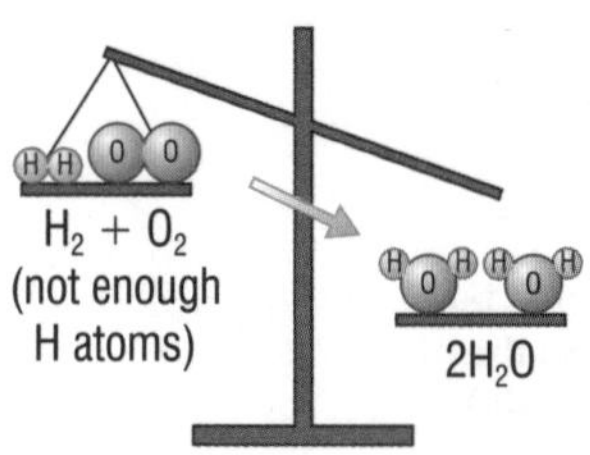

Still not balanced!

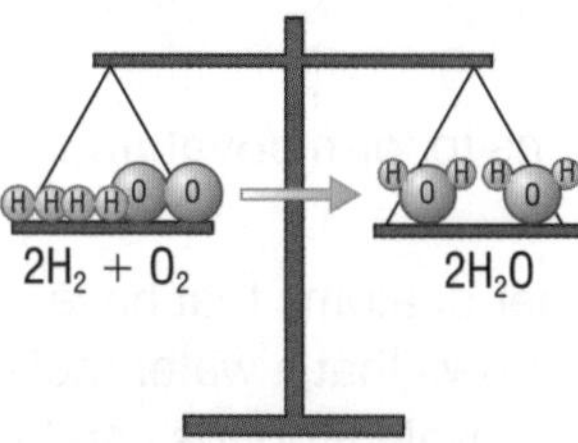

Balanced at last!

Making an equation balance

Study tip

Remember that in a balanced symbol equation a large number multiplies all of the atoms in the formula that follows.

- In chemical reactions the atoms in the reactants re-arrange themselves to form new substances, the products.
- Atoms are neither created nor destroyed in a chemical reaction. So the number and type of atoms remains the same before and after the reaction.
- This means that the mass of the **products** equals the mass of **reactants**.
- It also means that we can write chemical equations to represent reactions.
- Word equations only give the names of the reactants and products. Symbol equations show the numbers and types of atoms in the reactants and products.
- When symbol equations are written they should always be balanced.
- This means that the numbers of each type of atom should be the same on both sides of a symbol equation.

1 *Explain as fully as you can what this balanced symbol equation tells you:* $Mg + 2HCl \rightarrow MgCl_2 + H_2$

Making an equation balance

Symbol equations are balanced by changing the large numbers in front of the formulae of the reactants and products.

You should balance equations by changing only the large numbers. Never change the small (subscript) numbers because this changes the formula of the substance.

2 *Balance these equations:* **a** $H_2 + Cl_2 \rightarrow HCl$
b $Na + O_2 \rightarrow Na_2O$
c $Na_2CO_3 + HCl \rightarrow NaCl + H_2O + CO_2$

Bump up your grade

To improve your grade when taking the Higher Tier paper, learn how to balance a symbol equation given the formulae of the reactants and products.

Maths skills

In the formulae in symbol equations, small (subscript) numbers multiply only the atom they follow.

For example: In H_2SO_4 we have H_2 = 2 atoms of hydrogen, S = one atom of sulfur, O_4 = 4 atoms of oxygen.

If more than one atom within a formula has to be multiplied, brackets are used.

$Mg(NO_3)_2$ (one magnesium ion and two nitrate ions) is made from

one atom of magnesium   1 × 2 atoms of nitrogen   3 × 2 = 6 atoms of oxygen.

Large numbers multiply all atoms in the formula that follows. So $2CO_2$ (two molecules of carbon dioxide) shows a total of two carbon atoms and four oxygen atoms.

Key words: product, reactant

1 Sort these substances into elements and compounds: Ca, CH_4, H_2, HCl, MgO, Ne, O_2, SO_2.

2 What are the names and numbers of the particles in an atom of sodium (atomic number 11, mass number 23)?

3 What determines the order of the elements in the periodic table?

4 Draw a diagram to show the electronic structure of sulfur (atomic number 16).

5 Explain why boron and aluminium are both in the same group in the periodic table.

6 Name the type of bonds in each of these compounds: CaO, C_2H_6, H_2O, KCl, LiCl, $MgCl_2$, NH_3, Na_2O, PCl_3.

7 Explain what happens to the atoms when a sodium atom reacts with a chlorine atom.

8 The equation for a reaction of lead nitrate is:

$$Pb(NO_3)_2 + 2KI \rightarrow 2KNO_3 + PbI_2$$

a Write a word equation for this reaction.

b Give the name and number of each type of atom in the products.

9 Calcium carbonate decomposes when heated to produce calcium oxide and carbon dioxide. 20.0 g of calcium carbonate produced 11.2 g of calcium oxide. What mass of carbon dioxide would be produced?

10 Balance these symbol equations: [H]

a $Ca + O_2 \rightarrow CaO$

b $Na + H_2O \rightarrow NaOH + H_2$

c $CH_4 + O_2 \rightarrow CO_2 + H_2O$

Chapter checklist

✓ ✓ ✓

Tick when you have:

reviewed it after your lesson	✓	☐	☐
revised once – some questions right	✓	✓	☐
revised twice – all questions right	✓	✓	✓

Move on to another topic when you have all three ticks

Atoms, elements and compounds	☐	☐	☐
Atomic structure	☐	☐	☐
The arrangement of electrons in atoms	☐	☐	☐
Forming bonds	☐	☐	☐
Chemical equations	☐	☐	☐

Student Book pages 146–147 **C1**

2.1 Limestone and its uses

Key points

- Limestone is made mainly of calcium carbonate.
- Limestone is used as a building material and to make calcium oxide and cement.
- Cement mixed with sand, aggregate and water makes concrete.
- Calcium carbonate decomposes when heated to make calcium oxide and carbon dioxide.

- We quarry large amounts of limestone rock because it has many uses.
- Blocks of limestone can be used for building. Limestone is used to make calcium oxide and **cement**.
- We make **concrete** by mixing cement with sand, aggregate and water.
- Limestone is mainly **calcium carbonate**, $CaCO_3$.
- When heated strongly, calcium carbonate decomposes to make calcium oxide and carbon dioxide. This is done on a large scale in lime kilns. The equation for this reaction is:

$$\underset{\text{calcium carbonate}}{CaCO_3} \rightarrow \underset{\text{calcium oxide}}{CaO} + \underset{\text{carbon dioxide}}{CO_2}$$

- This type of reaction is called **thermal decomposition**.

1 *List the ways in which limestone and products made from limestone are used in the building industry.*

Study tip

Thermal decomposition means 'breaking down by heating'. You need to make both points – 'breaking down' and 'by heating' – to get full marks.

Key words: cement, concrete, calcium carbonate, thermal decomposition

Student Book pages 148–149 **C1**

2.2 Reactions of carbonates

Key points

- Metal carbonates decompose when heated to produce the metal oxide and carbon dioxide.
- Carbonates react with acids to produce a salt, water and carbon dioxide.
- Carbon dioxide turns limewater cloudy.

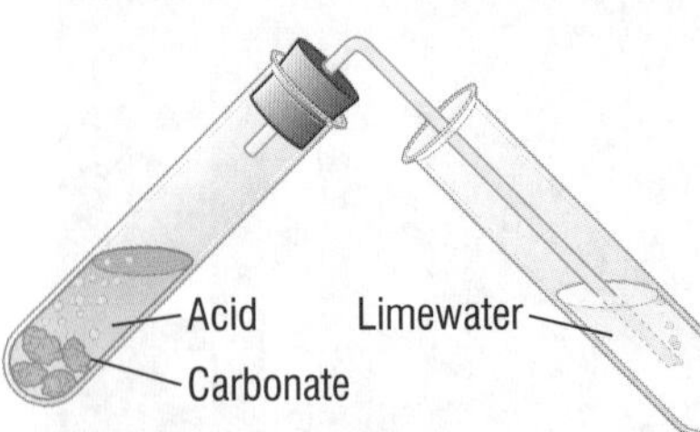

The test for carbonates

- All metal carbonates react in similar ways when heated or when reacted with acids.
- Metal carbonates decompose to the metal oxide and carbon dioxide when they are heated strongly enough.
- A Bunsen burner flame cannot get hot enough to decompose sodium carbonate or potassium carbonate.

1 *What are the products when zinc carbonate is heated strongly?*

- All carbonates react with acids to produce a salt, water and carbon dioxide gas. Limestone is damaged by acid rain because the calcium carbonate in the limestone reacts with acids in the rain.
- Calcium hydroxide solution is called limewater. **Limewater** is used to test for carbon dioxide. The limewater turns cloudy because it reacts with carbon dioxide to produce insoluble calcium carbonate.

2 *Write a word equation for the reaction of magnesium carbonate with hydrochloric acid.*

Key word: limewater

Student Book pages 150–151 **C1**

2.3 The 'limestone reaction cycle'

Key points

- Thermal decomposition of calcium carbonate produces calcium oxide and carbon dioxide.
- Calcium oxide reacts with water to produce calcium hydroxide.
- Calcium hydroxide is an alkali that can be used to neutralise acids.
- Calcium hydroxide reacts with carbon dioxide to produce calcium carbonate.

Bump up your grade

If you are taking the Higher Tier paper, you should be able to write balanced symbol equations for the three reactions in the 'limestone cycle'.

St Paul's Cathedral in London is built from limestone blocks

- When heated strongly the calcium carbonate in limestone decomposes to **calcium oxide** and carbon dioxide.
- When water is added to calcium oxide they react to produce **calcium hydroxide**.
- Calcium hydroxide is an alkali and so it can be used to neutralise acids. For example, it is used by farmers to neutralise acidic soils and in industry to neutralise acidic gases.
- Calcium hydroxide is not very soluble in water but dissolves slightly to make limewater.
- Calcium hydroxide reacts with carbon dioxide to produce calcium carbonate, the main compound in limestone.

1 *Write word equations for the three reactions in the 'limestone cycle'.*

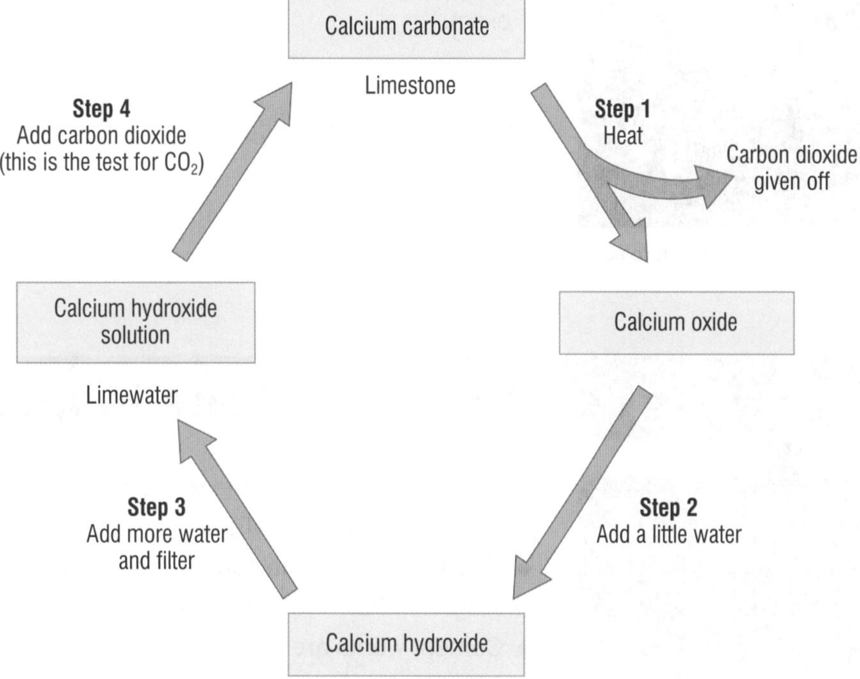

The 'limestone reaction cycle'

Key words: calcium oxide, calcium hydroxide

Student Book pages 152–153 **C1**

2.4 Cement and concrete

Key points

- Cement is made by heating limestone with clay in a kiln.
- Mortar is made by mixing cement and sand with water.
- Concrete is made by mixing aggregate with cement, sand and water.

Concrete is mixed, poured and left to set

- To make cement, limestone is mixed with clay and heated strongly in a kiln. The product is ground up to make a fine powder.
- Cement is mixed with sand and water to make **mortar**. The mortar is used to hold bricks and blocks together in buildings.
- Concrete is made by adding aggregate to cement, sand and water. Small stones or crushed rock are used as aggregate. The mixture can be poured into moulds before it sets to form a hard solid.

1 *What are the differences between cement, mortar and concrete?*

Study tip

You should have studied developments in using limestone, cement and concrete but you will not be tested on what you know about these developments in the exam.

Key word: mortar

Student Book pages 154–155 **C1**

2.5 Limestone issues 

Key points

- There are good and bad points about quarrying for limestone.
- Limestone, cement and concrete are needed as building materials.
- Quarrying and processing limestone and its products have negative impacts on the environment.

- We depend on limestone to provide building materials. Cement and concrete are needed in most buildings.
- Quarrying limestone can have negative impacts on the environment and on people living near to the quarries.
- Cement works are often close to limestone quarries. Making cement involves heating limestone with clay in large kilns. This uses a large area of land and a lot of energy.

1 *Sort the following into advantages and disadvantages for an area in which limestone is to be quarried.*

a *More employment opportunities for local people*
b *Dust and noise*
c *More traffic*
d *Loss of habitats for wildlife*
e *More customers and trade for local businesses*
f *Improved roads*

Study tip

You may be given information in the examination about building materials or the processes needed to make them so that you can consider their positive benefits and the negative aspects of their production and use.

1. **Which of these is the formula for the main compound in limestone?**
   $CaCl_2$, $CaCO_3$, $CaSO_4$, $Ca(OH)_2$

2. **How is cement made?**

3. **Name the four substances used to make concrete.**

4. **What is meant by 'thermal decomposition' of a compound?**

5. **Name the products formed when calcium carbonate is heated strongly.**

6. **Write a word equation for the reaction of calcium oxide with water.**

7. **Limewater goes cloudy when mixed with carbon dioxide. Explain why, using an equation in your answer.**

8. **Explain, as fully as you can, why acids damage limestone.**

9. **Farmers spread calcium hydroxide on fields with acidic soils. Explain why, naming the type of reaction that takes place and the property of calcium hydroxide on which this reaction depends.**

10. **Balance this symbol equation:**
    $K_2CO_3 + HCl \rightarrow KCl + H_2O + CO_2$ [H]

Chapter checklist ✓✓✓

Tick when you have:			
reviewed it after your lesson	✓	☐	☐
revised once – some questions right	✓	✓	☐
revised twice – all questions right	✓	✓	✓

Move on to another topic when you have all three ticks

Limestone and its uses	☐	☐	☐
Reactions of carbonates	☐	☐	☐
The 'limestone reaction cycle'	☐	☐	☐
Cement and concrete	☐	☐	☐
Limestone issues	☐	☐	☐

Student Book pages 158–159 **C1**

3.1 Extracting metals

Key points

- Metals are usually found in the Earth's crust. They are often combined chemically with other elements such as oxygen.
- An ore contains enough metal to make it worth extracting the metal.
- The method we use to extract a metal depends on its reactivity.
- Unreactive metals are found in the Earth as the metal.
- The oxides of metals less reactive than carbon can be reduced using carbon.

- Rock that contains enough of a metal or a metal compound to make it worth extracting the metal is called an **ore**.
- Mining ores often involves digging up large amounts of rock. The ore may need to be concentrated before the metal is extracted. These processes can produce large amounts of waste and may have major impacts on the environment.

1 *What is an ore?*

- A few unreactive metals, low in the **reactivity series**, such as gold are found in the Earth as the metal. Gold can be separated from rocks by physical methods. However, most metals are found as compounds. So then the metals have to be extracted by chemical reactions.
- Metals can be extracted from compounds by displacement using a more reactive element. Metals which are less reactive than carbon can be extracted from their oxides by heating with carbon. A **reduction** reaction takes place as carbon removes the oxygen from the oxide to produce the metal. This method is used commercially if possible.

2 **a** *Name two metals that have oxides that can be reduced by carbon?*
b *What do we call the removal of oxygen from a metal oxide?*

Bump up your grade

If you are taking the Higher Tier paper, you should be able to write a balanced symbol equation for the reduction of a named metal oxide by carbon.

Key words: ore, reactivity series, reduction

An open-cast copper mine

Student Book pages 160–161 **C1**

3.2 Iron and steels

Key points

- Iron oxide is reduced in a blast furnace to make iron.
- Iron from the blast furnace is too brittle for many uses.
- Most iron is converted into alloys called steels.
- Steels contain carefully controlled quantities of carbon and other elements.

- Many of the ores used to produce iron contain iron(III) oxide. Iron(III) oxide is reduced at high temperatures in a **blast furnace** using carbon. The iron produced contains about 96% iron. The impurities make it hard and brittle and so it has only a few uses as **cast iron**. Removing all of the carbon and other impurities makes pure iron, but this is too soft for many uses.

1 *Why does iron from the blast furnace have only a few uses?*

- Most iron is used to make **steels**. Steels are **alloys** of iron because they are mixtures of iron with carbon and other elements. Alloys can be made so that they have properties for specific uses.

Steels have many uses in modern buildings

- The amounts of carbon and other elements are carefully adjusted when making steels. Low-carbon steels are easily shaped and high-carbon steels are hard.
- Some steels, such as **stainless steels,** contain larger quantities of other metals. They resist corrosion.

2 *Why are steels more useful than pure iron?*

Key words: blast furnace, cast iron, steel, alloy, stainless steel

Student Book pages 162–163 C1

3.3 Aluminium and titanium

Key points

- Aluminium and titanium resist corrosion. They also have low densities compared with other strong metals.
- Aluminium and titanium cannot be extracted from their oxides using carbon.
- Aluminium and titanium are expensive because extracting them involves many stages and requires large amounts of energy.

- **Aluminium** has a low density and, although it is quite high in the reactivity series, it is resistant to corrosion.
- Aluminium is more reactive than carbon and so its oxide cannot be reduced using carbon.
- It has to be extracted by electrolysis of molten aluminium oxide. The process requires high temperatures and a lot of electricity. This makes aluminium expensive to extract.
- Pure aluminium is not very strong, but aluminium alloys are stronger and harder. They have many uses.

1 *Why is it expensive to extract aluminium from its ore?*

- **Titanium** is resistant to corrosion and is very strong. It also has a low density compared with other strong metals.
- Titanium oxide can be reduced by carbon, but the metal reacts with carbon making it brittle.
- Titanium is extracted from its ore by a process that involves several stages and large amounts of energy. The high costs of the process make titanium expensive.

2 *Why is titanium a very useful metal for making aircraft engines?*

Titanium turbine blades in a jet engine

Study tip

You do not need to remember any further details of the methods used to extract these metals.

Bump up your grade

Learn some of the properties and uses for each of the metals named in this chapter.

Key words: aluminium, titanium

Student Book pages 164–165 **C1**

3.4 Extracting copper

Key points

- Most copper is extracted from copper-rich ores by smelting.
- Copper can be purified by electrolysis.
- Bioleaching and phytomining are new ways to extract copper from low-grade ores.
- Copper can be obtained from solutions of copper salts by displacement or electrolysis.

- Copper can be extracted from **copper-rich ores** by **smelting**. This means heating the ore strongly in a furnace.
- Smelting produces impure copper, which can be purified by electrolysis.
- Smelting and purifying copper ore require huge amounts of heating and electricity.
- Copper-rich ores are a limited resource. Scientists are developing new ways of extracting copper from low-grade ores. These methods can have less environmental impact than smelting.
- **Phytomining** uses plants to absorb copper compounds from the ground. The plants are burned and produce ash from which copper can be extracted.
- **Bioleaching** uses bacteria to produce solutions containing copper compounds.

1 *Why are new ways of extracting copper being researched?*

Pure copper plates produced by electrolysis

- Solutions of copper compounds can be reacted with a metal that is more reactive than copper, such as scrap iron, to **displace** the copper.
- Copper can also be extracted from solutions of copper compounds by electrolysis.

2 *What three ways can be used to produce copper metal from its compounds?*

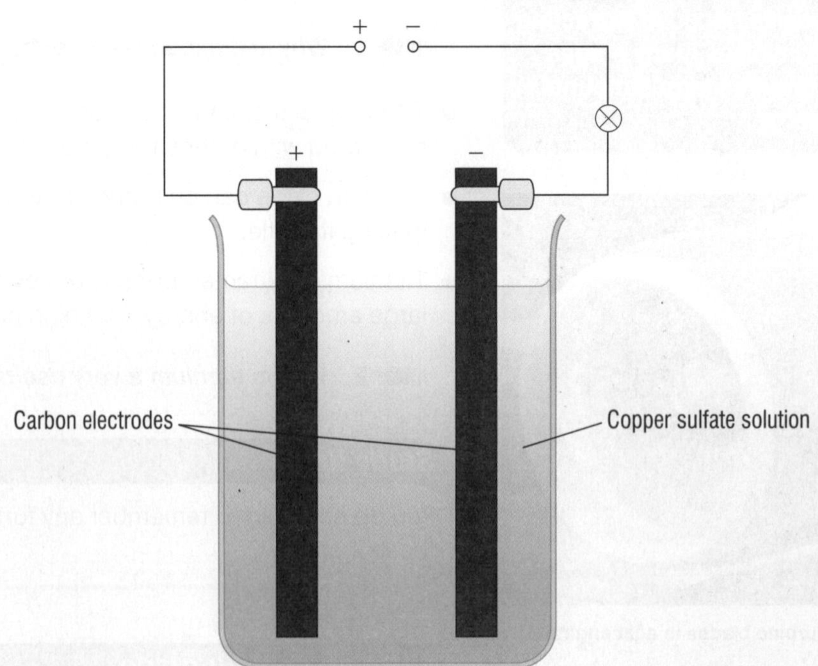

Extracting copper metal using electricity

Key words: copper-rich ore, smelting, phytomining, bioleaching, displace

Student Book pages 166–167 **C1**

3.5 Useful metals

Key points

- The transition metals are found in the central block of the periodic table.
- Transition metals have properties that make them useful for building and making things.
- Most of the metals we use are alloys.

Alloys are used to make some musical instruments

Study tip

When asked for the properties of alloys, many students include cost or cheapness but cost is not a property of a substance.

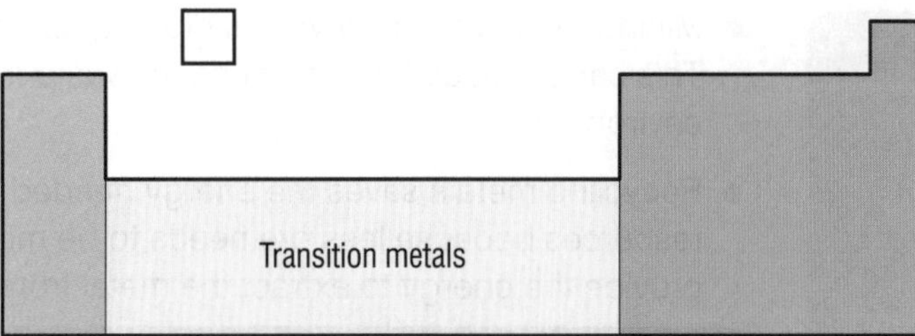

The position of the transition metals in the periodic table

- Elements from the central block of the periodic table are known as the **transition metals**.
- They are all metals and have similar properties.
- They are good conductors of heat and electricity.
- Many of them are strong, but can be bent or hammered into shape. These properties make them useful as materials for buildings, vehicles, containers, pipes and wires.

1 *What properties make transition metals useful materials for making things?*

- Copper is a very good conductor of heat and does not react with water. It can be bent but it is hard enough to keep its shape. These properties make it useful for making pipes and tanks in water and heating systems. It is a very good conductor of electricity as well and so it is used for electrical wiring.

2 *What properties are needed for electrical wiring?*

- Most of the metals we use are not pure elements.
- Pure iron, copper, gold and aluminium are soft and easily bent. They are often mixed with other elements to make alloys that are harder so that they keep their shape.
- Iron is made into steels (see C1 3.2).
- Gold used for jewellery is usually an alloy.
- Most of the aluminium used for buildings and aircraft is alloyed.
- Copper alloys include bronze and brass.

3 *Why is the gold used for wedding rings mixed with other metals?*

Key words: transition metal

Student Book pages 168–169 **C1**

3.6 Metallic issues

Key points

- There are social, economic and environmental issues associated with exploiting metal ores.
- Recycling saves energy and limited resources.
- There are drawbacks as well as benefits from the use of metals in structures.

Steel girders are used in many buildings

- Mining for metal ores involves digging up and processing large amounts of rock. This can produce large amounts of waste material and effect large areas of the environment.
- Recycling metals saves the energy needed to extract the metal. Recycling saves resources because less ore needs to be mined. Also, less fossil fuel is needed to provide the energy to extract the metal from its ore.

1 *Why should we recycle aluminium cans?*

- The benefits of using metals in construction should be carefully considered against the drawbacks. Some examples are shown in the table below.

Some benefits of using metals in construction	Some drawbacks of using metals in construction
• they are strong • they can be bent into shape • they can be made into flexible wires • they are good electrical conductors	• obtaining metals from ores causes pollution and uses up limited resources • metals are more expensive than other materials such as concrete • iron and steel can rust

2 ***Use the information in this chapter to explain the benefits and drawbacks of using steel for girders in buildings.***

Study tip

You do not need to remember details or specific examples of uses of metals beyond those given in C1 Topics 3.1 to 3.5, but you should be prepared to discuss and evaluate information you are given in the examination.

Bump up your grade

To gain the highest grade, you should be able to write a clear evaluation of information you are given about metals, identifying benefits and drawbacks and giving a conclusion.

1. What is the name for rock that is mined from which metal can be extracted economically?
2. Why is gold found in the Earth as the metal?
3. What are the typical properties of 'transition metals'?
4. Explain why most of the metals we use are not pure elements.
5. Describe a reaction that is used to get iron from iron oxide. Write a word equation for the reaction.
6. Name three types of steel and give an important property for each one.
7. Explain why all steels are alloys.
8. Give three properties that make aluminium a useful metal.
9. Give three reasons why titanium is expensive.
10. Suggest three reasons why we should recycle iron and steel.
11. Name two methods, other than smelting, of extracting copper from low-grade ores. Describe how one of these methods can be used to make copper.
12. Balance these equations:
    $Fe_2O_3 + C \rightarrow Fe + CO_2$
    $Na + TiCl_4 \rightarrow Ti + NaCl$ [H]

Chapter checklist ✓✓✓

Tick when you have:			
reviewed it after your lesson	✓	☐	☐
revised once – some questions right	✓	✓	☐
revised twice – all questions right	✓	✓	✓

Move on to another topic when you have all three ticks

Extracting metals	☐	☐	☐
Iron and steels	☐	☐	☐
Aluminium and titanium	☐	☐	☐
Extracting copper	☐	☐	☐
Useful metals	☐	☐	☐
Metallic issues	☐	☐	☐

Student Book pages 172–173 **C1**

4.1 Fuels from crude oil

Key points

- Crude oil is a mixture of many different compounds.
- Distillation can be used to separate mixtures of liquids.
- Most of the compounds in crude oil are hydrocarbons – they contain only hydrogen and carbon.
- Alkanes are saturated hydrocarbons. They contain as many hydrogen atoms as possible in their molecules.

Study tip

Remember that the boiling point of a substance is the temperature at which its liquid boils when it is heated. When its gas is cooled it condenses at the same temperature.

An oil refinery at night

- Crude oil contains many different compounds that boil at different temperatures. These burn under different conditions and so crude oil needs to be separated to make useful fuels.
- We can separate a **mixture** of liquids by **distillation**. Simple distillation of crude oil can produce liquids that boil within different temperature ranges. These liquids are called **fractions**.

1 *What are fractions?*

- Most of the compounds in crude oil are **hydrocarbons**. This means that their molecules contain only hydrogen and carbon. Many of these hydrocarbons are **alkanes**, with the general formula C_nH_{2n+2}. Alkanes contain only single carbon-carbon bonds, they do not contain any C=C double bonds. Therefore each carbon atom in an alkane molecule bonds to as many hydrogen atoms as is possible and no more hydrogen atoms can be added and so we call them **saturated hydrocarbons**.

2 *How can you tell that the substance with the formula C_5H_{12} is an alkane?*

- We can represent molecules in different ways. A molecular formula shows the number of each type of atom in each molecule, e.g. C_2H_6 represents a molecule of ethane. We can also represent molecules by a **displayed formula** that shows how the atoms are bonded together.

```
   H  H            H  H  H             H  H  H  H
   |  |            |  |  |             |  |  |  |
H—C—C—H         H—C—C—C—H          H—C—C—C—C—H
   |  |            |  |  |             |  |  |  |
   H  H            H  H  H             H  H  H  H
  Ethane          Propane              Butane
```

We can represent alkanes like this, showing all of the atoms and the covalent bonds in each molecule

3 *What is the molecular formula of butane?*

Key words: mixture, distillation, fraction, hydrocarbon, alkane, saturated hydrocarbon

4.2 Fractional distillation

Key points

- Crude oil is separated into fractions using fractional distillation.
- The properties of each fraction depend on the size of the hydrocarbon molecules.
- Fractions with lower boiling points are less viscous and burn more easily.

Study tip

Simple distillation is done in steps by heating the mixture to different temperatures. Fractional distillation is done continuously by vaporising the mixture and condensing the fractions at different temperatures.

- Crude oil is separated into fractions at refineries using **fractional distillation**. This can be done because the boiling point of a hydrocarbon depends on the size of its molecule. The larger the molecule, the higher the boiling point of the hydrocarbon.
- The crude oil is vaporised and fed into a fractionating column. This is a tall tower that is hot at the bottom and gets cooler going up the column.

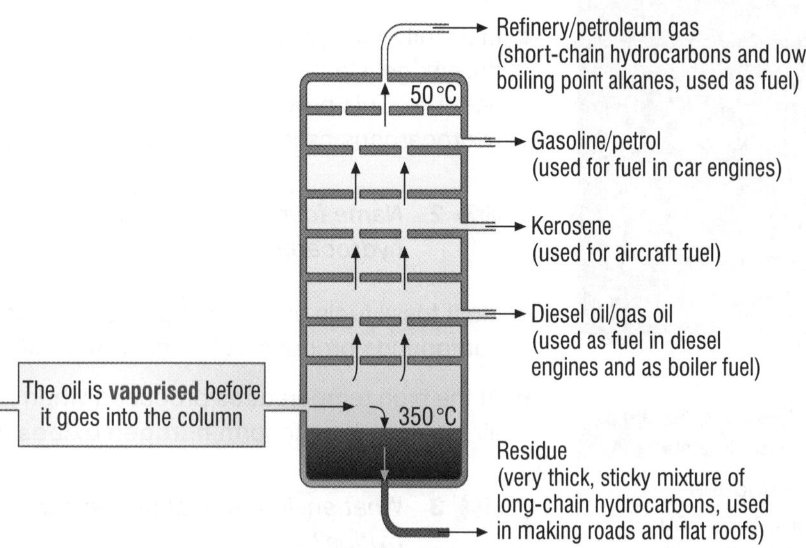

We use fractional distillation to separate crude oil into fractions. Each fraction contains compounds with similar boiling points.

- Inside the column there are many trays with holes to allow gases through. The vapours move up the column getting cooler as they go up. The hydrocarbons condense to liquids when they reach the level that is at their boiling point. Different liquids collect on the trays at different levels and there are outlets to collect the fractions.
- Hydrocarbons with the smallest molecules have the lowest boiling points and so are collected at the top of the column. The fractions collected at the bottom of the column contain hydrocarbons with the highest boiling points.

1 ***Why are different hydrocarbons collected at different levels of a fractional distillation column?***

- Fractions with low boiling ranges have low **viscosity** so they are runny liquids. They are very **flammable** so they ignite easily. They also burn with clean flames, producing little smoke. This makes them very useful as fuels.

2 ***What properties would you expect for a fraction that is collected one-third of the way up a fractionating column?***

Key words: fractional distillation, viscosity, flammable

Student Book pages 176–177 C1

4.3 Burning fuels

Key points

- Burning hydrocarbons in plenty of air produces carbon dioxide and water.
- Burning hydrocarbons in a limited supply of air may produce carbon monoxide and solid particles.
- Any sulfur compounds in the fuel burn to produce sulfur dioxide.
- Oxides of nitrogen can be formed when fuels burn under extreme conditions.

Bump up your grade

If you are taking the Higher Tier paper, you should be able to write balanced symbol equations for the complete and incomplete combustion of a hydrocarbon when given its formula.

- When pure hydrocarbons burn completely they are **oxidised** to carbon dioxide and water. However, the fuels we use are not always burned completely. They may also contain other substances.

1 *Write a word equation for the complete combustion of ethane.*

- In a limited supply of air **incomplete combustion** may produce **carbon monoxide**. Carbon may also be produced and some of the hydrocarbons may not burn. This produces solid particles that contain soot (carbon) and unburnt hydrocarbons called **particulates**.

2 *Name four possible products of the incomplete combustion of a hydrocarbon.*

- Most fossil fuels contain sulfur compounds. When the fuel burns these sulfur compounds produce **sulfur dioxide**. Sulfur dioxide causes acid rain.
- At the high temperatures produced when fuels burn, oxygen and nitrogen in the air may combine to form **nitrogen oxides**. Nitrogen oxides also cause acid rain.

3 *What environmental problem is caused by sulfur dioxide and nitrogen oxides?*

Key words: oxidised, incomplete combustion, carbon monoxide, particulate, sulfur dioxide, nitrogen oxide

Student Book pages 178–179 C1

4.4 Cleaner fuels

Key points

- Many scientists believe that carbon dioxide from burning fuels causes global warming.
- Sulfur dioxide and nitrogen oxides cause acid rain.
- Particulates cause global dimming.
- Pollutants can be removed from waste gases after the fuel is burned.
- Sulfur can be removed from fuels before they are burned so less sulfur dioxide is given off.

- We burn large amounts of fuels and this releases substances that spread throughout the atmosphere and affect the environment.
- Burning any fuel that contains carbon produces carbon dioxide. Carbon dioxide is a greenhouse gas that many scientists believe is the cause of **global warming**. Incomplete combustion of these fuels produces the poisonous gas carbon monoxide. It can also produce tiny solid particulates that reflect sunlight and so cause **global dimming**.

1 *Name the product of incomplete combustion that scientists believe causes global dimming.*

- Burning fuels also produces sulfur dioxide and nitrogen oxides. These gases dissolve in water droplets and react with oxygen in the air to produce acid rain.
- We can remove harmful substances from waste gases before they are released into the atmosphere. Sulfur dioxide is removed from the waste gases from power stations. Exhaust systems of cars are fitted with catalytic converters to remove carbon monoxide and nitrogen oxides. Filters can remove particulates.

A combination of many cars in a small area and the right weather conditions can cause smog to be formed. This is a mixture of SMoke and fOG.

- Sulfur can be removed from fuels before they are supplied to users so that less sulfur dioxide is produced when the fuel is burned.

2 *What two methods are used to reduce the amount of sulfur dioxide produced by burning fuels?*

Key words: global warming, global dimming

Student Book pages 180–181 **C1**

Key points

- Biodiesel can be made from vegetable oils.
- Biofuels are a renewable source of energy that could be used instead of fossil fuels.
- There are advantages and disadvantages of using biodiesel.
- Ethanol made from sugar is a biofuel.
- Hydrogen is a potential fuel for the future.

Study tip

You do not need to remember specific examples of advantages and disadvantages of biodiesel, but should be able to evaluate any information that is given in the examination.

Growing plants for biodiesel uses a lot of farmland

4.5 Alternative fuels

- **Biofuels** are made from plant or animal products and are renewable. **Biodiesel** can be made from vegetable oils extracted from plants.
- There are advantages to using biodiesel. For example, it makes little contribution to carbon dioxide levels. This is because the carbon dioxide given off when it burns was taken from the atmosphere by plants as they grew.
- There are also disadvantages, for example the plants that are grown for biodiesel use large areas of farmland.
- Ethanol made from sugar cane or sugar beet is a biofuel. It is a liquid and so can be stored and distributed like other liquid fuels. It can be mixed with petrol.

1 *Name two biofuels.*

How Science Works

- Using hydrogen as a fuel has the advantage that it produces only water when it is burned.
- However, it is a gas so it takes up a large volume. That makes it difficult to store in the quantities needed for combustion in engines.
- It can be produced from water by electrolysis but this requires large amounts of energy.

2 *Give one advantage and one disadvantage of hydrogen as a fuel.*

Cars run on biodiesel produce very little CO_2 overall, as CO_2 is absorbed by plants as the fuel is made

Key words: biofuel, biodiesel

End of chapter questions

1. Why is crude oil separated into fractions?
2. Name the products when ethane, C_2H_6, burns completely.
3. Give three reasons why fractions with lower boiling points are more useful as fuels.
4. Name two fuels that can be made from renewable sources.
5. Some exhaust fumes contain particulates. What are particulates and how are they produced?
6. Explain why burning some fuels produces sulfur dioxide.
7. Propane, C_3H_8, is used as a fuel for cookers. Explain why propane should always be burned in a plentiful supply of air.
8. Why are some scientists concerned about the carbon dioxide produced by burning fossil fuels?
9. Pentane has the formula C_5H_{12}. Draw a displayed formula for pentane and write down four facts about pentane that you can deduce from its formula.
10. Explain what happens in a fractional distillation column used to separate crude oil.
11. Write a balanced symbol equation for the complete combustion of ethanol, C_2H_6O. [H]
12. Write a balanced symbol equation for the reaction of hydrogen with oxygen. Explain why scientists are interested in using hydrogen as a fuel. [H]

Chapter checklist ✓✓✓

Tick when you have:							
reviewed it after your lesson	✓	☐	☐	Fuels from crude oil	☐	☐	☐
revised once – some questions right	✓	✓	☐	Fractional distillation	☐	☐	☐
revised twice – all questions right	✓	✓	✓	Burning fuels	☐	☐	☐
				Cleaner fuels	☐	☐	☐
Move on to another topic when you have all three ticks				Alternative fuels	☐	☐	☐

Student Book pages 184–185 **C1**

5.1 Cracking hydrocarbons

Key points

- Hydrocarbon molecules can be broken down by heating them with steam to a very high temperature or by passing their vapours over a hot catalyst.
- Cracking produces alkanes and alkenes.
- Alkenes are unsaturated hydrocarbons.
- Alkenes turn bromine water from orange to colourless.

$$\mathrm{H_2C{=}CH_2}$$
Ethene

$$\mathrm{CH_3{-}CH{=}CH_2}$$
Propene

Double bond

A molecule of ethene and a molecule of propene. These are both alkenes – each molecule has a carbon–carbon double bond in it.

In an oil refinery huge crackers like this are used to break down large hydrocarbon molecules into smaller ones

- Large hydrocarbon molecules can be broken down into smaller molecules by a process called **cracking**.
- Cracking can be done in two ways:
  - by heating a mixture of hydrocarbon vapours and steam to a very high temperature
  - by passing hydrocarbon vapours over a hot catalyst.
- During cracking thermal decomposition reactions produce a mixture of smaller molecules. Some of the smaller molecules are alkanes, which are saturated hydrocarbons with the general formula C_nH_{2n+2}. These alkanes with smaller molecules are more useful as fuels.

> **1** ***Give one reason why an oil company might want to crack large hydrocarbons to make smaller alkanes.***

- Some of the other smaller molecules formed are hydrocarbons with the general formula C_nH_{2n}. These are called **alkenes**. Alkenes are **unsaturated hydrocarbons** because they contain fewer hydrogen atoms than alkanes with the same number of carbon atoms.

$$\underset{\text{decane}}{C_{10}H_{22}} \xrightarrow{800\,^{\circ}\text{C} + \text{catalyst}} \underset{\text{pentane}}{C_5H_{12}} + \underset{\text{propene}}{C_3H_6} + \underset{\text{ethene}}{C_2H_4}$$

An example of a cracking reaction

- Alkenes have a **double bond** between two carbon atoms and this makes them more reactive than alkanes. Alkenes react with bromine water turning it from orange to colourless.

> **2** ***Give three ways in which alkenes are different from alkanes.***

Study tip

Different mixtures of alkanes and alkenes can be produced by cracking because different hydrocarbons can be used and the conditions for the reaction can be changed.

Key words: cracking, alkene, unsaturated hydrocarbon, double bond

Student Book pages 186–187 C1

5.2 Making polymers from alkenes

Key points

- Plastics are made of polymers.
- Polymers are large molecules made when many small molecules (monomers) join together.
- Alkenes can be used to make polymers such as poly(ethene) and poly(propene).

Containers like these are made from poly(ethene) and poly(propene)

Study tip

Double bonds in the monomer become single bonds in the polymer when the molecules have joined together.

- Plastics are made of very large molecules called **polymers**. Polymers are made from many small molecules joined together. The small molecules used to make polymers are called **monomers**. The reaction to make a polymer is called **polymerisation**.

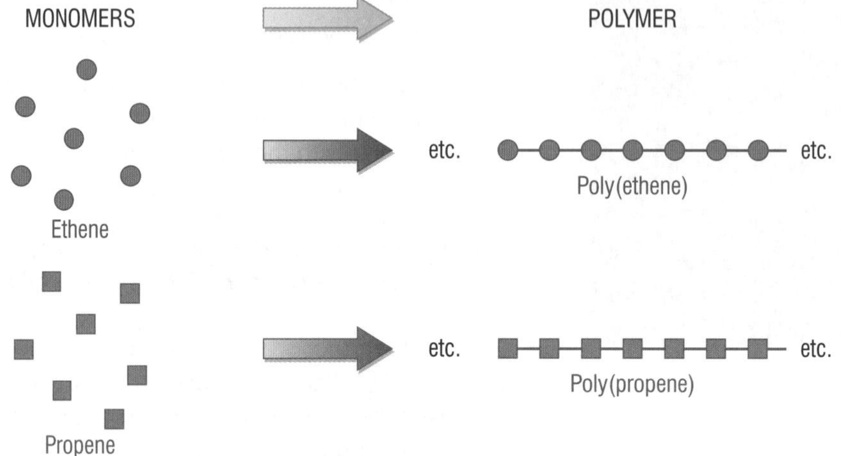

Polymers are made from many smaller molecules called monomers

1 *How are polymers made?*

- Lots of **ethene** (C_2H_4) molecules can join together to form poly(ethene), commonly called polythene. In the polymerisation reaction the double bond in each ethene molecule becomes a single bond and thousands of ethene molecules join together in long chains.

$$n\,\mathrm{CH_2{=}CH_2} \longrightarrow \left(\mathrm{-CH_2-CH_2-}\right)_n$$

Many single ethene monomers → Long chain of poly(ethene)

where n is a large number

2 *How many monomers are there in a poly(ethene) molecule?*

- Other alkenes can polymerise in a similar way. For example, **propene** (C_3H_6), can form poly(propene).
- Many of the plastics we use as bags, bottles, containers and toys are made from alkenes.

3 *Why can we make polymers from alkenes but not from alkanes?*

Bump up your grade

Learn to recognise monomers and polymers from diagrams. You should be able to draw the structure of the polymer made from a given monomer.

Key words: polymer, monomer, polymerisation, ethene, propene

Student Book pages 188–189 **C1**

5.3 New and useful polymers

Key points

- New polymers are being developed all the time.
- Polymers are designed to have properties that make them specially suited for certain uses.
- We are now recycling more plastics and finding new uses for them.

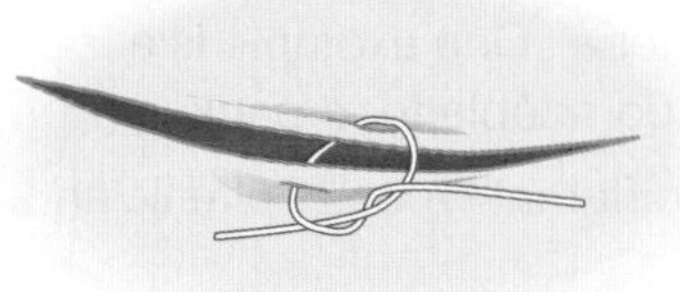

A shape-memory polymer uses the temperature of the body to make the thread tighten and close the wound

Recycling bottles like these can produce fibres for clothes or duvets

- Materials scientists can design new polymers to make materials with special properties for particular uses. Many of these materials are used for packaging, clothing and medical applications.
- New polymer materials for dental fillings have been developed to replace fillings that contain mercury. Light-sensitive polymers are used in sticking plasters to cover wounds so the plasters can be easily removed. Hydrogels are polymers that can trap water and have many uses including dressings for wounds.
- Shape-memory polymers change back to their original shape when temperature or other conditions are changed. An example of this type of **smart polymer** is a material used for stitching wounds that changes shape when heated to body temperature.

1 *What is a shape-memory polymer?*

- The fibres used to make fabrics can be coated with polymers to make them waterproof and breathable.
- The plastic used to make many drinks bottles can be recycled to make polyester fibres for clothing as well as filling pillows and duvets.

2 *Give two medical uses and two non-medical uses for polymers.*

Study tip

You should know some of the ways that polymers are used but you do not have to remember the names of specific polymers.

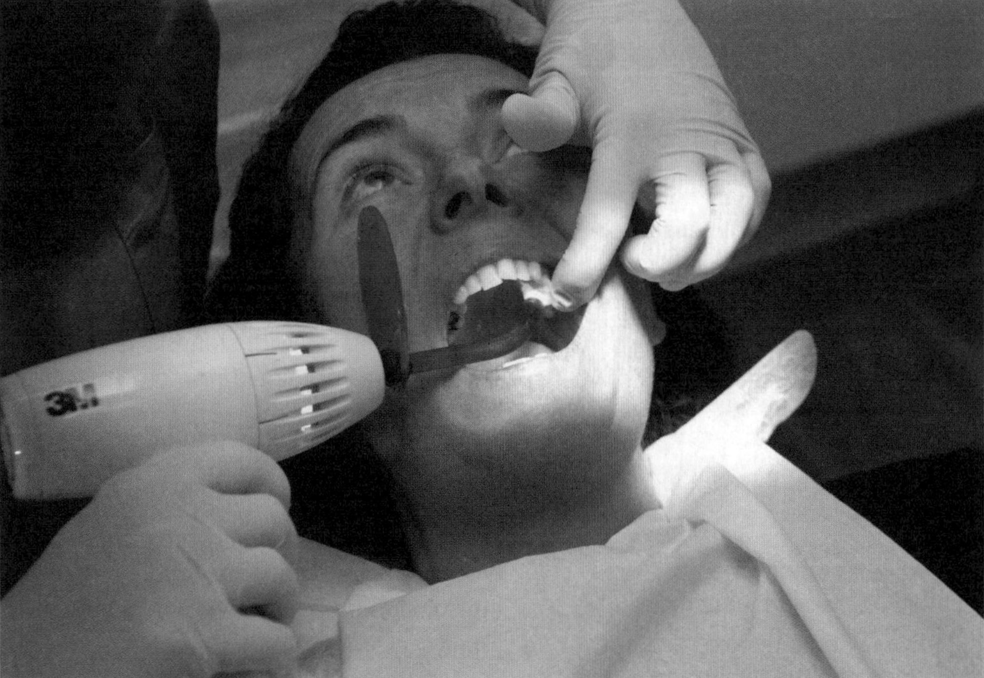

A dentist using UV light to set a filling made from a light-sensitive polymer

Key words: smart polymer

Student Book pages 190–191 **C1**

Key points

- Non-biodegradable plastics cause unsightly rubbish, can harm wildlife and take up space in landfill sites.
- Biodegradable plastics are decomposed by the action of microorganisms in soil.
- Making plastics with starch granules in their structure helps the microorganisms break down a plastic.
- We can make biodegradable plastics from plant material such as cornstarch.

5.4 Plastic waste

- Many polymers are not **biodegradable**. This means that plastic waste is not broken down when left in the environment. Unless disposed of properly, plastic rubbish gets everywhere. It is unsightly and can harm wildlife. Even when put into landfill sites it takes up valuable space.
- We are using more plastics that are biodegradable. Microorganisms can break down biodegradable plastics. These plastics break down when in contact with soil.

1 ***How would using biodegradable plastics help with the problems of plastic litter?***

- Plastics made from non-biodegradable polymers can have cornstarch mixed into the plastic. Microorganisms break down the cornstarch so the plastic breaks down into very small pieces that can be mixed with soil or compost.
- Biodegradable plastics can be made from plant material. One example is a polymer made from cornstarch that is used as biodegradable food packaging.
- Some plastics can be recycled but there are many different types of plastic and sorting is difficult.

2 ***Describe the two ways that cornstarch can be used to help with problems of disposal of plastic waste.***

Key word: biodegradable

Student Book pages 192–193 **C1**

Key points

- Ethanol can be made by fermenting sugar using enzymes in yeast.
- Ethanol can also be made by hydration of ethene with steam in the presence of a catalyst.
- Using ethene to make ethanol needs non-renewable crude oil whereas fermentation uses renewable plant material.

Bump up your grade

You should be able to describe the two ways of making ethanol and write balanced symbol equations for the reactions.

5.5 Ethanol

- Ethanol has the formula C_2H_6O. It is often written as C_2H_5OH. This shows the OH group in the molecule and that means it is an alcohol.
- Ethanol can be produced by the **fermentation** of sugar from plants using yeast.
- Enzymes in the yeast cause the sugar to convert to ethanol and carbon dioxide. This method is used to make alcoholic drinks.

1 ***Write a word equation for the fermentation of sugar using yeast.***

- Ethanol can also be made by the hydration of ethene.
- Ethene is reacted with steam at a high temperature in the presence of a catalyst. The ethene is obtained from crude oil by cracking.

2 ***Write a word equation for the hydration of ethene.***

- Ethanol produced by fermentation uses a renewable resource, sugar from plants.
- Fermentation is done at room temperature. However, fermentation can only produce a dilute aqueous solution of ethanol. The ethanol must be separated from the solution by fractional distillation to give pure ethanol.
- Ethanol produced from ethene uses a non-renewable resource, crude oil.
- The reaction can be run continuously and produces pure ethanol, but requires a high temperature.

Key word: fermentation

1. Give two reasons why fractions from crude oil are cracked.

2. Describe two ways that are used to crack hydrocarbons.

3. Sort these formulae into alkanes and alkenes:

   C_3H_6, C_5H_{12}, C_4H_{10}, C_4H_8, C_6H_{14}

4. Poly(ethene) is a polymer. Explain what is meant by 'a polymer'.

5. Describe one use of a smart polymer.

6. Some plastics are biodegradable. What does 'biodegradable' mean?

7. Suggest three ways of reducing the problems of plastic rubbish.

8. Outline the two ways that can be used to make ethanol and give an advantage and a disadvantage of each method.

9. a Write an equation using displayed formulae showing the bonds for the polymerisation of propene.

   b Write a balanced equation showing the hydration of ethene. [H]

10. Copy and complete this equation for cracking a hydrocarbon:

    $C_{12}H_{26} \rightarrow C_6H_{14} + C_4H_8 + \ldots\ldots\ldots$ [H]

Chapter checklist ✓✓✓

Tick when you have:

reviewed it after your lesson ✓ ☐ ☐

revised once – some questions right ✓ ✓ ☐

revised twice – all questions right ✓ ✓ ✓

Move on to another topic when you have all three ticks

Topic			
Cracking hydrocarbons	☐	☐	☐
Making polymers from alkenes	☐	☐	☐
New and useful polymers	☐	☐	☐
Plastic waste	☐	☐	☐
Ethanol	☐	☐	☐

Student Book pages 196–197 C1

6.1 Extracting vegetable oil

Key points

- Vegetable oils can be extracted from seeds, nuts and fruits by pressing or by distillation.
- Vegetable oils provide nutrients and a lot of energy. They are important foods and can be used to make biofuels.
- Unsaturated oils contain carbon–carbon double bonds (C=C) and so they decolourise bromine water.

- Some seeds, nuts and fruits are rich in **vegetable oils**. The oils can be extracted by crushing and pressing the plant material, followed by removing water and other impurities. Some oils are extracted by distilling the plant material mixed with water. This produces a mixture of oil and water from which the oil can be separated.

1 *What two methods are used to extract vegetable oils?*

- When eaten, vegetable oils provide us with a lot of energy and important nutrients. Vegetable oils also release a lot of energy when they burn in air and so can be used as fuels. They are used to make biofuels such as biodiesel.

2 *Why are vegetable oils important foods?*

- The molecules in vegetable oils have hydrocarbon chains. Those with carbon–carbon double bonds (C=C) are unsaturated. If there are several double bonds in each molecule, they are called polyunsaturated. **Unsaturated oils** react with bromine water, turning it from orange to colourless.

3 *Why are some vegetable oils described as unsaturated?*

Key words: vegetable oil, unsaturated oil

Student Book pages 198–199 C1

6.2 Cooking with vegetable oils

Key points

- Vegetable oils are useful in cooking because of their high boiling points.
- Cooking in oil increases the energy content of foods and changes the flavour, colour and texture of the food.
- Vegetable oils can be hardened by reacting them with hydrogen at 60 °C with a nickel catalyst. This makes them solids at room temperature that are suitable for spreading. [H]

- The boiling points of vegetable oils are higher than water, so food is cooked at higher temperatures in oil. This means it cooks faster. It also changes the flavour, colour and texture of the food. Some of the oil is absorbed and so the energy content of the food increases.

1 *Why are many of the foods from fast food outlets cooked in oil?*

Unsaturated oils can be reacted with hydrogen so that some or all of the carbon-carbon double bonds become single bonds. This reaction is called hydrogenation and is done at about 60 °C using a nickel catalyst. The **hydrogenated oils** have higher melting points because they are more saturated. The reaction is also called **hardening** because the hydrogenated oils are solids at room temperature. This means they can be used as spreads and to make pastries and cakes that require solid fats.

2 *What is meant by hardening vegetable oils?*

Study tip

Increasing the temperature makes chemical reactions go faster, so food cooks faster in oil than in water.

Key words: hydrogenated oil, hardening

Student Book **pages 200–201** **C1**

6.3 Everyday emulsions

Key points

- Oils do not dissolve in water but oils and water can be used to produce emulsions. These have special properties.
- Emulsions made from vegetable oils are used in many foods.
- Emulsifiers stop oil and water from separating into layers.
- Emulsifiers have molecules in which one part is hydrophobic and one part is hydrophilic. [H]

Ice cream is a frozen emulsifier

- Oil and water do not mix and usually separate from each other, forming two layers. If we shake, stir or beat the liquids together tiny droplets form that can be slow to separate. This type of mixture is called an **emulsion**.
- Emulsions are opaque and thicker than the oil and water they are made from. This improves their texture, appearance and their ability to coat and stick to solids. Milk, cream, salad dressings and ice cream are examples of emulsions. Some water-based paints and many cosmetic creams are also emulsions.

1 *How can you recognise an emulsion?*

- **Emulsifiers** are substances that help stop the oil and water from separating into layers. Most emulsions contain emulsifiers to keep the emulsion stable.

Higher

Emulsifier molecules have a small **hydrophilic** part and a long **hydrophobic** part. The hydrophilic part or 'head' is attracted to water. The hydrophobic part or 'tail' is attracted to oil. The hydrophobic parts of many emulsifier molecules go into each oil droplet, and so the droplets become surrounded by the hydrophilic parts. This keeps the droplets apart in the water, preventing them from joining together and separating out.

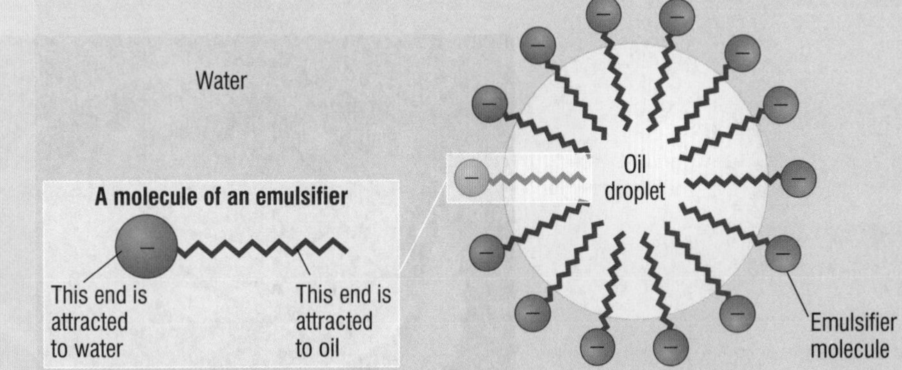

The structure of a typical emulsifier molecule with its water-loving (hydrophilic) head and its water-hating (hydrophobic) tail

2 *What is an emulsifier?*

Bump up your grade

Try to describe how an emulsifier works using the words 'hydrophobic' and 'hydrophilic'.

Study tip

You cannot see through an emulsion because the liquids remain as tiny droplets and do not dissolve. In a solution the substances dissolve, which means they mix completely, and the solution is clear.

Key words: emulsion, emulsifier, hydrophilic, hydrophobic

Student Book **pages 202–203** **C1**

6.4 Food issues

Key points

- Vegetable oils are high in energy and provide nutrients.
- Vegetable oils are believed to be better for health than saturated fats.
- Emulsifiers improve the texture of foods enabling water and oil to mix. This makes fatty foods more palatable and tempting to eat.

- There are benefits and drawbacks to using vegetable oils and emulsifiers in foods.
- Vegetable oils are high in energy and contain important nutrients. They contain unsaturated fats that are believed to be better for your health than saturated fats.
- Animal fats and hydrogenated vegetable oils contain saturated fats and are used in many foods. Saturated fats have been linked to heart disease.
- Emulsifiers stop oil and water separating into layers. This makes foods smoother, creamier and more palatable. However, because they taste better and it is less obvious that they are high in fat, you may be tempted to eat more.

1 *Give one benefit and one drawback from eating foods that contain vegetable oils.*

2 *Why should you be aware of emulsifiers in the food you eat?*

Study tip

You should be aware of the issues in this section to help you answer questions about information you are given in the exam, but you do not need to remember names of specific fats, oils or emulsifiers.

Emulsified fats can be very tempting

1. Why are vegetable oils used as food and fuels?
2. What type of fuel is produced from vegetable oils?
3. What is used to test for an unsaturated oil? Give the result of the test.
4. Why are some foods cooked in vegetable oils?
5. Describe how to make an emulsion from cooking oil and water.
6. Mayonnaise is made from oil, vinegar and egg yolk. What is the purpose of the egg yolk?
7. Why are emulsions more useful than separate oil and water?
8. Why should you know what type of fats are in the food you eat?
9. Sunflower seeds contain vegetable oil. Outline a method you could use to separate some oil from the seeds.
10. a Describe the reaction and conditions used to hydrogenate vegetable oils.
    b Why is this done? [H]
11. Describe how an emulsifier works. [H]

Chapter checklist ✓✓✓

Tick when you have:
reviewed it after your lesson ✓ ☐ ☐
revised once – some questions right ✓ ✓ ☐
revised twice – all questions right ✓ ✓ ✓
Move on to another topic when you have all three ticks

Extracting vegetable oil	☐	☐	☐
Cooking with vegetable oils	☐	☐	☐
Everyday emulsions	☐	☐	☐
Food issues	☐	☐	☐

Student Book pages 206–207 **C1**

7.1 Structure of the Earth

Key points

- The Earth is made of layers called the core, mantle and crust with the atmosphere around the outside.
- The Earth's limited resources come from its crust, the oceans and the atmosphere.

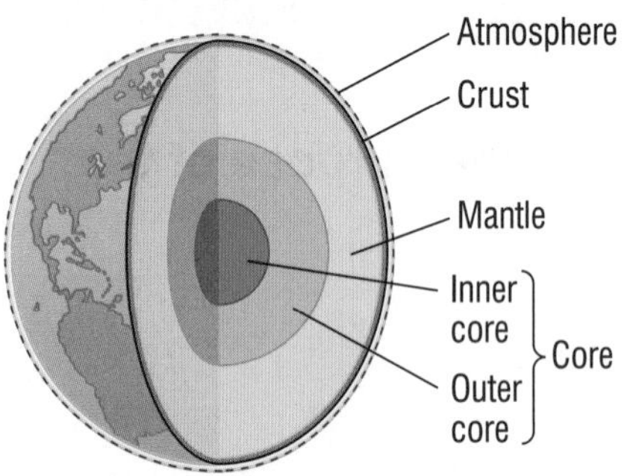

The structure of the Earth

- The Earth is almost spherical, with a diameter of about 12 800 km. At the surface is a thin, solid **crust**. The crust is a very thin layer that varies in thickness between about 5 km and 70 km.
- The **mantle** is under the crust and is about 3000 km thick. It goes almost halfway to the centre of the Earth. The mantle is almost entirely solid but parts of it can flow very slowly.
- The **core** is about half the diameter of the Earth. It has a high proportion of the magnetic metals iron and nickel. It has a liquid outer part and a solid inner part.
- The **atmosphere** surrounds the Earth. Most of the air is within 10 km of the surface and most of the atmosphere is within 100 km of the surface.

1 *Name the layers of the Earth that are solid.*

- All of the raw materials and other resources that we depend on come from the crust, the oceans and the atmosphere. This means the resources available to us are limited.

Study tip

You should have an idea of the size of the Earth and the relative size of its layers. You do not have to remember the diameter or thickness of the layers.

Key words: crust, mantle, core, atmosphere

Student Book pages 208–209 **C1**

7.2 The restless Earth

Key points

- The Earth's crust and upper mantle is cracked into tectonic plates which are constantly moving.
- The tectonic plates move because of convection currents in the mantle that are caused by radioactive decay.
- Earthquakes and volcanoes happen where tectonic plates meet, but it is difficult to predict accurately when and where earthquakes will happen.
- Wegener's theory of continental drift was not accepted for many years.

- Scientists now believe the Earth's crust and upper part of the mantle is cracked into massive pieces called **tectonic plates**. Tectonic plates move a few centimetres a year because of **convection currents** in the mantle beneath them. The convection currents are caused by energy released by the decay of radioactive elements heating up the mantle.

1 *What causes tectonic plates to move?*

- Where the plates meet, huge forces build up. Eventually the rocks give way, changing shape or moving suddenly causing earthquakes, volcanoes or mountains to form. Scientists still do not know enough about what is happening inside the Earth to predict exactly when and where earthquakes or volcanic eruptions will happen.

2 *Why can scientists not predict when and where earthquakes will happen?*

- Alfred Wegener put forward the idea of continental drift in 1915. Other scientists at that time did not accept his ideas, mainly because he could not explain why the continents moved. They believed that the Earth was shrinking as it cooled. In the 1960s scientists found new evidence and the theory of plate tectonics was developed.

3 *Why were Wegener's ideas not accepted for many years?*

Bump up your grade

You should be able to explain how and why tectonic plates move.

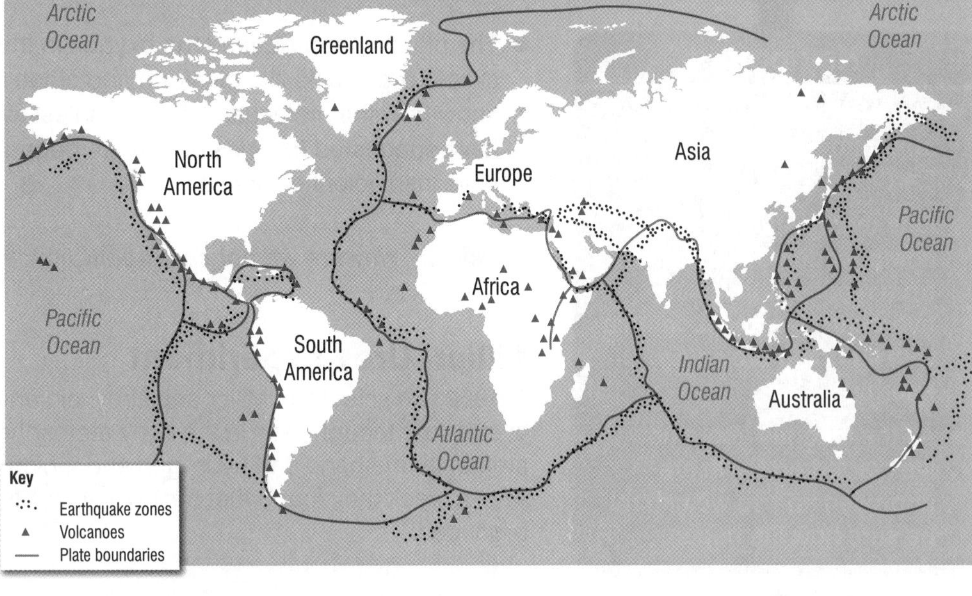

The distribution of volcanoes and earthquakes around the world largely follows the boundaries of the Earth's tectonic plates

Key words: tectonic plate, convection current

Student Book pages 210–211 **C1**

7.3 The Earth's atmosphere in the past

Key points

- The Earth's early atmosphere was formed by volcanic activity.
- It probably consisted mainly of carbon dioxide. There may also have been water vapour together with traces of methane and ammonia.
- As plants spread over the Earth, the levels of oxygen in the atmosphere increased

The surface of one of Jupiter's moons, called Io, with its active volcanoes releasing gases into its atmosphere. This gives us an idea of what our Earth was like billions of years ago.

- Scientists think that the Earth was formed about 4.5 billion years ago. In the first billion years the surface was covered with volcanoes that released carbon dioxide, water vapour and nitrogen.
- As the Earth cooled most of the water vapour condensed to form the oceans. So the early atmosphere was mainly carbon dioxide with some water vapour. Some scientists believe there was also nitrogen and possibly some methane and ammonia.

1 ***Where did most of the carbon dioxide, nitrogen and water vapour in the Earth's early atmosphere come from?***

- In the next two billion years bacteria, algae and plants evolved. Algae and plants used carbon dioxide for photosynthesis and this released oxygen. As the number of plants increased the amount of carbon dioxide in the atmosphere decreased and the amount of oxygen increased.

2 ***What produced the oxygen in the atmosphere?***

Study tip

You may find other theories about the Earth's formation and its early atmosphere, but you are only expected to know about this one for the examination.

Bump up your grade

Try to memorise the main gases that were probably in the Earth's early atmosphere.

Student Book
pages 212–213 **C1**

7.4 Life on Earth

Key points

- There are many theories about how life began on Earth.
- One theory states that the compounds needed came from reactions involving hydrocarbons and ammonia with lightning providing energy. [H]
- All the theories about how life started on Earth are unproven and so we cannot be sure how life began. [H]

Study tip

Although there are many theories about how life began you do not need to remember the details of any of them, except for Higher Tier candidates, who should be aware of the Miller–Urey experiment and the idea of 'primordial soup'.

- The plants that produced the oxygen in the atmosphere probably evolved from simple organisms like plankton and algae in the ancient oceans. But we do not know how the molecules of the simplest living things were formed. Many scientists have suggested theories of how life began but no one knows for sure because we have insufficient evidence.

1 ***Why are we not sure about how life began?***

Miller–Urey experiment

In 1952 two scientists, Miller and Urey, did an experiment based on what scientists at that time thought was in the early atmosphere. They used a mixture of water, ammonia, methane and hydrogen and a high voltage spark to simulate lightning. After a week they found that amino acids, the building blocks for proteins, had been produced.

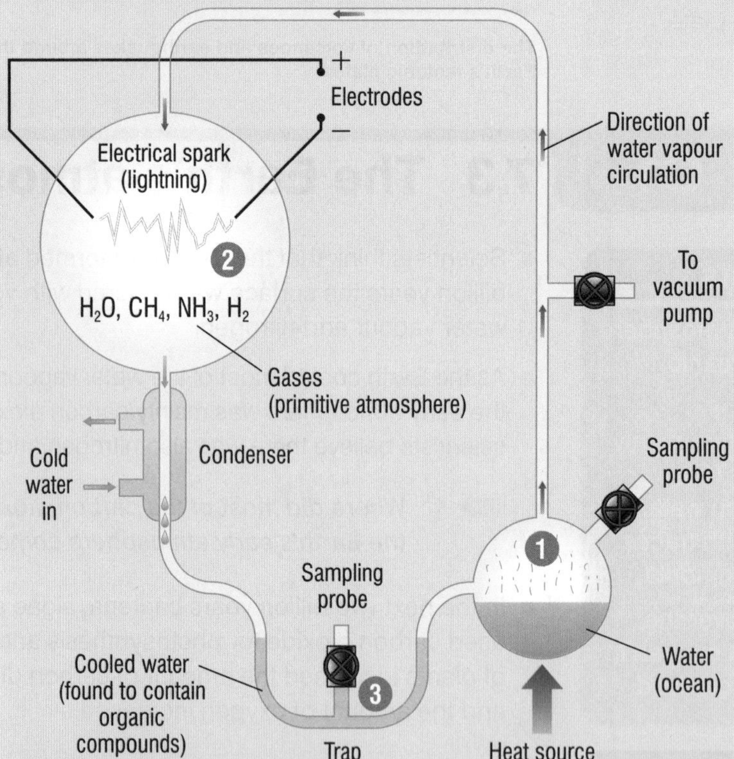

The classic Miller–Urey experiment

Other theories

Since the 1950s theories about what was in the early atmosphere have changed, but scientists have been able to produce amino acids using other mixtures of gases. One theory suggests that these organic molecules formed a 'primordial soup' and that the amino acids in this mixture combined to make proteins from which life began. Many other theories have been proposed, but there is no evidence that proves any theory.

2 ***Amino acids are made from the elements carbon, hydrogen, oxygen and nitrogen. Suggest why Miller and Urey used a mixture of water, ammonia, methane and hydrogen in their experiment.***

Student Book pages 214–215 **C1**

7.5 Gases in the atmosphere

Key points

- Most of the carbon dioxide in the early atmosphere became locked up in sedimentary rocks.
- About four-fifths (almost 80%) of the atmosphere is nitrogen, and about one-fifth (just over 20%) is oxygen.
- The main gases in the air can be separated by fractional distillation. These gases are used in industry as raw materials. [H]

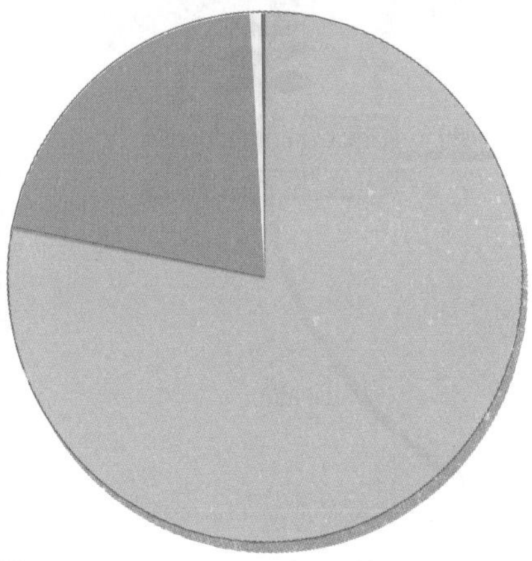

The relative proportions of nitrogen, oxygen and other gases in the Earth's atmosphere

Bump up your grade

To get maximum marks, you should be able to explain the fractional distillation of liquid air, given the boiling points of nitrogen and oxygen.

- Plants took up much of the carbon dioxide in the Earth's early atmosphere. Animals ate the plants and much of the carbon ended up in plant and animal remains as sedimentary rocks and fossil fuels. Limestone was formed from the shells and skeletons of marine organisms. Fossil fuels contain carbon and hydrogen from plants and animals.
- Carbon dioxide dissolves in the oceans and some probably formed insoluble carbonate compounds that were deposited on the seabed and became sedimentary rocks.

1 *In what ways did carbon from carbon dioxide become 'locked up'?*

- By 200 million years ago the proportions of gases in the atmosphere had stabilised and were much the same as today. The atmosphere is now almost four-fifths nitrogen and just over one-fifth oxygen. Other gases, including carbon dioxide, water vapour and noble gases, make up about 1% of the atmosphere.

2 *What are the approximate percentages of nitrogen and oxygen in the air?*

Higher

Separating the gases in air

The gases in the air have different boiling points and so can be separated from liquid air by **fractional distillation**. Fractional distillation of liquid air is done industrially to produce pure oxygen and liquid nitrogen, which have important uses. The air is cooled to below –200 °C and fed into a fractional distillation column. Nitrogen is separated from oxygen and argon and further distillation is used to produce pure oxygen and argon.

3 *Why can the gases in air be separated by fractional distillation?*

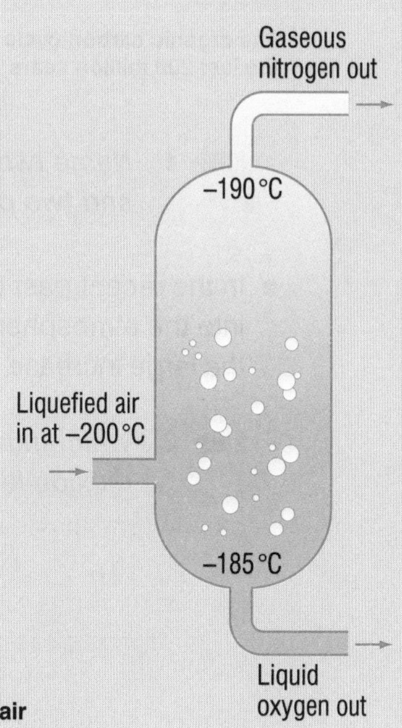

Fractional distillation of liquid air

Student Book pages 216–217 **C1**

7.6 Carbon dioxide in the atmosphere

Key points

- Carbon moves into and out of the atmosphere due to plants, animals, the oceans and rocks.
- The amount of carbon dioxide in the Earth's atmosphere has risen in the recent past largely due to the amount of fossil fuels we now burn.

Study tip

Questions on this topic will test your understanding of the main processes that add or remove carbon dioxide and how they affect its amount in the atmosphere. You only need to know those included in the AQA specification. There are other processes involved, and you may be given information about these in the exam, but you will not be expected to remember their details.

- For about 200 million years the amount of carbon dioxide in the atmosphere has remained about the same.
- This is because various natural processes that move carbon dioxide into and out of the atmosphere had achieved a balance.
- These processes involve carbon compounds in plants, animals, the oceans and rocks. The organic carbon cycle shows some of these processes.
- Carbon dioxide dissolves in water, particularly the oceans, and reactions of inorganic carbonate compounds are also important in maintaining a balance.

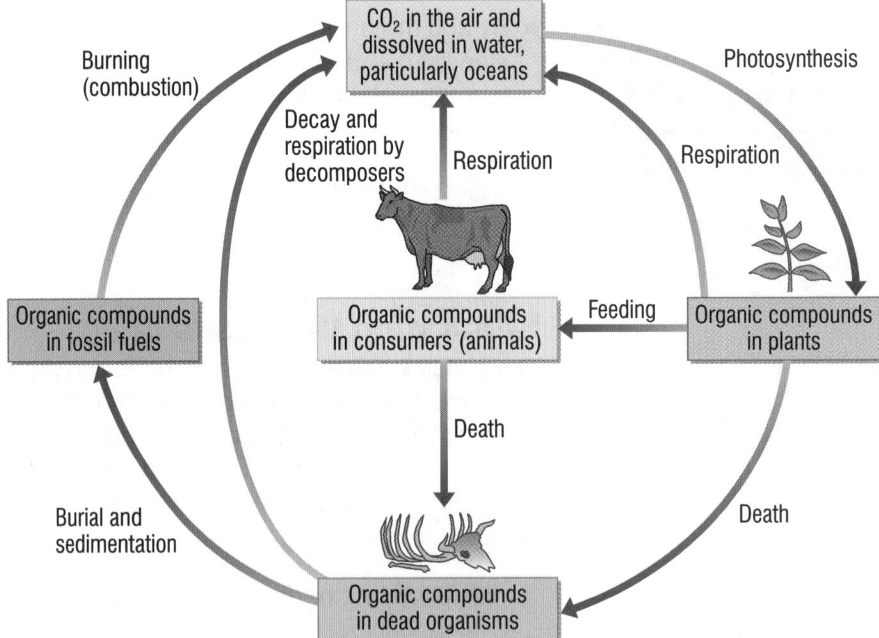

The organic carbon cycle has helped to keep the level of carbon dioxide in the atmosphere steady for the last 200 million years

1 ***Name two processes that release carbon dioxide into the atmosphere and two processes that remove it from the atmosphere.***

- In the recent past the amount of carbon dioxide that human activity has released into the atmosphere has increased dramatically. This has been mainly caused by the large increase in the amount of fossil fuels that we burn.

2 ***Which human activity has been the main cause of increased carbon dioxide levels in the atmosphere?***

1. Name the main parts of the Earth, starting from its centre.
2. Why should we be careful not to waste the Earth's resources?
3. Name three gases that scientists think were in the Earth's early atmosphere.
4. Name four gases that are now in the atmosphere.
5. How did the oceans form?
6. What was the effect of algae and plants on the early atmosphere?
7. a What are tectonic plates?
   b Why do tectonic plates move?
   c About how much do they move in a year?
   d What happens at plate boundaries?
8. a Why have the amounts of gases in the atmosphere been almost the same for the last 200 million years?
   b What has been the main cause of a change in this balance in recent years?
9. Why were Wegener's ideas not accepted until the 1960s?
10. Why are there so many theories about how life began?
11. a Outline the Miller and Urey experiment. [H]
    b What is meant by 'primordial soup'?
12. a Why is the fractional distillation of liquid air done commercially? [H]
    b Explain briefly how it works.

Chapter checklist

Tick when you have:

reviewed it after your lesson	✓	☐	☐
revised once – some questions right	✓	✓	☐
revised twice – all questions right	✓	✓	✓

Move on to another topic when you have all three ticks

	✓	✓	✓
Structure of the Earth	☐	☐	☐
The restless Earth	☐	☐	☐
The Earth's atmosphere in the past	☐	☐	☐
Life on Earth	☐	☐	☐
Gases in the atmosphere	☐	☐	☐
Carbon dioxide in the atmosphere	☐	☐	☐

1 The symbol for the element phosphorus is P and its atomic number is 15.

a How many protons are in an atom of phosphorus? *(1 mark)*

b How many electrons are in an atom of phosphorus? *(1 mark)*

c The mass number of an atom of phosphorus is 31. How many neutrons are in this atom? *(1 mark)*

d Copy and complete the electronic structure of phosphorus: 2,8, ….. *(1 mark)*

e In which group of the periodic table is phosphorus? *(1 mark)*

f Phosphorus reacts with chlorine to form phosphorus chloride, PCl_3. The equation for the reaction is:

$$2P + 3Cl_2 \rightarrow 2PCl_3$$

i Write a word equation for the reaction. *(1 mark)*

ii How many atoms of chlorine combine with two atoms of phosphorus? *(1 mark)*

iii What type of bond holds the atoms together in PCl_3? *(1 mark)*

2 Limestone is mainly calcium carbonate, $CaCO_3$.

a When limestone is heated strongly the calcium carbonate breaks down.

i Write a word equation for this reaction. *(1 mark)*

ii What type of reaction is this? *(1 mark)*

b When water is added to the solid product, calcium hydroxide, $Ca(OH)_2$, is produced. Adding more water and filtering produces a solution of calcium hydroxide.

i Some universal indicator solution was added to calcium hydroxide solution. The indicator turned blue. What does this tell you about calcium hydroxide? *(1 mark)*

ii When carbon dioxide is bubbled into calcium hydroxide solution the solution turns cloudy. Explain why. *(2 marks)*

3 a Copper can be extracted from copper-rich ores by smelting. This is done by heating the ore in a furnace to about 1100 °C and blowing air through it. An equation for a reaction in the furnace is:

copper sulfide + oxygen → copper + sulfur dioxide

i Copper ore and air are needed for this process. What other resource is needed? *(1 mark)*

ii Why should sulfur dioxide not be allowed to escape into the air? *(1 mark)*

iii The copper that is produced is impure. Name the method used to purify the copper. *(1 mark)*

b Copper can be extracted from low-grade ores by bioleaching. A solution containing water, bacteria and sulfuric acid is added to the top of a heap of ore. The leachate solution that is collected from the bottom of the heap contains copper sulfate. Copper is extracted from the solution using scrap iron. The solution can be re-used.

i What is the purpose of the bacteria in this process? *(1 mark)*

ii Write a word equation for the reaction between iron and copper sulfate. *(1 mark)*

iii What is the name of this type of reaction? *(1 mark)*

iv The solution from which the copper has been extracted should not be allowed to escape without further treatment. Explain why. *(2 marks)*

4 Oil companies crack some of the fractions from crude oil. The equation shows an example of a reaction that happens during cracking.

$$C_{12}H_{26} \rightarrow C_7H_{16} + C_2H_4 + C_3H_6$$

a What conditions are used for cracking? *(2 marks)*

b Draw a diagram to show all of the bonds in C_3H_6. *(2 marks)*

c C_3H_6 can be used to make a polymer. Which other product of the reaction can be used to make a polymer? *(1 mark)*

d *In this question you will be assessed on using good English, organising information clearly and using specialist terms where appropriate.*

Plastic waste that contains polymers made from C_3H_6 and similar monomers causes environmental problems. Explain why. *(6 marks)*

5 The table shows the percentages of the four most abundant gases in dry air.

Name of gas	Percentage (%) by volume in dry air
Nitrogen	78.08
Oxygen	20.95
Argon	0.93
Carbon dioxide	0.03

a Which of these gases is believed to have been the most abundant in the Earth's early atmosphere? *(1 mark)*

b Name **one** other gas that was probably in the Earth's early atmosphere. *(1 mark)*

c What produced the oxygen that is in the air? *(1 mark)*

d Why are there many theories about how life began on Earth? *(1 mark)*

e In the Miller–Urey experiment electric sparks were passed through a mixture of gases. The gases were those that scientists believed were in the early atmosphere. After several days amino acids were produced. The simplest amino acid has the formula $C_2H_5O_2N$. Suggest a mixture of three gases that could have been in the Earth's early atmosphere that could combine to form amino acids. **[H]** *(3 marks)*

f The table shows the boiling points of the three most abundant elements in air.

Name of element	Boiling point in °C
Argon	–186
Nitrogen	–196
Oxygen	–183

To separate these elements, air is cooled to –200 °C, so that the gases become liquids. The liquid mixture is then put into a fractional distillation column that is colder at the bottom than the top. From which part of the column is each element is collected? **[H]** *(2 marks)*

Study tip

In questions that assess the quality of written communication, like 4d, there is not a mark for each scientific point you make. It is the overall quality of the answer that you write that decides the mark. However, you will need to have enough chemistry in your answer to get the highest marks.

Study tip

Many questions will give you some information or data. It is important that you read this carefully and that your answer relates to this information, and not to some other context that you may have studied.

Study tip

When a question uses the word 'suggest', as in 5e, there may be lots of possible answers. You only need to give the number that the question asks for, but make sure they are relevant.

Student Book pages 222–223 **P1**

1.1 Infrared radiation

Key points

- Infrared radiation is energy transfer by electromagnetic waves.
- All objects emit infrared radiation.
- The hotter an object is the more infrared radiation it emits in a given time.

Study tip

Remember that the transfer of energy by infrared radiation does **not** involve particles.

- Infrared waves are part of the electromagnetic spectrum. They are the part of the spectrum just beyond visible red light. We can detect **infrared radiation** with our skin – it makes us feel warm.
- All objects **emit** (give off) infrared radiation.
- The hotter an object is the more infrared radiation it emits in a given time.

1 ***How does the temperature of an object affect the rate at which it emits infrared radiation?***

- Infrared radiation can travel through a vacuum, as in travelling through space. This is how we get energy from the Sun.

2 ***What is a vacuum?***

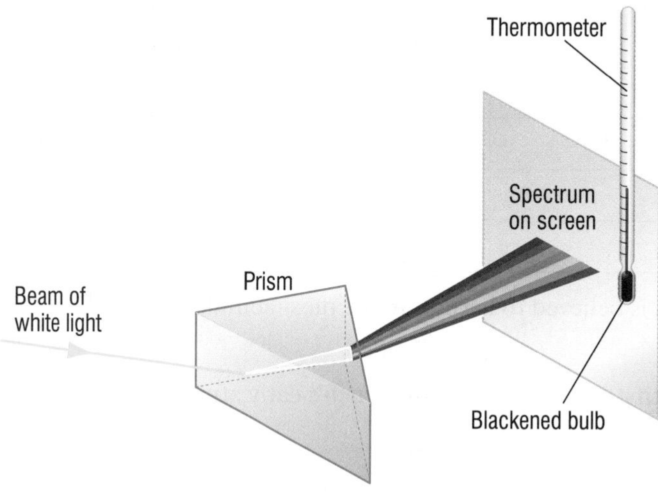

Detecting infrared radiation

Key words: infrared radiation, emit

Student Book pages 224–225 **P1**

1.2 Surfaces and radiation

Key points

- Dark, matt surfaces emit infrared radiation more quickly than light, shiny surfaces.
- Dark, matt surfaces absorb infrared radiation more quickly than light, shiny surfaces.
- Light, shiny surfaces reflect more infrared radiation than dark, matt surfaces.

- Dark, matt surfaces are good **absorbers** of infrared radiation. An object painted dull black and left in the Sun will become hotter than the same object painted shiny white.

1 ***Why are houses in hot countries often painted white?***

- Dark, matt surfaces are also good **emitters** of infrared radiation. So an object that is painted dull black will transfer energy and cool down more quickly than the same object painted shiny white.

2 ***Why are the pipes on the back of a fridge usually painted black?***

- Light, shiny surfaces are good **reflectors** of infrared radiation.

Key words: absorber, emitter, reflector

Student Book pages 226–227 **P1**

1.3 States of matter

Key points

- Flow, shape, volume and density are the properties used to describe each state of matter.
- The particles in a solid are held next to each other, vibrating in their fixed positions.
- The particles in a liquid move about at random and are in contact with each other.
- The particles in a gas move about randomly and are much farther apart than particles in a solid or liquid.

Bump up your grade

Make sure that you can describe the arrangement of the particles in each of the three states of matter.

- The three states of matter are **solid**, **liquid** and **gas**. We can make a substance change between these states by heating or cooling it.
- In a solid, the particles vibrate about fixed positions so the solid has a fixed shape.
- In a liquid, the particles are in contact with each other but can move about at random, so a liquid doesn't have a fixed shape and can flow.

1 *How is the arrangement of the particles in a liquid different from that in a solid?*

- In a gas, the particles are usually far apart and move at random much faster, so a gas doesn't have a fixed shape and can flow. The density of a gas is much less than that of a solid or liquid.

2 *How is the arrangement of the particles in a gas different from that in a liquid?*

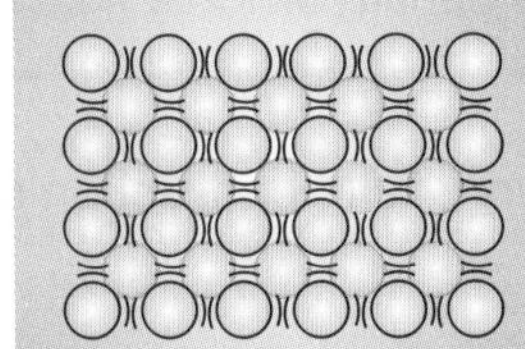
a
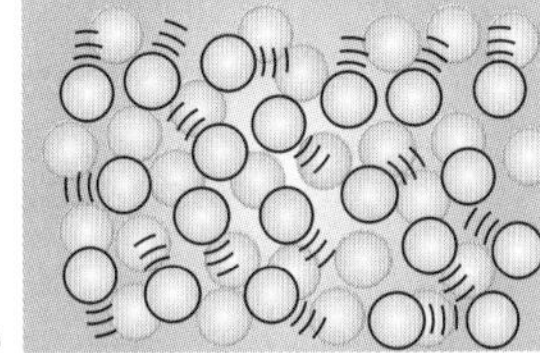
b
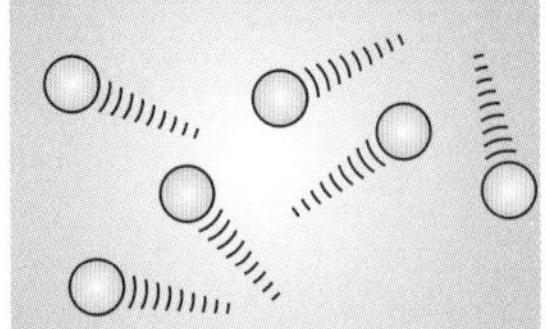
c

The arrangement of particles in a a solid, b a liquid and c a gas

Key words: solid, liquid, gas

Student Book pages 228–229 **P1**

1.4 Conduction

Key points

- Metals are the best conductors.
- Materials such as wool and fibreglass are good insulators.
- Conduction in a metal is mainly due to free electrons transferring energy inside the metal.
- Non-metals are poor conductors because they do not contain free electrons.

Study tip

Know some examples of insulators and how they are used.

- **Conduction** occurs mainly in solids. Most liquids and all gases are poor **conductors**.
- If one end of a solid is heated, the particles at that end gain kinetic energy and vibrate more. This energy is passed to neighbouring particles and in this way the energy is transferred through the solid.
- This process occurs in metals.
- In addition, when metals are heated their **free electrons** gain kinetic energy and move through the metal, transferring energy by colliding with other particles. Hence all metals are good conductors.

1 *Why are saucepans often made of metal with wooden handles?*

- Poor conductors are called **insulators**. Materials such as wool and fibreglass are good insulators because they contain trapped air.

2 *Why are materials that trap air good insulators?*

Key words: conduction, conductor, free electron, insulator

Student Book
pages 230–231
P1

1.5 Convection

Key points

- Convection is the circulation of a fluid (liquid or gas) caused by heating it.
- Convection takes place only in liquids and gases (fluids).
- Heating a liquid or a gas makes it less dense so it rises and causes circulation.

Study tip

Remember that convection cannot occur in solids.

- **Convection** occurs in **fluids**. Fluids are liquids and gases.
- When a fluid is heated it expands. The fluid becomes less dense and rises. The warm fluid is replaced by cooler, denser fluid. The resulting **convection current** transfers energy throughout the fluid.

1 Why doesn't convection occur in solids?

- Convection currents can be on a very small scale, such as heating water in a beaker, or on a very large scale, such as heating the air above land and sea. Convection currents are responsible for onshore and offshore breezes.

2 Why does a fluid become less dense when it is heated?

Bump up your grade

Make sure that you can explain how convection currents are set up, in terms of the changes in density when a fluid is heated.

Key words: convection, fluid, convection current

Student Book
pages 232–233
P1

1.6 Evaporation and condensation

Key points

- Evaporation is when a liquid turns into a gas.
- Condensation is when a gas turns into a liquid.

Bump up your grade

Make sure you know the factors that affect the rate of evaporation and condensation.

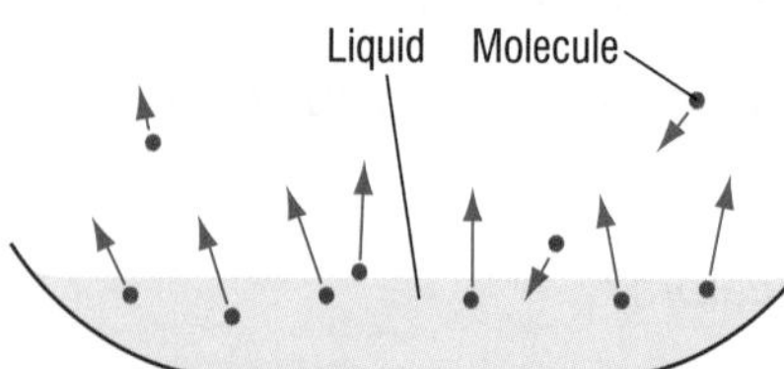

Water molecules escaping from a liquid

- **Evaporation** is when a liquid turns into a gas. Evaporation takes place because the most energetic liquid molecules escape from the liquid's surface and enter the air. Therefore, the average kinetic energy of the remaining molecules is less, so the **temperature** of the liquid decreases. This means that evaporation causes cooling.
- The rate of evaporation is increased by:
  - increasing the surface area of the liquid
  - increasing the temperature of the liquid
  - creating a draught of air across the liquid's surface.

1 What effect would decreasing the surface area of a liquid have on its rate of evaporation?

- **Condensation** is when a gas turns into a liquid. This often takes place on cold surfaces such as windows and mirrors.
- The rate of condensation is increased by:
  - increasing the surface area
  - reducing the surface temperature.

2 What effect would decreasing the surface area of a liquid have on its rate of condensation?

Key words: evaporation, temperature, condensation

Student Book pages 234–235 **P1**

1.7 Energy transfer by design

Key points

- The rate of energy transfer to or from an object depends on:
  - the shape, size and type of material of the object
  - the materials the object is in contact with
  - the temperature difference between the object and its surroundings.

Motorcycle engine fins

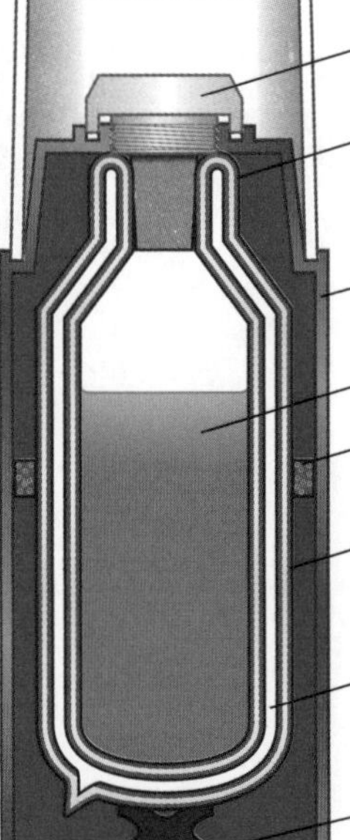

A vacuum flask

- The greater the **temperature difference** between an object and its surroundings, the greater the rate at which energy is transferred.
- The rate at which energy is transferred also depends on:
  - the materials the object is in contact with
  - the object's shape
  - the object's surface area.
- Sometimes we want to **maximise** the rate of energy transfer to keep things cool. To do this we may use things that:
  - are good conductors
  - are painted dull black
  - have the air flow around them maximised.

1 *Why does painting an object dull black maximise the rate of energy transfer?*

- Sometimes we want to **minimise** the rate of energy transfer to keep things warm. To do this we need to minimise the transfer of energy by conduction, convection and radiation. We may use things that:
  - are good insulators
  - are white and shiny
  - prevent convection currents by trapping air in small pockets.

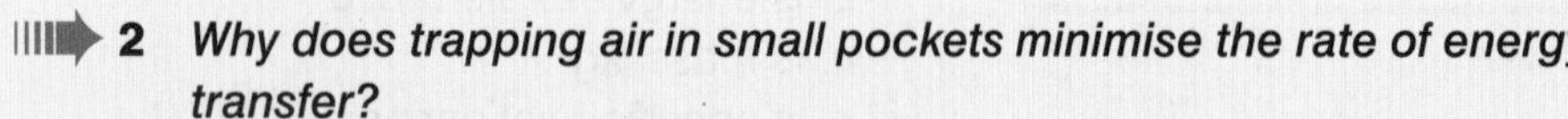

2 *Why does trapping air in small pockets minimise the rate of energy transfer?*

Study tip

Be prepared to apply your knowledge of energy transfer to different situations. These might include animal adaptations to hot or cold climates.

Bump up your grade

A vacuum flask is an application that often comes up in examination questions. Make sure that you can relate the structure of a vacuum flask to minimising energy transfer by conduction, convection and radiation. A vacuum flask reduces the rate of energy transfer to keep hot things hot and cold things cold.

Key words: temperature difference, maximise, minimise

Student Book
pages 236–237

P1

1.8 Specific heat capacity

Key points

- The greater the mass of an object, the more slowly its temperature increases when it is heated.
- The rate of temperature change in a substance when heated depends on the energy transferred to it, its mass and its specific heat capacity.

Study tip

Note that in the equation, θ is the temperature change. In an exam question it may be necessary to work out the change in temperature by subtracting the initial temperature from the final temperature.

- When we heat a substance, we transfer energy to it which will increase its temperature. The **specific heat capacity** of a substance is the amount of energy required to raise the temperature of 1 kilogram of the substance by 1 degree Celsius.
- Different substances have different specific heat capacities. The greater the specific heat capacity, the more energy required for each degree temperature change. For example, the specific heat capacity of aluminium is 900 J/kg°C and of copper is 490 J/kg°C. If we wanted to raise the temperature of 1 kg of aluminium, we would need to transfer almost twice the energy needed to raise the temperature of 1 kg of copper by the same amount.

1 ***The specific heat capacity of oil is 2100 J/kg°C. How much energy is needed to raise the temperature of 1 kg of oil by 1 °C?***

- The greater the **mass** of substance being heated the more energy required for each degree temperature change. If we had a 2 kg piece of copper, we would need to transfer twice the energy needed to raise the temperature of 1 kg of copper by the same amount.

2 ***The specific heat capacity of water is 4200 J/kg°C. How much energy is needed to raise the temperature of 2 kg of water by 1 °C?***

- The equation for specific heat capacity is: $\boldsymbol{E = m \times c \times \theta}$
  Where:
  E is energy transferred, J
  m is mass, kg
  c is specific heat capacity, J/kg°C
  θ is temperature change, °C.

Key words: specific heat capacity, mass

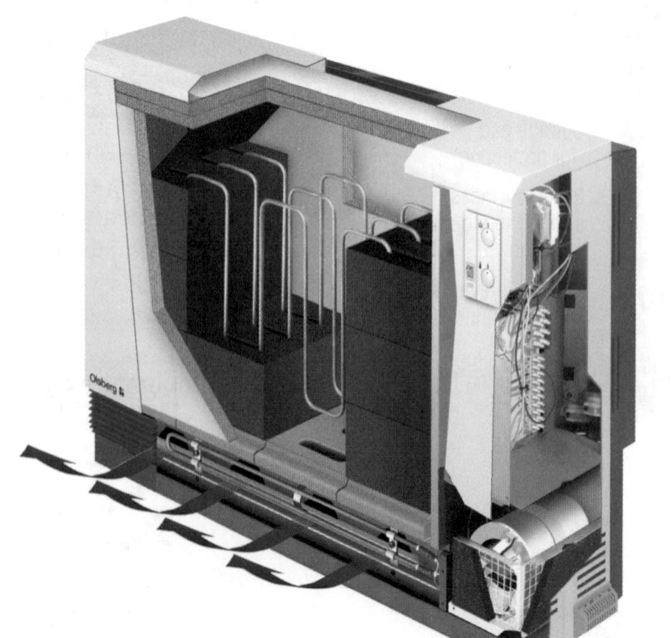

Storage heater

Student Book pages 238–239 **P1**

1.9 Heating and insulating buildings

Key points

- The rate of energy transfer to or from our homes can be reduced.
- U-values tell us how much energy per second passes through different materials. The lower the U-value the better the material is as an insulator.
- Solar heating panels do not use fuel to heat water but they are expensive to buy and install.

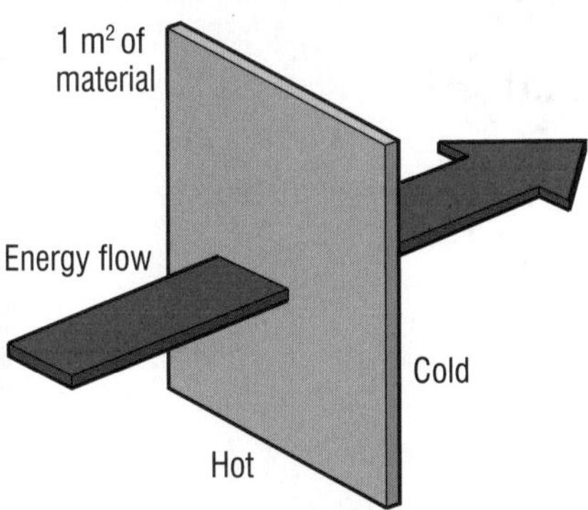

U-values

Bump up your grade

Be prepared to look at tables of U-values and decide which would be the best material to use in a particular situation. You may also have to take into account other things such as cost-effectiveness and payback time.

How Science Works

- Most people want to minimise the rate of **energy transfer** out of their homes to reduce fuel bills. This can be done by fitting:
  - fibreglass loft insulation to reduce energy transfer by conduction
  - cavity wall insulation that traps air in small pockets to reduce energy transfer by convection
  - double glazing to reduce energy transfer by conduction through windows
  - draught proofing to reduce energy transfer by convection
  - aluminium foil behind radiators to reflect infrared radiation back into the room.

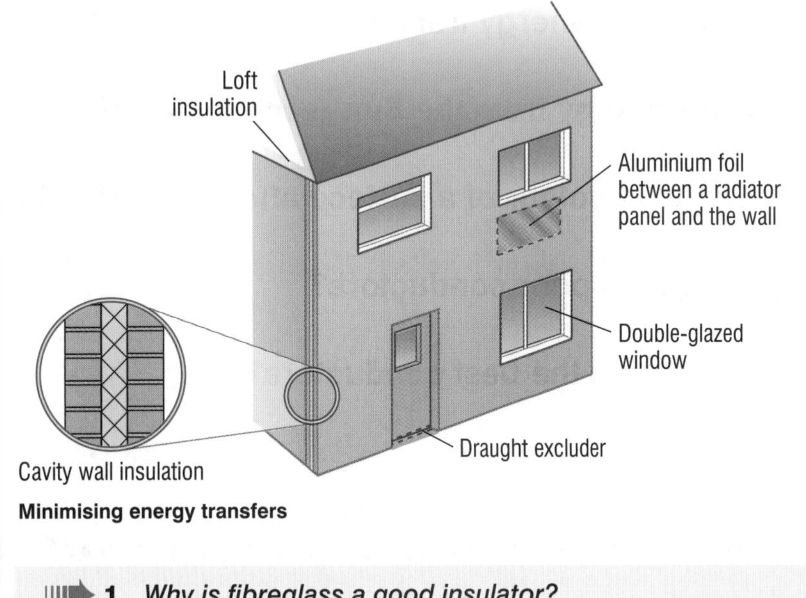

Minimising energy transfers

1 *Why is fibreglass a good insulator?*

- The U-value of a material tells us how much energy per second passes through it. Knowing the U-values of different materials allows us to compare them. The lower the U-value the better the material is as an insulator.
- **Solar heating panels** contain water that is heated by radiation from the Sun. This water may then be used to heat buildings or provide domestic hot water. Solar heating panels are cheap to run because they do not use fuel. However, they are expensive to buy and install, and the water is not heated at night.

2 *Why are the pipes that contain the water in a solar heating panel often painted black?*

Key words: energy transfer, solar heating panel

1. What is the best colour for a central heating radiator, glossy white or dull black?
2. Why does a solid have a fixed volume?
3. When a liquid evaporates, why is the average kinetic energy of the remaining molecules reduced?
4. What happens to the rate of energy transfer between an object and its surroundings if the temperature difference between them is reduced?
5. Which types of energy transfer involve particles?
6. How does energy from the Sun reach the Earth?
7. How does the colour of a surface affect the rate of conduction?
8. Why are gases poor conductors?
9. Why are metals the best conductors?
10. What is convection?
11. How does cavity wall insulation reduce energy transfer from a house?
12. The specific heat capacity of water is 4200 J/kg °C. How much energy is needed to raise the temperature of 3 kg of water by 4 °C?

Chapter checklist

Tick when you have:

reviewed it after your lesson	✓	☐	☐
revised once – some questions right	✓	✓	☐
revised twice – all questions right	✓	✓	✓

Move on to another topic when you have all three ticks

	✓	✓	✓
Infrared radiation	☐	☐	☐
Surfaces and radiation	☐	☐	☐
States of matter	☐	☐	☐
Conduction	☐	☐	☐
Convection	☐	☐	☐
Evaporation and condensation	☐	☐	☐
Energy transfer by design	☐	☐	☐
Specific heat capacity	☐	☐	☐
Heating and insulating buildings	☐	☐	☐

Student Book pages 242–243 **P1**

2.1 Forms of energy

Key points

- Energy exists in different forms.
- Energy can be transferred from one form into another form.
- When an object falls and gains speed, its gravitational potential energy decreases and its kinetic energy increases.

- Energy exists in different forms such as: light, sound, **kinetic** (movement), nuclear, **electrical**, **gravitational potential**, **elastic potential** and **chemical**.
- The last three are forms of stored energy.

1 *What form of energy does a compressed spring have?*

- Energy can be transferred from one form to another.
- Any object above the ground has gravitational potential energy.
- A falling object transfers gravitational potential energy to kinetic energy.

2 *Where does the chemical energy stored in your muscles come from?*

Bump up your grade

Make sure that you are familiar with the different forms that energy can take and know some examples of each of them.

Key words: kinetic energy, electrical energy, gravitational potential energy, elastic potential energy, chemical energy

Student Book pages 244–245 **P1**

2.2 Conservation of energy

Key points

- Energy can be transferred from one form to another, or from one place to another.
- Energy cannot be created or destroyed.
- Conservation of energy applies to all energy changes.

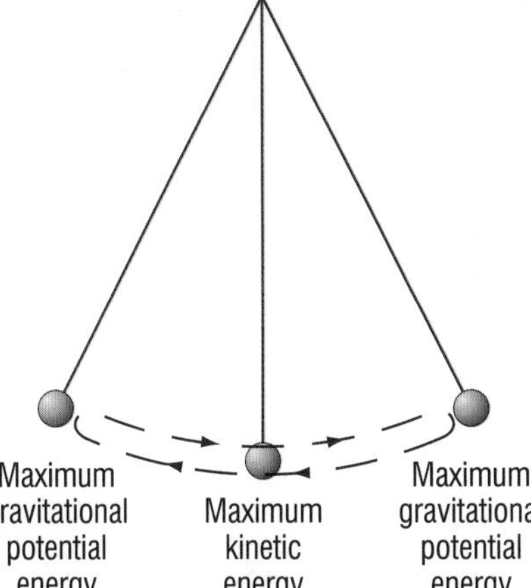

A pendulum in motion

- It is not possible to create or destroy energy. It is only possible to transfer it from one form to another, or from one place to another.
- This means that the total amount of energy is always the same. This is called the **conservation of energy** and it applies to all energy transfers.

1 *What energy transfers take place when you turn on a torch?*

- For example, when an object falls, gravitational potential energy is transferred to kinetic energy.
- Similarly, stretching an elastic band transfers chemical energy to elastic potential energy.
- In a solar cell, light energy is transferred to electrical energy.

2 *In terms of energy, what happens when you burn a fuel?*

- A swinging pendulum transfers energy from gravitational potential energy to kinetic energy and back again as it swings.

Study tip

Conservation of energy is an extremely important idea in physics, so it will often come up in examination questions.

Key words: conservation of energy

Student Book pages 246–247 **P1**

2.3 Useful energy

Key points

- Useful energy is energy in the place we want it and the form we need it.
- Wasted energy is energy that is not useful energy.
- Useful energy and wasted energy both end up being transferred to the surroundings, which become warmer.
- As energy spreads out, it gets more and more difficult to use for further energy transfers.

- A **machine** is something that transfers energy from one place to another or from one form to another.
- The energy we get out of a machine consists of:
  - **useful energy**, which is transferred to the place we want and in the form we want it
  - **wasted energy**, which is not usefully transferred.

1 *What happens to the wasted energy from a light bulb?*

- Both the useful energy and the wasted energy will eventually be transferred to the surroundings, and make them warm up. As the energy spreads out, it becomes more difficult to use for further energy transfers.
- Energy is often wasted because of friction between the moving parts of a machine. This energy warms the machine and the surroundings.
- Sometimes friction may be useful, for example in the brakes of a bicycle or a car. Some of the kinetic energy of the vehicle is transferred to energy heating the brakes.

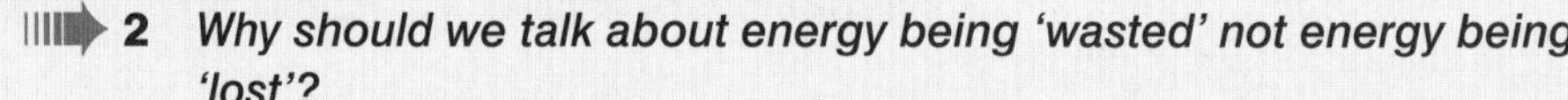

2 *Why should we talk about energy being 'wasted' not energy being 'lost'?*

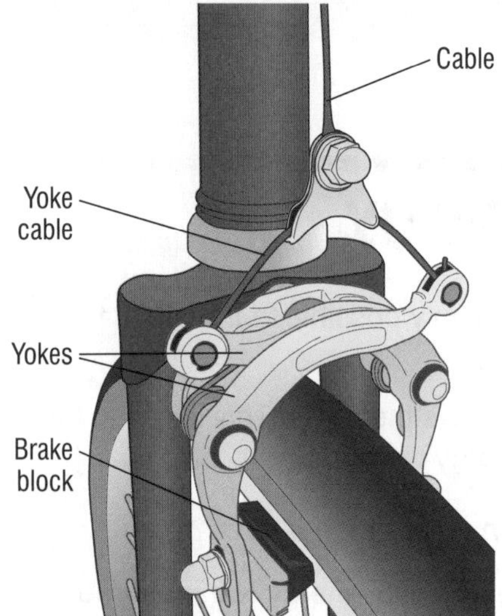

Braking on a bicycle

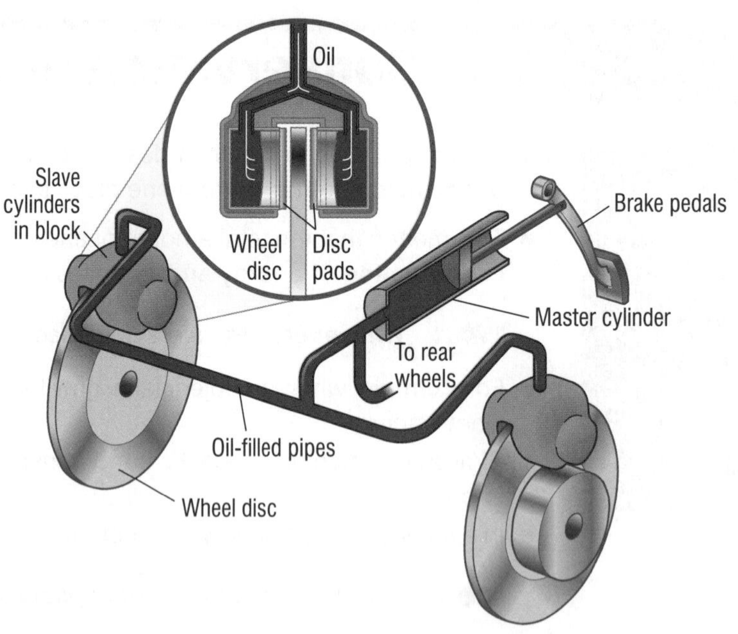

Disc brakes

Key words: machine, useful energy, wasted energy

Bump up your grade

Sometimes wasted energy is transferred as sound, but the amount of energy is usually very small. Remember that this energy will also eventually be transferred to the surroundings making them warmer.

Student Book pages 248–249 **P1**

2.4 Energy and efficiency

Key points

- The efficiency of an appliance = useful energy transferred by the appliance ÷ total energy supplied to the appliance (×100%).
- No machine can be more than 100% efficient.
- Measures to make machines more efficient include reducing:
  - friction
  - air resistance
  - electrical resistance
  - noise due to vibrations.

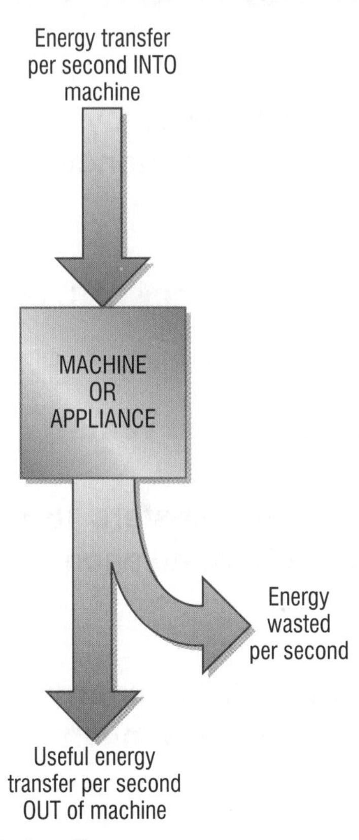

A Sankey diagram

- Energy is measured in **joules (J)**. This unit is used for all forms of energy.
- The energy supplied to a machine is often called the **input energy**. From the conservation of energy we know that:

  input energy (energy supplied) = useful energy transferred + energy wasted

- The less energy that is wasted by a machine, the more efficient the machine.
- We can calculate the **efficiency** of any appliance that transfers energy, using the equation:

$$\text{Efficiency} = \frac{\text{useful energy transferred by the appliance}}{\text{total energy supplied to the appliance}} \ (\times\ 100\%)$$

1 *In a light bulb, for every 25 joules of energy that are supplied to the bulb, 5 joules are usefully transferred into light energy. What is the efficiency of the bulb?*

- The efficiency can be left as a fraction or multiplied by 100 to give a percentage.
- No appliance can be 100% efficient, except an electric heater, which usefully transfers all of the electrical energy supplied to it by heating its surroundings.

2 *A machine is adjusted so that it wastes less energy because of friction. What happens to the efficiency of the machine?*

- The energy transfer through an appliance can be represented with a **Sankey diagram**.

Study tip

Remember that no appliance can be more than 100% efficient. So if you do an efficiency calculation and the answer is greater than 1 (or 100%), you have made an error and should check your working.

Bump up your grade

Efficiency is a ratio. That means it does not have a unit.

Key words: joule (J), input energy, efficiency, Sankey diagram

1. What form of energy does a moving car have?
2. What form of energy does a stretched spring have?
3. When is electrical energy transferred?
4. What are the useful energy transfers that take place in a hairdryer?
5. What are the useful energy transfers that take place in a television?
6. What energy transfers take place when you lift a ball into the air and then drop it so it falls to the ground?
7. Wear and tear causes a particular machine to waste more energy. What happens to the efficiency of this machine?
8. In an electric motor, 250 J of energy are transferred to the surroundings by heating, for every 1000 J of electrical energy supplied. What is the efficiency of the motor as a fraction?
9. Why is an electric heater the only appliance that may have an efficiency of 1, or 100%?
10. Why do electrical appliances such as televisions and computers have vents?
11. 60 J of energy are supplied each second to a light bulb. The bulb transfers 18 J of energy to light each second. How much energy does the bulb waste each second?
12. When a kettle full of cold water is brought to boiling point, 720 000 J of energy are transferred to the water. If the kettle has an efficiency of 96%, how much energy is supplied to the kettle to boil the water?

Chapter checklist

Tick when you have:			
reviewed it after your lesson	✓	☐	☐
revised once – some questions right	✓	✓	☐
revised twice – all questions right	✓	✓	✓

Move on to another topic when you have all three ticks

	✓	✓	✓
Forms of energy	☐	☐	☐
Conservation of energy	☐	☐	☐
Useful energy	☐	☐	☐
Energy and efficiency	☐	☐	☐

Student Book pages 252–253 **P1**

3.1 Electrical appliances

Key points

- Electrical appliances can transfer electrical energy into useful energy at the flick of a switch.
- Uses of everyday electrical appliances include heating, lighting, making objects move and creating sound and visual images.
- An electrical appliance is designed for a particular purpose and should waste as little energy as possible.

- **Electrical appliances** are extremely useful. They transfer electrical energy into whatever form of energy we need at the flick of a switch.
- Common electrical appliances include:
  - lamps, to produce light
  - electric mixers, to produce kinetic energy
  - speakers, to produce sound energy
  - televisions, to produce light and sound energy.

1 *What useful energy transfer takes place in an electric drill?*

- Many electrical appliances transfer energy by heating. This may be a useful transfer, for example in a kettle, but energy is often wasted. Appliances should be designed to waste as little energy as possible.

2 *Which electrical appliance usefully transfers electrical energy into light energy and sound energy?*

Key words: electrical appliance

Student Book pages 254–255 **P1**

3.2 Electrical power

Key points

- Power is rate of transfer of energy.
- $P = \frac{E}{t}$
- Efficiency = $\frac{\text{useful power out}}{\text{total power in}}$ (×100%)

Rocket power

- The **power** of an appliance is the rate at which it transfers energy.
- The unit of power is the **watt**, symbol W. An appliance with a power of 1 watt transfers 1 joule of electrical energy to other forms of energy every second.
- Often a watt is too small a unit to be useful, so power may be given in **kilowatts (kW)**. 1 kilowatt = 1000 watts.

1 *How many watts are equivalent to 12 kilowatts?*

- Power is given by the equation: $P = \frac{E}{t}$

  Where:

  P is the power in watts, W

  E is the energy in joules, J

  t is the time taken (in seconds) for the energy to be transferred.
- Power is the energy per second transferred or supplied, so we can write the efficiency equation in terms of power:

$$\textbf{Efficiency} = \frac{\textbf{useful power out}}{\textbf{total power in}} \ (\times 100\%)$$

2 *An electric motor transfers 48 kJ of electrical energy into kinetic energy in 2 minutes. What is the useful power output of the motor?*

Bump up your grade

Be sure that you practise efficiency calculations using both fractions and percentages.

Key words: power, watt, kilowatt (kW)

Student Book
pages 256–257

P1

3.3 Using electrical energy

Key points

- The kilowatt-hour is the energy supplied to a 1 kW appliance in 1 hour.
- $E = P \times t$
- Total cost = number of kW h × cost per kW h.

An electricity meter

Study tip

Remember that the kilowatt-hour is a unit of energy.

- Companies that supply mains electricity charge customers for the amount of electrical energy used. Because of the large numbers involved, the joule is not a suitable unit. The amount of energy used is measured in **kilowatt-hour (kW h)**.
- A kilowatt-hour is the amount of energy that is transferred by a one-kilowatt appliance when used for one hour.
- The amount of energy transferred to a mains appliance can be found using the equation: $\boldsymbol{E = P \times t}$

  Where:
  E is the energy transferred in kilowatt-hours, kW h
  P is the power of the appliance in kW
  t is the time taken (in hours) for the energy to be transferred.

1 *How much electrical energy, in kW h, is transferred when a 9 kW shower is used for 15 minutes?*

- The electricity meter in a house records the number of kW h of energy used. If the previous meter reading is subtracted from the current reading, the electrical energy used between the readings can be calculated.

An electricity meter will record the energy usage of all appliances in use

- The cost of the electrical energy supplied is found using the equation:

  total cost = number of kW h × cost per kW h

- The cost per kW h is given on the electricity bill.

2 *The price of 1 kW h of electrical energy is 9p. How much does it cost to use a 60 W electric light for 4 hours?*

Key words: kilowatt-hour (kW h)

Student Book
pages 258–259

P1

3.4 Cost effectiveness matters 

Key points

- Cost effectiveness means getting the best value for money.
- To compare the cost effectiveness of different appliances, we need to take account of a number of different costs.

Study tip

In the examination you may be given data on different appliances and asked to compare the data to decide which appliance is the most cost effective.

- To compare the **cost effectiveness** of different appliances we must consider a number of different costs.
- These may include:
  - the cost of buying the appliance
  - the cost of installing the appliance
  - the running costs
  - the maintenance costs
  - environmental costs
  - the interest charged on a loan to buy the appliance.

1 *What might environmental costs include?*

- Many householders want to reduce their energy bills. To do this they may buy newer, more efficient appliances (such as a new fridge). They could also install materials designed to reduce energy wastage (such as loft insulation).
- The **payback time** is the time it takes for an appliance or installation to pay for itself in terms of energy savings.

2 ***Loft insulation costs £600 including installation. It saves £80 per year on the fuel bill. How long is the payback time?***

Bump up your grade

Make sure that you can work out the payback time for different appliances or methods of insulation.

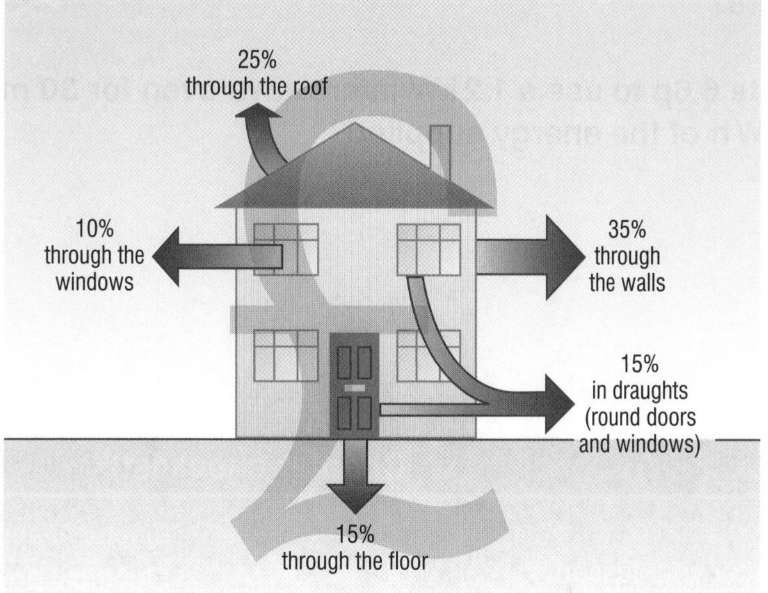

Energy loss from a house

Key words: cost effectiveness, payback time

1. What is the useful energy transfer in an electric toaster?
2. How may energy be wasted in an electric heater?
3. How may energy be wasted in an electric kettle?
4. How many kilowatts are equivalent to 30 000 watts?
5. Which is more powerful, a 2000 W hairdryer or a 2.2 kW hairdryer?
6. What quantity is measured in kilojoules?
7. An electric light bulb transfers 6000 J of energy in 1 minute. What is its power?
8. How much electrical energy, in kW h, is transferred when a 2 kW iron is used for 30 minutes?
9. Why is the electrical energy supplied by the mains measured in kilowatt-hours?
10. A machine has an input power rating of 100 kW and a useful output power of 40 kW. What is its percentage efficiency?
11. Electricity costs 12p per kW h. What is the cost of using a 2.5 kW h heater for 2 hours?
12. It costs 6.6p to use a 1.2 kW microwave oven for 30 minutes. What is the cost per kW h of the energy supplied? [H]

Chapter checklist

Tick when you have:

reviewed it after your lesson	✓	☐	☐
revised once – some questions right	✓	✓	☐
revised twice – all questions right	✓	✓	✓

Move on to another topic when you have all three ticks

	✓	✓	✓
Electrical appliances	☐	☐	☐
Electrical power	☐	☐	☐
Using electrical energy	☐	☐	☐
Cost effectiveness matters	☐	☐	☐

4.1 Fuel for electricity

Key points

- Electricity generators in power stations are driven by turbines.
- Coal, oil and natural gas are burned in fossil-fuel power stations.
- Uranium or plutonium is used as the fuel in a nuclear power station.
- Biofuels are renewable sources of energy which can generate electricity.

Bump up your grade

Most power stations burn fuels to produce energy to heat water. In a nuclear power station uranium is not burned; the energy comes from the process of nuclear fission.

- In most power stations, water is heated to produce steam. The steam drives a **turbine**, which is coupled to an electrical **generator** that produces the electricity.
- The energy can come from burning a **fossil fuel** such as coal, oil or gas. Fossil fuels are obtained from long-dead biological material.
- In some gas-fired power stations, hot gases may drive the turbine directly. A gas-fired turbine may be switched on very quickly.
- A **biofuel** is any fuel obtained from living or recently living organisms. Some biofuels can be used in small-scale, gas-fired power stations. Biofuels are renewable sources of energy.

1 *Name three fossil fuels.*

- In a nuclear power station, the fuel used is uranium (or sometimes plutonium).
- The nucleus of a uranium atom can undergo a process called **nuclear fission**. This process releases energy.
- There are lots of uranium nuclei, so lots of fission reactions take place, releasing lots of energy. This energy is used to heat water, turning it into steam.

2 ***What is the process by which energy is produced in a nuclear power station?***

How Science Works

- Much more energy is released per kilogram of uranium undergoing fission reactions than from each kilogram of fossil fuel that we burn.
- Nuclear power stations do not release any greenhouse gases, unlike fossil-fuel power stations. However, nuclear power stations do produce radioactive waste that must be safely stored for a long period of time.

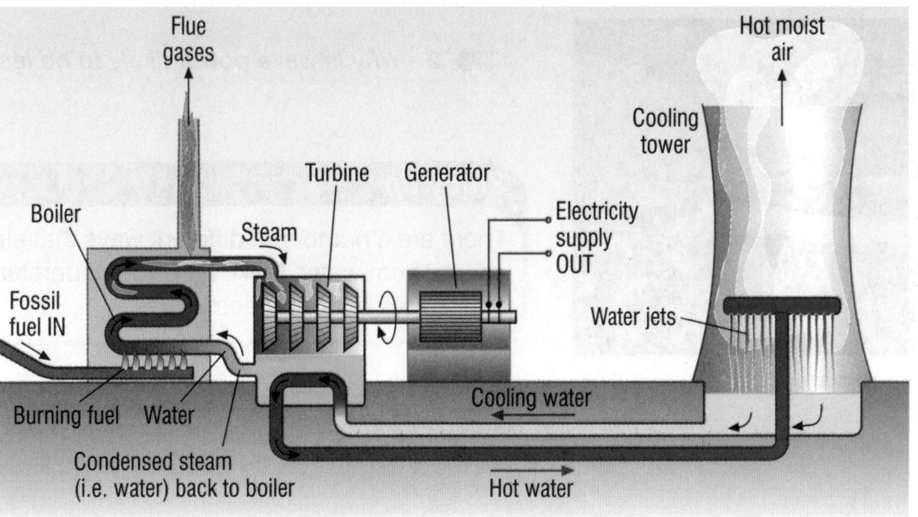

Inside a fossil fuel power station

Key words: turbine, generator, fossil fuel, biofuel, nuclear fission

4.2 Energy from wind and water

Key points

- A wind turbine is an electricity generator on top of a tall tower.
- Waves generate electricity by turning a floating generator.
- Hydroelectricity generators are turned by water running downhill.
- A tidal power station traps each high tide and uses it to turn generators.

A wind farm

A tidal power station

Energy from wind, waves and tides is called **renewable energy**. That's because these sources of energy can never be used up, unlike fossil fuels or nuclear fuels.

Wind

- We can use energy from **wind** and water to drive turbines directly.
- In a wind turbine, the wind passing over the blades makes them rotate and drive a generator at the top of a narrow tower.

Water

- Electricity can be produced from energy obtained from **falling water**, **waves** or **tides**.
- **Hydroelectric power.** At a hydroelectric power station, water is collected in a reservoir. This water is allowed to flow downhill and turn turbines at the bottom of the hill.
- In a pumped storage system, surplus electricity is used, at times of low demand, to pump the water back up the hill to the top reservoir. This means that the energy is stored. Then at times of high demand the water can be released to fall through the turbines and transfer the stored energy to electrical energy.

1 *What form of energy is stored in the water in the top reservoir of a pumped storage scheme?*

- **Wave power.** We can use the movement of the waves on the sea to generate electricity. The movement drives a floating turbine that turns a generator. Then the electricity is delivered to the grid system on shore by a cable.
- **Tidal power.** The level of the sea around the coastline rises and falls twice each day. These changes in sea level are called tides. If a barrage is built across a river estuary, the water at each high tide can be trapped behind it. When the water is released to fall down to the lower sea level, it drives turbines.

2 *Why is wave power likely to be less reliable than tidal power?*

Study tip

There are a number of different ways that electricity can be generated using energy from water. Make sure you understand them and can describe the differences between them.

Key words: renewable energy, wave, tide

Student Book pages 266–267 **P1**

4.3 Power from the Sun and the Earth

Key points

- Solar cells transfer solar energy directly into electricity.
- Solar heating panels use the Sun's energy to heat water directly.
- Geothermal energy comes from inside the Earth.

Bump up your grade

Know some examples of where solar energy is particularly useful for producing electricity.

- **Solar energy** from the Sun travels through space to the Earth as electromagnetic radiation.
- A **solar cell** can transfer this energy into electrical energy. Each cell only produces a small amount of electricity, so they are useful to power small devices such as watches and calculators.
- We can also join together large numbers of the cells to form a solar panel.
- Water flowing through a **solar heating panel** is heated directly by energy from the Sun.
- A **solar power tower** uses thousands of mirrors to reflect sunlight onto a water tank to heat the water and produce steam.

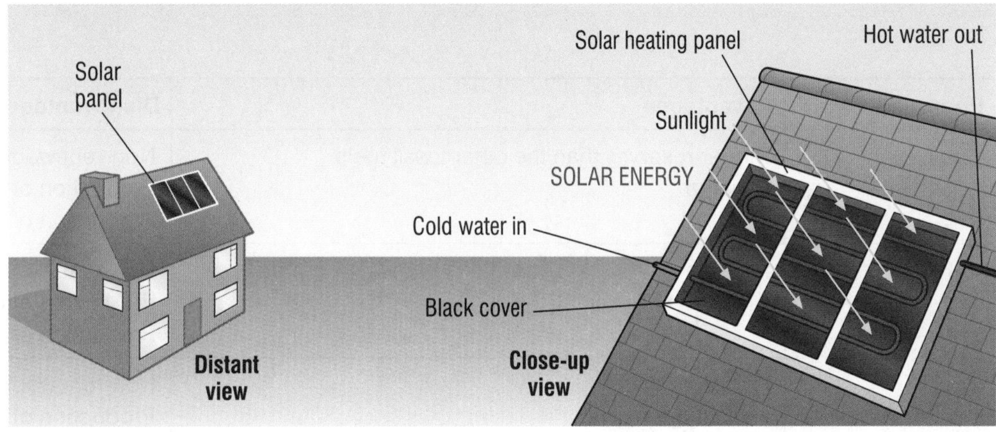

Solar water heating

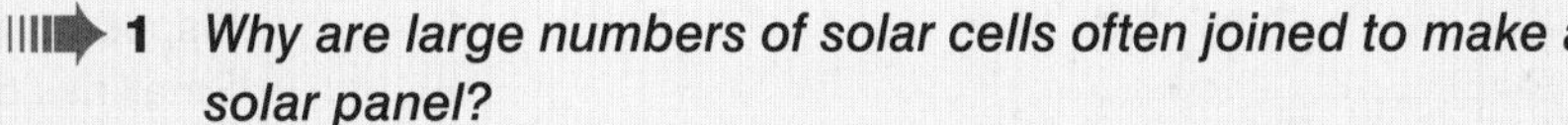

1 *Why are large numbers of solar cells often joined to make a solar panel?*

- **Geothermal energy** is produced inside the Earth by radioactive processes and this heats the surrounding rock. In volcanic or other suitable areas, very deep holes are drilled and cold water is pumped down to the hot rocks. There it is heated and comes back to the surface as steam. The steam is used to drive turbines that turn generators and so electricity is produced.
- In a few parts of the world, hot water comes up to the surface naturally and can be used to heat buildings nearby.

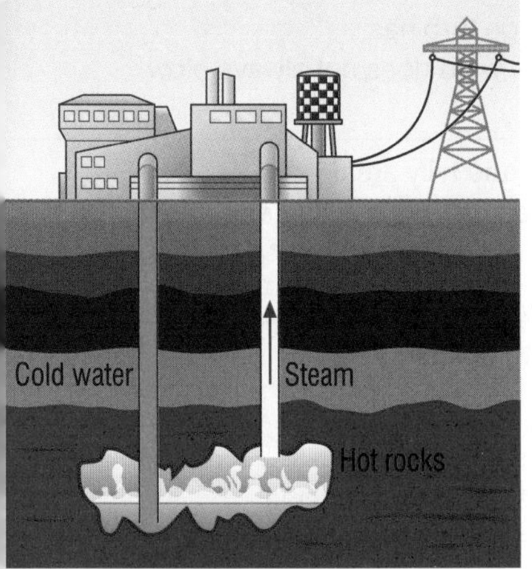

A geothermal power station

2 *Why are only a few places in the world able to have geothermal power stations?*

Key words: solar energy, solar cell, solar power tower, geothermal energy

Student Book pages 268–269 **P1**

4.4 Energy and the environment

Key points

- Burning fossil fuels produces greenhouse gases that cause global warming.
- Nuclear fuels produce radioactive waste.
- Using renewable energy resources can affect plant and animal life.

- Coal, oil, gas and uranium are **non-renewable** energy resources. The rate at which they are being used up is very much faster than the rate at which they are produced.
- Oil and gas will probably run out in the next fifty years or so, although coal will last much longer.
- **Renewable** energy resources will not run out. They can be produced as fast as they are used.
- Scientists are investigating ways to reduce the environmental impact of using fossil fuels. For example sulfur may be removed from fuel before burning. Instead of allowing carbon dioxide to be released into the atmosphere from power stations, it could be captured and stored in old oil and gas fields.
- There are advantages and disadvantages to using each type of energy resource.

Energy resource	Advantages	Disadvantages
Coal	Bigger reserves than the other fossil fuels Reliable	Non-renewable Production of CO_2, a greenhouse gas Production of SO_2, causing acid rain
Oil	Reliable	Non-renewable Production of CO_2, a greenhouse gas Production of SO_2, causing acid rain
Gas	Reliable	Non-renewable Production of CO_2, a greenhouse gas
Nuclear	No production of polluting gases Reliable	Non-renewable Produces hazardous nuclear waste, which is difficult to dispose of safely Small risk of a big nuclear accident
Wind	Renewable No production of polluting gases Free energy resource	Requires many large turbines Not reliable, as the wind does not always blow
Falling water	Renewable No production of polluting gases Reliable in wet areas Free energy resource	Only works in wet and hilly areas Damming the areas causes flooding and affects the local ecology
Waves	Renewable No production of polluting gases Free energy resource	Can be a hazard to boats Not reliable
Tides	Renewable No production of polluting gases Reliable, always tides twice a day Free energy resource	Only a few river estuaries are suitable Building a barrage affects the local ecology
Solar	Renewable No production of polluting gases Reliable in hot countries, in the daytime Free energy resource	Solar cells only produce a small amount of electricity Unreliable in less sunny countries
Geothermal	Renewable No production of polluting gases Free energy resource	Only economically viable in a very few places Drilling through large depth of rock is difficult and expensive

Study tip

If you are asked to discuss energy resources, remember that they all have advantages and disadvantages and you must include both.

1 *What type of area would be most suitable for a wind farm?*
2 *What is the difference between a renewable energy resource and a non-renewable energy resource?*
3 *Which gas, released by the burning of coal, causes acid rain?*

Key words: non-renewable

Student Book pages 270–271 P1

Key points

- The National Grid distributes electricity from power stations to our homes.
- Step-up and step-down transformers are used in the National Grid.
- A high grid voltage reduces energy wastage and makes the system more efficient.

Bump up your grade

Remember that step-up transformers increase the voltage and step-down transformers decrease the voltage.

4.5 The National Grid

- In Britain, electricity is distributed through the **National Grid**. This is a network of pylons and cables that connects power stations to homes, schools, factories and other buildings. Since the whole country is connected to the system, power stations can be switched in or out of the grid according to demand.
- The cables are carried long distances across the countryside supported by overhead pylons. In towns and close to homes the cables are buried underground.

1 *Give two advantages of overhead cables compared to underground cables.*

- The National Grid's voltage is 132 000 V or more. Power stations produce electricity at a voltage of 25 000 V.
- In power stations, electricity is generated at a particular voltage. The voltage is increased by **step-up transformers** before the electricity is transmitted across the National Grid. This is because transmission at high voltage reduces the energy wasted in the cables, making the system more efficient.
- It would be dangerous to supply electricity to consumers at these very high voltages. So, at local sub-stations, **step-down transformers** are used to reduce the voltage to 230 V for use in homes and offices.

2 *What sort of transformers are used at local sub-stations?*

Study tip

You do not need to remember the voltage of the power stations or the National Grid. But you need to know that the mains voltage in homes is 230 V.

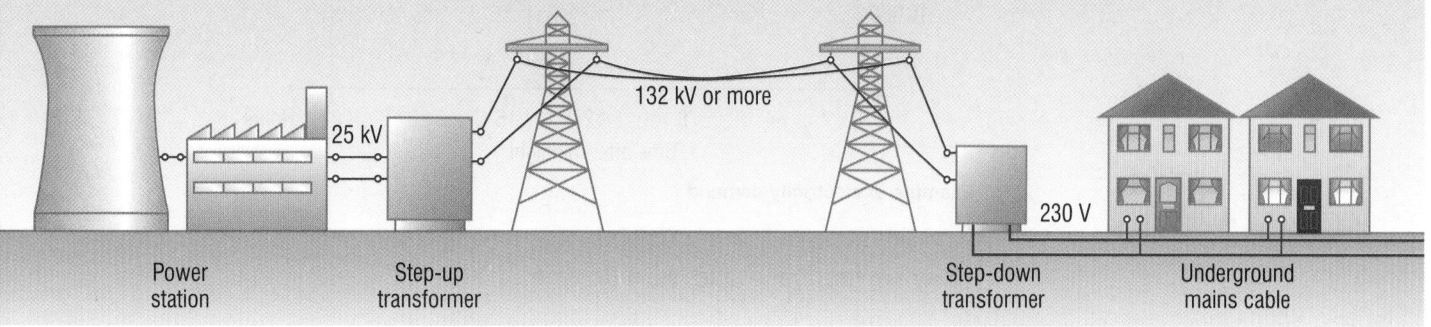

The National Grid

Key words: National Grid, step-up transformer, step-down transformer

Student Book pages 272–273 P1

4.6 Big energy issues

Key points

- Gas-fired power stations and pumped-storage stations can meet variations in demand.
- Nuclear, coal and oil power stations can meet base-load demand.
- Nuclear power stations, fossil-fuel power stations using carbon capture and renewable energy are all likely to contribute to future energy supplies.

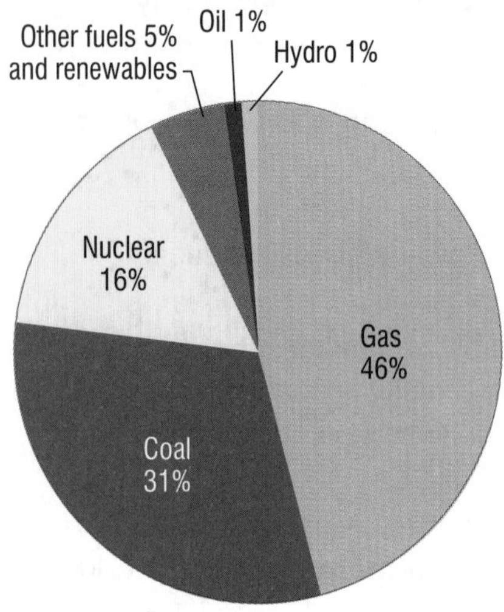

Energy sources for electricity

- A constant amount of electricity is provided by nuclear, coal-fired and oil-fired power stations. This is called the **base load** demand.
- The demand for electricity varies during the day and between summer and winter.

1 *Why does the demand for electricity vary between summer and winter?*

- This variable demand is met using gas-fired power stations, pumped-storage schemes and renewable energy sources.
- When demand is low, energy is stored by pumping water to the top reservoir of pumped storage schemes.
- Different types of power station have different **start-up times**. Gas-fired power stations have the shortest start-up times and nuclear power stations have the longest.

2 *In what form is energy stored in the top reservoir of a pumped storage scheme?*

Study tip

You may be asked to argue for or against a particular type of power station in an exam question. If data on the power station is provided in the question, make sure that you use it in your answer.

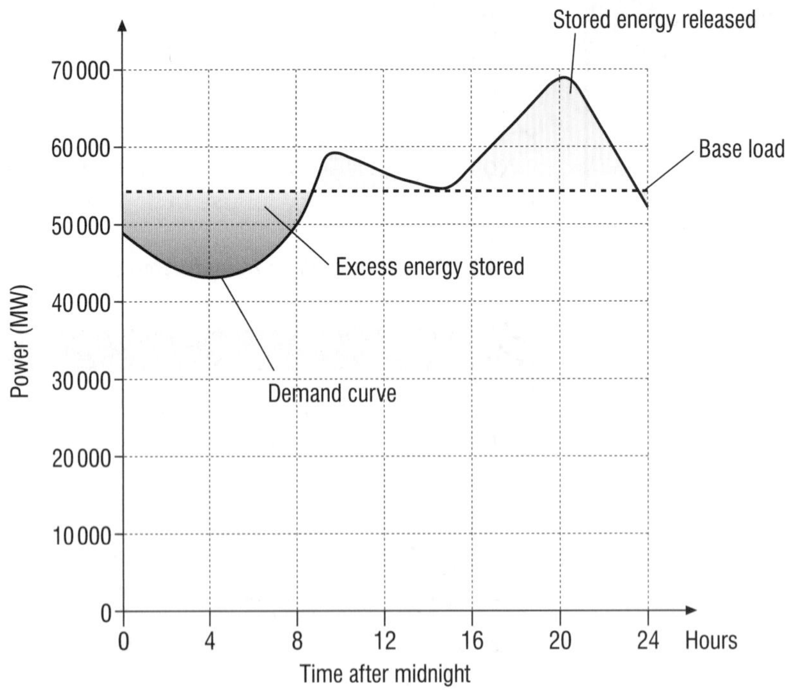

Example of electricity demand

Key words: base load, start-up time

1. Give three examples of biofuels.
2. Why do hydroelectric power stations have to be built in hilly areas?
3. Give three situations in which energy can be obtained from water to produce electricity.
4. What is a fossil fuel?
5. Where does geothermal energy come from?
6. Give two examples of where solar energy is particularly useful for producing electricity.
7. What is a solar cell?
8. What is a solar heating panel?
9. Are renewable or non-renewable energy sources the most reliable?
10. What are the disadvantages of using fossil fuels in power stations to produce electricity?
11. What colour are the pipes in a solar heating panel usually painted?
12. State three advantages of geothermal energy.

Chapter checklist ✓✓✓

Tick when you have:

reviewed it after your lesson	✓	☐	☐
revised once – some questions right	✓	✓	☐
revised twice – all questions right	✓	✓	✓

Move on to another topic when you have all three ticks

Fuel for electricity	☐	☐	☐
Energy from wind and water	☐	☐	☐
Power from the Sun and the Earth	☐	☐	☐
Energy and the environment	☐	☐	☐
The National Grid	☐	☐	☐
Big energy issues	☐	☐	☐

Student Book pages 276–277 **P1**

5.1 The nature of waves

Key points

- We use waves to transfer energy and to transfer information.
- Transverse waves vibrate at right angles to the direction of energy transfer. All electromagnetic waves are transverse waves.
- Longitudinal waves vibrate parallel to the direction of energy transfer. A sound wave is a longitudinal wave.
- Mechanical waves, which need a medium (substance) to travel through, may be transverse or longitudinal waves.

Study tip

If you are asked to show what is meant by longitudinal and transverse waves, you may find it easier to draw labelled diagrams than to give descriptions in words.

- We use waves to transfer energy and information. The direction of travel of the wave is the direction in which the wave transfers energy.
- There are different types of wave:
- For a **transverse wave** the **oscillation** (vibration) of the particles is **perpendicular** (at right angles) to the direction in which the wave travels.

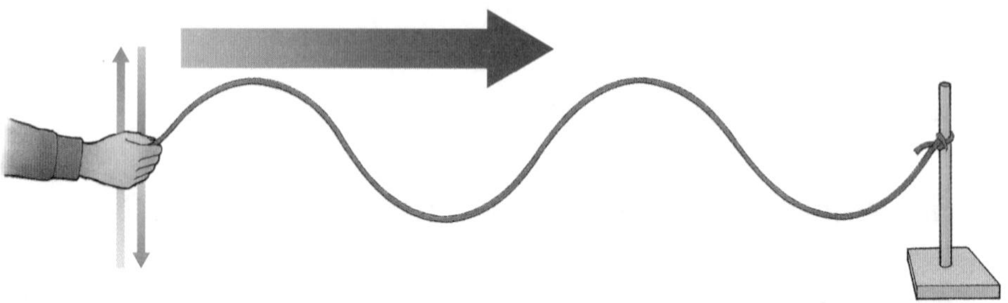

Transverse waves

- For a **longitudinal wave** the oscillation of the particles is parallel to the direction of travel of the wave.
- A longitudinal wave is made up of **compressions** and **rarefactions**.

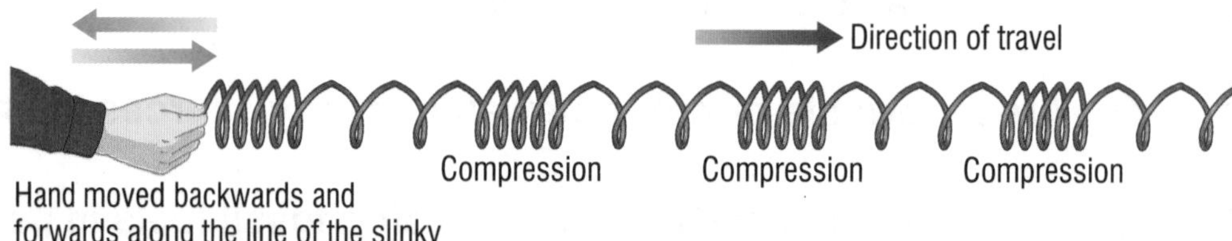

Longitudinal waves on a slinky

> **1** *When a longitudinal wave passes through air, what happens to the air particles at a compression?*

- **Electromagnetic waves**, e.g. light waves and radio waves, can travel through a vacuum. There are no particles moving in an electromagnet wave, as these waves are oscillations in electric and magnetic fields. The oscillations are perpendicular to the direction of travel of the wave. So all electromagnetic waves are transverse waves.
- **Mechanical waves**, e.g. waves on springs, and sound waves, travel through a medium (substance). Mechanical waves may be transverse or longitudinal.
- Sound waves are longitudinal waves.

> **2** *What type of wave can be produced on a stretched string?*

Key words: transverse wave, oscillation, perpendicular, longitudinal wave, compression, rarefaction, electromagnetic wave, mechanical wave

Student Book pages 278–279 **P1**

5.2 Measuring waves

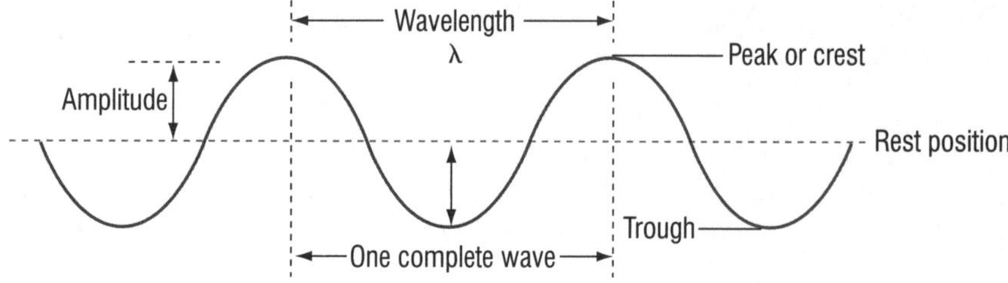

A transverse wave

- The **amplitude** of a wave is the height of the wave crest or the depth of the wave trough from the position at rest.
- The greater the amplitude of a wave the more energy it carries.
- The **wavelength** of a wave is the distance from one crest to the next crest, or from one trough to the next trough.
- The **frequency** of a wave is the number of wave crests passing a point in one second. The unit of frequency is the hertz (Hz). This unit is equivalent to per second (s).
- The **speed** of a wave is given by the equation: $v = f \times \lambda$

Where:
v is the wave speed in metres per second, m/s
f is the frequency in hertz, Hz
λ is the wavelength in metres, m.

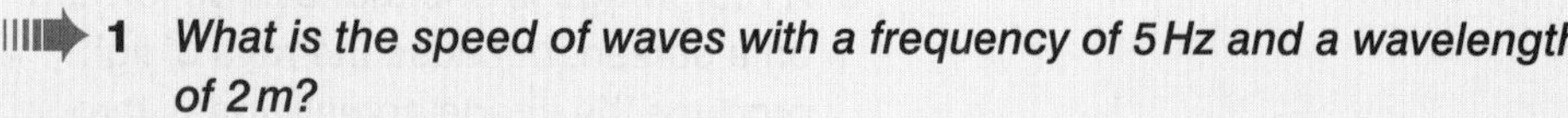

1 *What is the speed of waves with a frequency of 5 Hz and a wavelength of 2 m?*

- The diagram shows a transverse wave, but the same terms apply to a longitudinal wave.
- The wavelength of a longitudinal wave is the distance from the middle of one compression to the middle of the next compression. This is the same as the middle of one rarefaction to the middle of the next rarefaction.
- The frequency of a longitudinal wave is the number of compressions passing a point in one second.

2 *What is the unit of frequency?*

Key words: amplitude, wavelength, frequency, speed

Key points

- For any wave, its amplitude is the height of the wave crest or the depth of the wave trough, from the position at rest.
- For any wave, its frequency is the number of wave crests passing a point in one second.
- For any wave, its wavelength is the distance from one wave crest to the next wave crest. This is the same as the distance from one wave trough to the next wave trough.
- $v = f \times \lambda$

Bump up your grade

Make sure that you know what the wave terms mean and can mark them on a diagram.

Student Book pages 280–281 **P1**

5.3 Wave properties: reflection

Key points

- The normal at a point on a surface is a line drawn perpendicular to the surface.
- Angles are always measured between the light ray and the normal.
- The law of reflection states that: the angle of incidence is equal to the angle of reflection.

Study tip

Practise drawing neat diagrams to show reflection in a plane mirror. Remember to put arrows on the rays.

- The image seen in a mirror is due to the **reflection** of light.
- The diagram shows how an image is formed by a **plane** (flat) **mirror**. The incident ray is the ray that goes towards the mirror. The reflected ray is the one coming away from the mirror.
- We draw a line, called the **normal**, perpendicular to the mirror at the point where the incident ray hits the mirror.
- The **angle of incidence** is the angle between the incident ray and the normal.

The law of reflection

- The **angle of reflection** is the angle between the reflected ray and the normal.
- For any reflected ray the angle of incidence is equal to the angle of reflection.

1 *What is the normal?*

- The image in a plane mirror is:
  - the same size as the object
  - upright
  - the same distance behind the mirror as the object is in front.
  - virtual.
- A **real image** is one that can be formed on a screen, because the rays of light that produce the image actually pass through it.
- A **virtual image** cannot be formed on a screen, because the rays of light that produce the image only appear to pass through it.

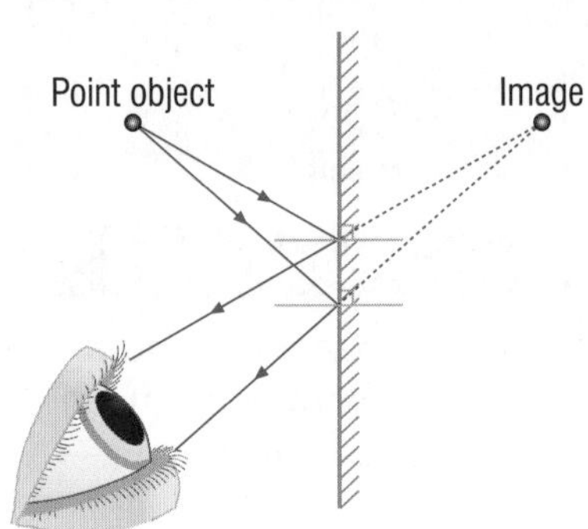

Image formation by a plane mirror

2 *What size is the image in a plane mirror?*

Bump up your grade

Make sure that you understand the difference between a real image and a virtual image.

Key words: plane mirror, normal, angle of incidence, angle of reflection, real image, virtual image

Student Book
pages 282–283

P1

5.4 Wave properties: refraction

Key points

- Refraction of light is the change of direction of a light ray when it crosses a boundary between two transparent substances.
- If the speed is reduced, refraction is towards the normal (e.g. air to glass).
- If the speed is increased, refraction is away from the normal (e.g. glass into air).

Refraction by a prism

- Waves change speed when they cross a **boundary** between different substances. The wavelength of the waves also changes, but the frequency stays the same.
- **Refraction** is a property of all waves, including light and sound. For example, a light ray refracts when it crosses a boundary between two substances such as air and glass, or air and water.
- The change in speed of the waves causes a change in direction.
- When light enters a more dense substance, such as going from air to glass, it slows down and the ray changes direction towards the normal.
- When light enters a less dense substance, such as going from glass to air, it speeds up and the ray changes direction away from the normal.
- However, if the wave is travelling along a normal, then it will not change direction.

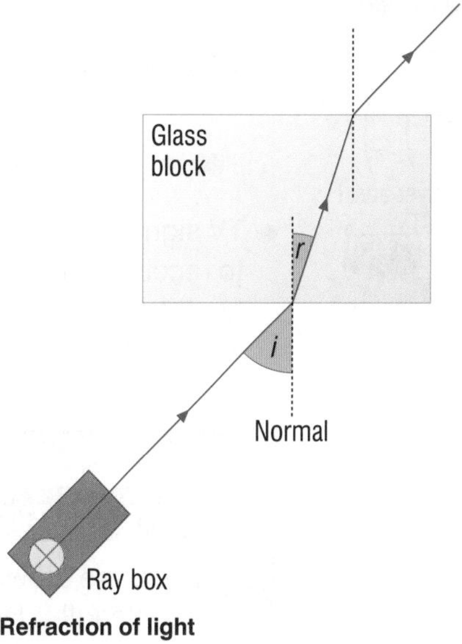

Refraction of light

1 *Why does refraction take place?*

- Different colours of light have different wavelengths, and are refracted by slightly different amounts. When a ray of white light is shone onto a triangular glass prism we can see this because a spectrum is produced. This is called dispersion.
- Violet light is refracted the most.
- Red light is refracted the least.

2 *Why does light split up into different colours when it passes through a triangular prism?*

Study tip

Take care not to confuse reflection and refraction.

Bump up your grade

Remember that a ray of light travelling along a normal is **not** refracted.

Key words: boundary, refraction

Student Book pages 284–285 **P1**

5.5 Wave properties: diffraction

Key points

- Diffraction is the spreading out of waves when they pass through a gap or round the edge of an obstacle.
- The narrower a gap the greater the diffraction.
- If radio waves do not diffract enough when they go over hills, radio and TV reception will be poor.

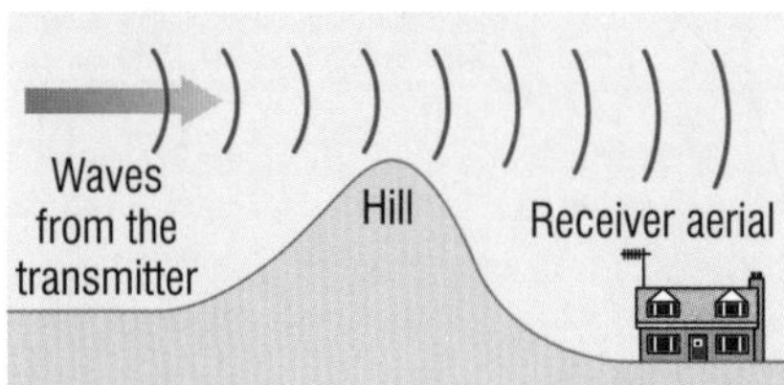

Poor reception

- **Diffraction** is a property of all waves, including light and sound. It is the spreading of waves when they pass through a gap or round an obstacle.
- The effect is most noticeable if the wavelength of the waves is about the same size as the gap or the obstacle.

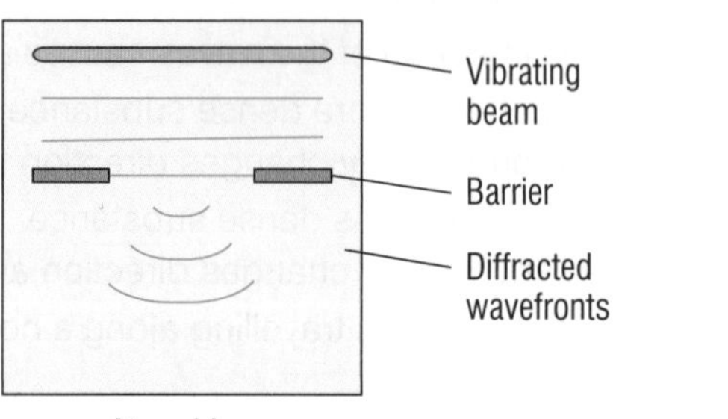

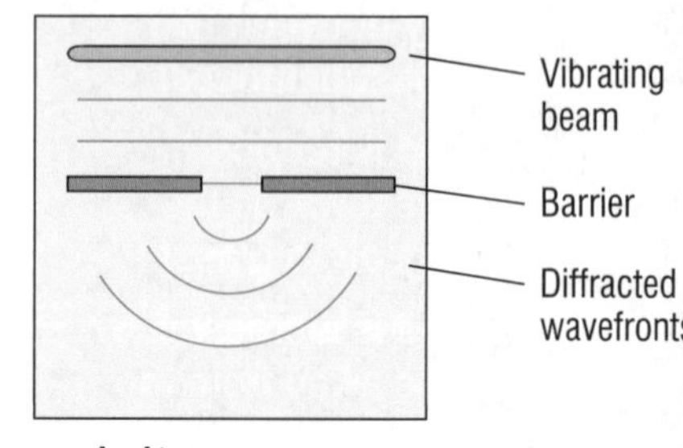

Diffraction of waves by a gap: a a wide gap b a narrow gap

1 *Why don't we often observe the diffraction of light during everyday life?*

- TV signals are carried by radio waves. People living in hilly areas may not be able to receive a signal because it is blocked by a hill. Radio waves passing the hill will be diffracted round the hill. If they do not diffract enough, the radio and TV signals will be poor.

2 *What sort of waves are diffracted?*

Bump up your grade

If you are drawing a diagram to show diffraction, make sure that the wavelength of the waves stays the same.

Key words: diffraction

Student Book pages 286–287 **P1**

5.6 Sound

Key points

- The frequency range of the normal human ear is from about 20 Hz to about 20 kHz.
- Sound waves are longitudinal.
- Sound waves need a medium in which to travel.
- Reflections of sound are called echoes.

- **Sound** is caused by mechanical vibrations in a substance, and travels as a wave.
- It can travel through liquids, solids and gases. Sound waves generally travel fastest in solids and slowest in gases.
- They cannot travel through a vacuum (like space). This can be tested by listening to a ringing bell in a 'bell jar'. As the air is pumped out of the jar, the ringing sound fades away.
- Sound waves are longitudinal waves. The direction of the vibrations is the same as the direction in which the wave travels.
- The range of frequencies that can be heard by the human ear is from 20 Hz to 20 000 Hz. The ability to hear the higher frequencies declines with age.

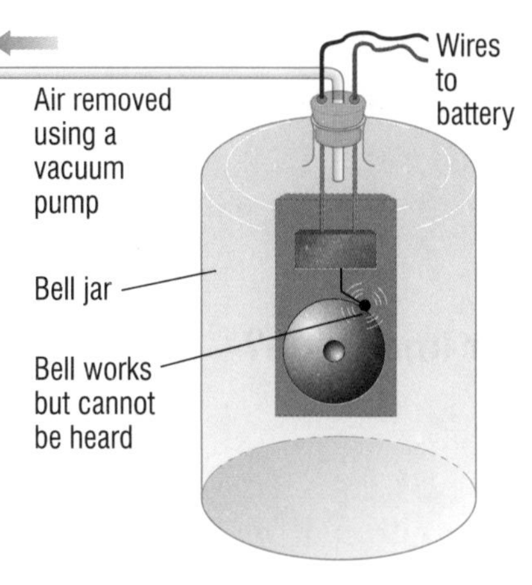

A sound test

- Sound waves can be reflected to produce **echoes**:
  - Only hard, flat surfaces such as flat walls and floors reflect sound.
  - Soft things like carpets, curtains and furniture absorb sounds.
  - An empty room will sound different once carpets, curtains and furniture are put into it.
- Sound waves can be refracted. Refraction takes place at the boundaries between layers of air at different temperatures.
- Sound waves can also be diffracted.

1 *What is the range of frequencies that can be heard by the human ear?*
2 *What is the reflection of a sound called?*

Key words: sound, echo

Student Book pages 288–289 **P1**

5.7 Musical sounds

Key points

- The pitch of a note increases if the frequency of the sound waves increases.
- The loudness of a note depends on the amplitude of the sound waves.
- Vibrations created in an instrument when it is played produce sound waves.

- The **pitch** of a note depends on the frequency of the sound waves. The higher the frequency of the wave, the higher the pitch of the sound.
- The loudness of a sound depends on the amplitude of the sound waves. The greater the amplitude the more energy the wave carries and the louder the sound.
- Differences in **waveform** can be shown on an oscilloscope.

1 *What happens to the pitch of a note as the frequency decreases?*

- Tuning forks and signal generators produce 'pure' waveforms.
- The quality of a note depends on the waveform.
- Different instruments produce different waveforms, which is why they sound different from each other.
- Vibrations created in an instrument when it is played produce sound waves.
- In some instruments (e.g. a saxophone) a column of air vibrates. In others (e.g. a violin) a string vibrates. Some instruments vibrate when they are struck, e.g. a xylophone.

2 *Why do different instruments sound different when they play the same note?*

Bump up your grade

Practise sketching waveforms, e.g. sketch a wave with twice the frequency and half the amplitude of the original.

Key words: pitch

a Loud and high-pitched

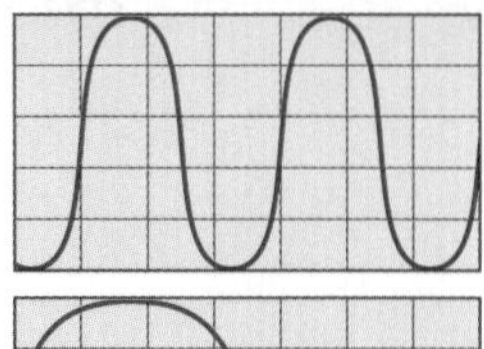

b Loud and low-pitched

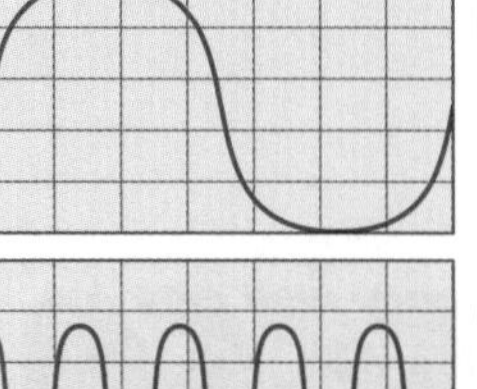

c Quiet and high-pitched (higher pitch than **a**)

Different sounds

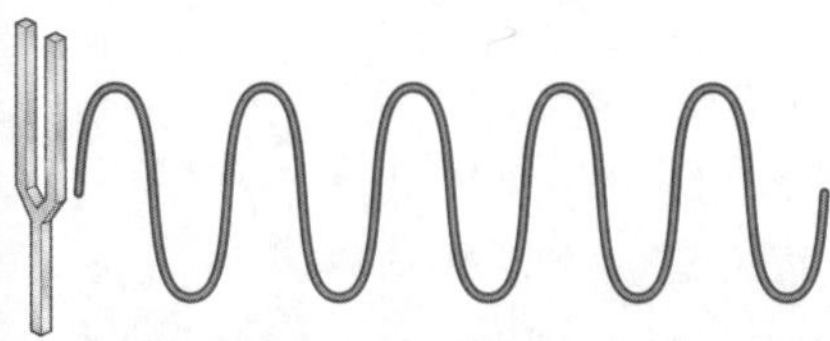

Tuning fork waves as they appear on an oscilloscope

1. What is the unit of wavelength?
2. What type of image is produced by a plane mirror?
3. If you stand 1.5 m in front of a plane mirror, where will your image be?
4. Which colour of light is refracted the most?
5. What is an echo?
6. What is a rarefaction?
7. What happens when light waves cross a boundary between two transparent substances?
8. What is diffraction?
9. How does a flute produce sound?
10. What does the pitch of a note depend on?
11. What is the speed of a sound wave of frequency 330 Hz and wavelength 1 cm?
12. What is the frequency of a wave if it travels at 400 m/s and its wavelength is 20 m? [H]

Chapter checklist ✓✓✓

Tick when you have:

reviewed it after your lesson	☑	☐	☐
revised once – some questions right	☑	☑	☐
revised twice – all questions right	☑	☑	☑

Move on to another topic when you have all three ticks

The nature of waves	☐	☐	☐
Measuring waves	☐	☐	☐
Wave properties: reflection	☐	☐	☐
Wave properties: refraction	☐	☐	☐
Wave properties: diffraction	☐	☐	☐
Sound	☐	☐	☐
Musical sounds	☐	☐	☐

Student Book pages 292–293 **P1**

6.1 The electromagnetic spectrum

Key points

- The electromagnetic spectrum (in order of increasing wavelength) is: gamma rays, X-rays, ultraviolet, visible, infrared, microwaves, radio waves.
- $v = f \times \lambda$ can be used to calculate the frequency or wavelength of electromagnetic waves.

Study tip

Remember that electromagnetic waves transfer energy, not matter.

Bump up your grade

Exam questions often come up about the electromagnetic spectrum. Make sure that you can put the different parts of the spectrum in the correct order. The order can be asked for in either decreasing or increasing wavelength, frequency or energy.

- Electromagnetic radiations are electric and magnetic disturbances. They travel as waves and move energy from place to place.
- All electromagnetic waves travel through space (a vacuum) at the same speed but they have different wavelengths and frequencies.
- All of the waves together are called the **electromagnetic spectrum**. We group the waves according to their **wavelength** and **frequency**:
  - Gamma rays have the shortest wavelength and highest frequency.
  - Gamma rays can have wavelengths as short as 10^{-15} m (= 0.000 000 000 000 001 m).
  - Radio waves have the longest wavelength and lowest frequency.
  - Radio waves can have wavelengths of more than 10 000 m.
- The spectrum is continuous. The frequencies and wavelengths at the boundaries are approximate as the different parts of the spectrum are not precisely defined.
- Different wavelengths of electromagnetic radiation are reflected, absorbed or transmitted differently by different substances and types of surface.
- The higher the frequency of an electromagnetic wave the more energy it transfers.

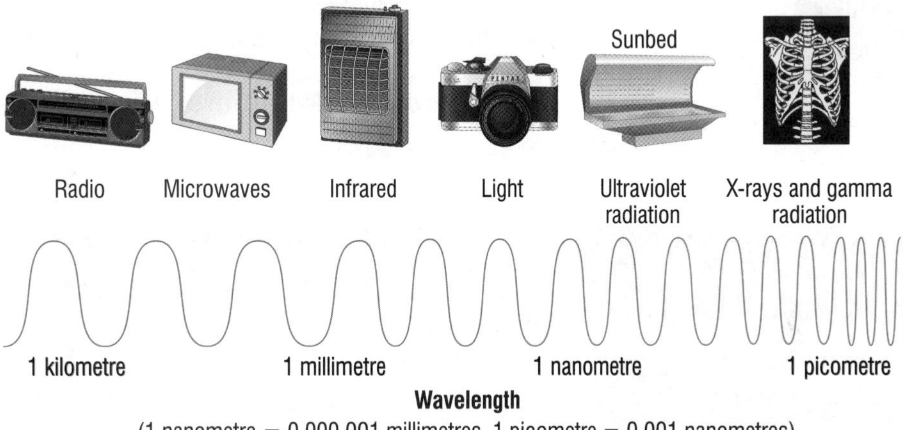

The electromagnetic spectrum

- All electromagnetic waves travel through space at a **wave speed** of 300 million m/s. We can link the speed of the waves to their wavelength and frequency using the equation:

$$v = f \times \lambda$$

Where:

v is the wave speed = 300 000 000 m/s

f is the frequency in hertz, Hz

λ is the wavelength in metres, m.

1 *What is the unit of frequency?*

2 *Which part of the electromagnetic spectrum transfers the most energy?*

Key words: gamma rays, X-rays, ultraviolet radiation, electromagnetic spectrum, wave speed

Student Book pages 294–295 **P1**

6.2 Light, infrared, microwaves and radio waves

Key points

- White light contains all the colours of the spectrum.
- Visible light, infrared radiation, microwaves and radio waves are all used for communication.

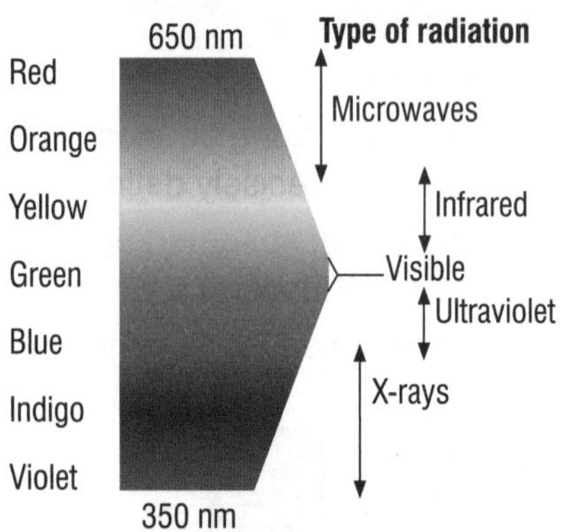

Parts of the electromagnetic spectrum

- **Visible light** is the part of the electromagnetic spectrum that is detected by our eyes. We see the different wavelengths within it as different colours.
- The wavelength increases across the spectrum from violet to red. We see a mixture of all the colours as white light.
- Visible light can be used for photography.
- Infrared (IR) radiation is given out by all objects. The hotter the object, the more IR it emits. Remote controls for devices such as TVs and CD players use IR.
- **Microwaves** are used in communications. Microwave transmitters produce wavelengths that are able to pass through the atmosphere. They are used to send signals to and from satellites and within mobile phone networks.
- **Radio waves** transmit radio and TV programs and carry mobile phone signals.

1 *Which have the longer wavelengths, microwaves or radio waves?*

- Microwave radiation and radio waves penetrate your skin and are absorbed by body tissue. This can heat internal organs and may damage them.
- Infrared radiation is absorbed by skin; too much will burn your skin.

Key words: visible light, microwave, radio wave

Student Book pages 296–297 **P1**

6.3 Communications

Key points

- Radio waves of different frequencies are used for different purposes.
- Microwaves are used for satellite TV signals.
- Research is needed to evaluate whether or not mobile phones are safe to use.
- Optical fibres are very thin fibres that are used to transmit signals by light and infrared radiation.

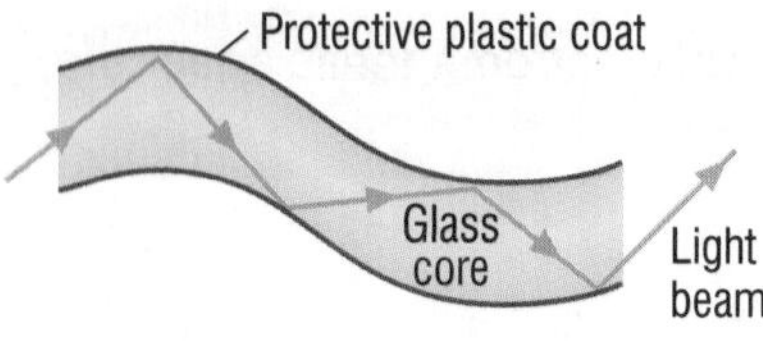

An optical fibre

- An alternating voltage applied to an aerial emits radio waves with the same frequency as the alternating voltage. When the waves are received they produce an alternating current in the aerial with the same frequency as the radiation received.
- The radio and microwave spectrum is divided into different **bands**. The different bands are used for different communications purposes.
- The shorter the wavelength of the waves the more information they carry, the shorter their range, the less they spread out.

1 *How are radio waves produced?*

- Mobile phones communicate with a local mobile phone mast using wavelengths just on the border between radio waves and microwaves. They are usually referred to as microwaves.
- Some scientists think that the radiation from mobile phones may affect the brain, especially in children.
- **Optical fibres** are very thin glass fibres. We use them to transmit signals carried by **visible light** or **infrared radiation**. The signals travel down the fibre by repeated total internal reflection.
- Optical fibres carrying visible light or infrared are useful in communications because they carry much more information and are more secure than radio wave and microwave transmissions.

Key words: band, optical fibre

Student Book pages 298–299 **P1**

6.4 The expanding universe

Key points

- Light from distant galaxies is red-shifted.
- Red-shift provides evidence that the universe is expanding.

Study tip

Remember that light is shifted towards the red end of the spectrum; it is **not** turned into red light.

- Imagine a wave source is moving relative to an observer. The wavelength and frequency of the waves detected by the observer will have changed (shifted) from the original produced by the source. This is called the **Doppler effect**.
- When the source moves away from the observer, the observed wavelength increases and the frequency decreases.
- When the source moves towards the observer, the observed wavelength decreases and the frequency increases.
- The Doppler effect can be demonstrated with sound waves. For example, an ambulance siren will sound different depending on whether it is moving away from you (pitch is lower) or towards you (pitch is higher).

1 *What happens to the wavelength if a wave source is moving away from you?*

- Galaxies are large collections of stars. Light observed from distant galaxies has been 'shifted' towards the red end of the spectrum. This is known as **red-shift** and means that the frequency has decreased and the wavelength increased.
- A **blue-shift** would indicate that a galaxy is moving towards us. We are able to see these effects by observing dark lines in the spectra from galaxies.

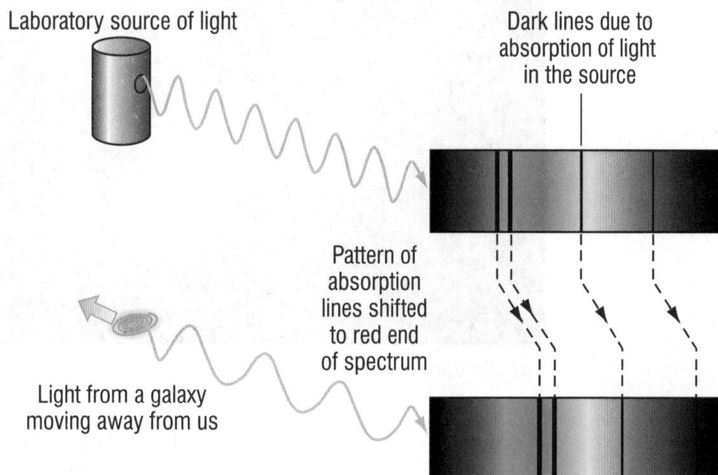

Red-shift

- The further away the galaxy, the bigger the red-shift. This suggests that distant galaxies are moving away from us, and the most distant galaxies are moving the fastest. This is true of galaxies no matter which direction you look.
- All the distant galaxies are moving away from each other, so the whole universe is expanding.

2 *Which galaxies are moving fastest?*
3 *How does red-shift show that the universe is expanding?*

Key words: Doppler effect, red-shift, blue-shift

Student Book pages 300–301 **P1**

6.5 The Big Bang

Key points

- The universe started with the Big Bang; a massive explosion from a very small initial point.
- The universe has been expanding ever since the Big Bang.
- Cosmic microwave background radiation (CMBR) is electromagnetic radiation created just after the Big Bang.
- At present CMBR can only be explained by the Big Bang theory.

- Red-shift gives us evidence that the universe is expanding outwards in all directions.
- We can imagine going back in time to see where the universe came from. If it is now expanding outwards, this suggests that it started with a massive explosion at a very small initial point. This is known as the **Big Bang theory**.

1 *What is the Big Bang theory?*

The Big Bang

- If the universe began with a Big Bang, then high energy gamma radiation would have been produced. As the universe expanded, this would have become lower-energy radiation.
- Scientists discovered microwaves coming from every direction in space. This is **cosmic microwave background radiation** (CMBR), the radiation produced by the Big Bang.
- The Big Bang theory is so far the only way to explain the existence of CMBR.

2 ***What happens to the wavelength of radiation as it changes from gamma to microwave?***

Bump up your grade

Be sure that you can explain why red-shift is evidence for an expanding universe and the Big Bang.

Key words: Big Bang theory, cosmic microwave background radiation

1 Which part of the electromagnetic spectrum has the longest wavelengths?

2 Which part of the electromagnetic spectrum is between X-rays and visible light?

3 The wave speed for all electromagnetic waves is 300 million m/s. What is the frequency of electromagnetic waves with a wavelength of 300 m?

4 Which part of the electromagnetic spectrum transfers the least energy?

5 Which part of the electromagnetic spectrum is used to transmit signals to and from satellites?

6 How does visible light travel along an optical fibre?

7 What is the Doppler effect?

8 What is a galaxy?

9 What has happened to the frequency of light that reaches Earth from distant galaxies?

10 How can we tell if light from a distant galaxy has been red-shifted?

11 What has happened to the gamma radiation produced at the time of the Big Bang?

12 What piece of evidence can only be explained by the Big Bang theory?

Chapter checklist ✓✓✓

Tick when you have:

reviewed it after your lesson	✓	☐	☐
revised once – some questions right	✓	✓	☐
revised twice – all questions right	✓	✓	✓

Move on to another topic when you have all three ticks

The electromagnetic spectrum	☐	☐	☐
Light, infrared, microwaves and radio waves	☐	☐	☐
Communications	☐	☐	☐
The expanding universe	☐	☐	☐
The Big Bang	☐	☐	☐

1 An electric kettle is used to heat water. When the kettle is switched on, the energy is transferred to the water by a heating element at the bottom of the kettle.

a State the process that transfers energy from the heating element to the water at the bottom of the kettle. *(1 mark)*

b Eventually all of the water in the kettle becomes hot. Explain how energy is transferred from the water at the bottom of the kettle to the rest of the water. *(4 marks)*

c The kettle contains 1.2 kg of water. The temperature of the water is increased by 80 °C. Calculate the energy supplied to the water by the heating element.
The specific heat capacity of the water is 4200 J/kg °C.
Write down the equation you use. Show clearly how you work out your answer and give the unit. *(3 marks)*

d Not all of the energy supplied to the kettle is transferred to the water. Explain what happens to the energy not transferred to the water. *(3 marks)*

2 *In this question you will be assessed on using good English, organising information clearly and using specialist terms where appropriate.*
There are three states of matter: solid, liquid and gas. The kinetic theory of matter tells us that solids, liquids and gases consist of particles. Use the kinetic theory to describe and explain the properties of solids, liquids and gases. *(6 marks)*

3 A food processor contains an electric motor.

a i What is the useful energy transfer that takes place in the motor? *(1 mark)*

ii How is some energy wasted in the motor? *(1 mark)*

b i The motor wastes 300 J of energy for every 1000 J of energy supplied to it. How much useful energy is transferred? *(1 mark)*

ii Calculate the percentage efficiency of the motor.
Write down the equation you use. Show clearly how you work out your answer and give the unit. *(3 marks)*

c The power of the motor is 800 W. If electricity costs 12p per kW h, calculate the cost of using the food processor for 15 minutes. *(4 marks)*

4 Energy can be produced using renewable and non-renewable energy sources. In a nuclear power station, energy is produced from uranium by nuclear fission.

a Is uranium a renewable or a non-renewable energy source? *(1 mark)*

b Explain how the energy from nuclear fission is used to generate electricity. *(4 marks)*

c Wind turbines use a renewable energy source to produce electricity.

i Explain the advantages of using a nuclear power station, compared to using a wind turbine, to generate electricity. *(2 marks)*

ii Explain the disadvantages of using a nuclear power station, compared to using a wind turbine, to generate electricity. *(2 marks)*

Study tip

Qu 1b There are four marks for explaining how the energy is transferred, so to get four marks make sure you make four points.

Study tip

Qu 3bii Be careful with percentages – this question has asked for the answer to be converted to a percentage, so you must multiply your answer by 100.

5 A student is investigating the reflection of light. He stands a plane mirror on a piece of paper and marks the position of the back of the mirror with a line.

a Why should he mark the position of the back of the mirror? *(1 mark)*

b He pushes a pin into the paper in front of the mirror. The image of the pin in the mirror is virtual.

i Explain what is meant by a virtual image. *(2 marks)*

ii The pin is 6 cm from the line and 4 cm tall. Describe the image of the pin. *(3 marks)*

c The diagram shows the positions of the mirror and the pin.

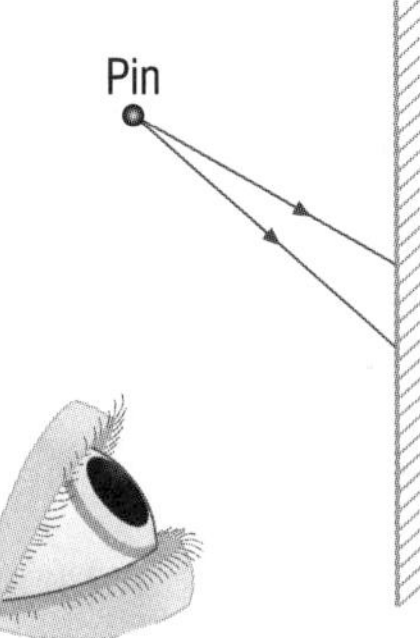

Copy and complete the diagram to show how the virtual image is formed. *(3 marks)*

6 A teacher uses a tuning fork to produce a note.

a Describe how a sound wave from the tuning fork travels through the air. *(3 marks)*

b The teacher uses a microphone and an oscilloscope to produce a trace of the note from the tuning fork. The trace is shown below.

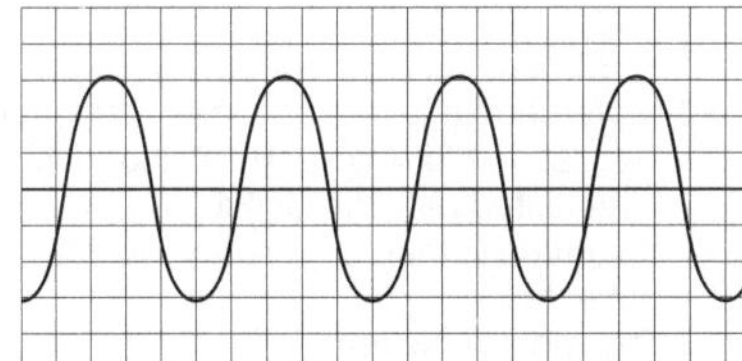

i Copy and complete the diagram below to show what the trace would look like for a note that had the same pitch as the original note, but was louder. *(3 marks)*

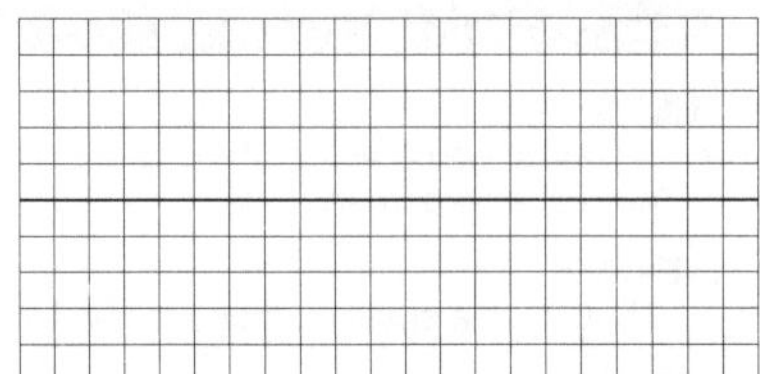

ii Copy and complete the diagram below to show what the trace would look like for a note that had the same volume as the original note, but a higher pitch. *(3 marks)*

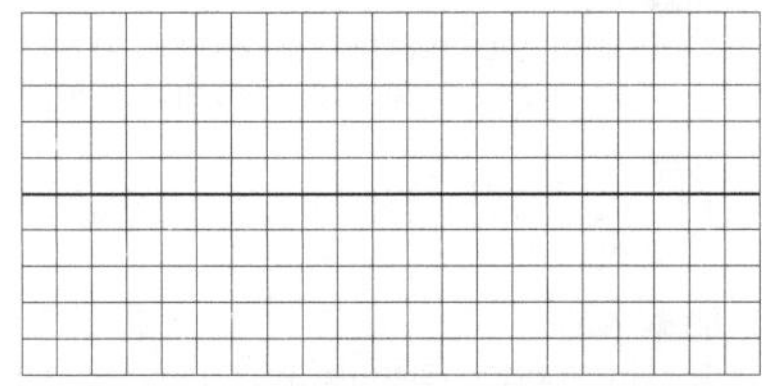

Study tip

Make sure that you use a sharp pencil and ruler to complete the diagram as neatly as you can. Add arrows to show the direction of the rays and use dashed lines to represent virtual rays.

Answers

B1 Answers

1 Keeping healthy

1.1

1 You become malnourished. Too much energy – gain weight; too few vitamins – develop deficiency disease.

1.2

1 They have taken in more energy than they have used.
2 They have too little energy/may have a disease.

1.3

1 They can increase exercise/reduce saturated fat intake.

1.4

1 They produce toxins/damage cells.
2 No-one knew about bacteria and viruses.

1.5

1 The skin stops them (also mucus and stomach acid).
2 They ingest pathogens/produce antibodies/ produce antitoxins.

1.6

1 Viruses are inside the body cells.

1.7

1 The bacteria will grow at a faster rate.
2 Heat all equipment, boil solutions and cover Petri dishes or flasks.

1.8

1 Very few people are immune to the new pathogen.
2 The antibiotics kill the non-resistant strains which allows the resistant ones to survive and to multiply (no competition). [H]

1.9

1 Injection (or oral drops) of a dead or inactive pathogen to stimulate the white blood cells to produce antibodies.

1.10

1 Advantages – protects the individual and society from serious diseases which may cause death. Disadvantages – may cause side effects in a few people.
2 Some pathogens are resistant to drugs. New pathogens arise by mutation.

Answers to end of chapter questions

1 A balanced diet contains the correct amounts of all the nutrients needed for healthy functioning of the body.
2 They may take in too much energy; they may have too little food; particular nutrients may be missing from their diet
3 Three from: Size of the person, sex of the person, the amount of exercise they do, the outside temperature, pregnancy, breast feeding
4 Metabolic rate is a measure of how quickly the chemical reactions in cells release energy from food. Exercise/proportion of fat to muscle/ inherited factors affect the rate.
5 a A pathogen is an organism that causes disease.
  b An antibiotic is a drug that kills bacteria.
6 Viruses reproduce inside body cells. The drugs would also damage the cells or tissues.
7 Everyone in a hospital should wash their hands or use hand gels to prevent transfer of pathogens.
8 A mutation is a change in a gene.
9 A pandemic occurs when a disease spreads between different countries, an epidemic occurs within one country.
10 Mild throat infections can get better quickly without antibiotics. Overuse of antibiotics results in the development of antibiotic resistant bacteria.
11 Some bacteria mutate and become resistant to an antibiotic. Antibiotics kill the non-resistant strains. The resistant strains multiply. Each time antibiotics are used more of the resistant strains survive until the whole population of bacteria is resistant to the antibiotic. [H]
12 White blood cells respond to the vaccine by producing antibodies. If the body is infected with the pathogen, the white blood cells respond quickly by producing more antibodies.

2 Coordination and control

2.1

1 Light, sound, chemicals, touch, pain and temperature changes
2 As electrical impulses along a sensory neuron

2.2

1 It links the sensory and motor neurons.

2.3

1 FSH and LH

2.4

1 FSH

2.5

1 So that the enzymes work properly

2.6

1 Unequal distribution of auxin causes unequal growth of the shoot.

2.7

1 Contraceptives prevent unwanted pregnancies. Allows couples to plan their family. Gives woman control over her life. Fertility drugs used in IVF – allows infertile women to have babies.
2 Much older women have babies. Extra embryos may be produced and stored.
3 The hormones might kill trees or other plants as well as weeds.

Answers to end of chapter questions

1 Glands and muscles
2 Three of: Light, sound, chemicals, touch, pain and temperature changes
3 It inhibits the release of FSH.
4 Two of: water, mineral ions, temperature, sugar
5 By means of a chemical
6 Receptor
7 Auxin
8 Response of a root to gravity
9 The growth hormone auxin causes the side of the shoot away from the light to grow more so it becomes longer.
10 It contains hormones which inhibit FSH so that the egg does not mature.
11 FSH causes the egg to mature. LH stimulates ovulation (egg release).
12 Stimulus → receptor → sensory neuron → relay neuron → motor neuron → effector → response

3 Medicine and drugs

3.1

1 To find out if they work, if they are toxic, to find the best dose, for side effects.

3.2

1 To reduce cholesterol levels and reduce the risk of heart disease.
2 To check that they work as well as a tested drug like Prozac

3.3

1 They change the body's chemistry.

3.4

1 They affect the nervous system, particularly the brain.

3.5

1 They are in contact with drug dealers who may 'push' hard drugs.

3.6

1 They want to win so badly.

Answers to end of chapter questions

1 Against the law
2 a It was found to be useful at treating morning sickness.
  b It caused limb abnormalities in babies whose mothers were treated when pregnant.
3 Cocaine and heroin
4 Drugs which are taken for pleasure rather than to cure a disease or symptom
5 To build muscle mass
6 Neither the doctor nor the patient know who has been given the drug or the placebo.
7 Depression – a mental health problem
8 The drugs change the chemical processes in the body
9 The brain, nervous system and liver.
10 More people take medicines and legal recreational drugs such as alcohol and tobacco.
11 First tested on cells, tissue and organs; then on animals; then on healthy volunteers; finally patients
12 The most likely reason is that the drug pushers offer them more expensive drugs when they buy cannabis.

4 Adaptation for survival

4.1

1 A feature which allows the organism to live in its normal environment.

4.2

1 They have a small surface area : volume ratio

4.3

1 Three of: curled leaves, stomata situated away from heat and wind, waxy leaves, small leaves and water storage in stems

4.4

1 So that they can find enough food and water. They also need space to protect and rear their young.

4.5

1 To avoid competition for water, light and mineral ions

4.6

1 The wasps pollinate the fig tree with the right sort of pollen.

2 The mole is sensitive to touch and smell so detects food underground. The Venus fly trap is brightly coloured and produces sticky nectar to attract and trap flies.

4.7

1 Three of: temperature, rainfall, light, oxygen levels, carbon dioxide levels, pH, pollution levels (e.g. sulfur dioxide)

4.8

1 Climate change has caused it to become warm enough further north for the birds to nest and possibly too warm further south.

Answers to end of chapter questions

1 Three of: light, water, nutrients (mineral ions), space
2 So they are camouflaged against the snow and ice and their prey find it more difficult to see them.
3 Three of: smaller leaves, water storage tissue, e.g. swollen stem, stomata situated away from light and wind, curled leaves, waxy leaves
4 The colour signals that they are poisonous or have an awful taste. Once the animal eats it they won't try again!
5 The climate further south gets too warm in the summer. It is too cold for them in the northern winter.
6 So that they are able to use the sunlight to photosynthesise and grow. Once the trees have their leaves the smaller plants will receive much less light. They will also have more competition for water and nutrients from the soil as the trees begin to grow.
7 A data logger – a computer attached to sensors
8 So their prey find them more difficult to see. This means that the predator can get closer to its prey before attacking. This makes them more successful at obtaining food.
9 It will transfer energy slowly. This is why elephants have a folded skin which increases the total surface area and its large ears will also transfer energy effectively.
10 When the plants are grown closer together there is more competition for light, water and nutrients. This means that individual plants may not grow as well and the overall yield is the same or lower.
11 To keep cool/stay out of the Sun and to feed. They are also less easily seen by a predator.
12 There are so many possible variables. It may be obvious that the climate has got warmer but this might lead to other changes. For example, if a plant flowers earlier in the year the insects which feed on it may not be around to pollinate the flowers. This could lead to a fall in the number of plants and also in the number of insects which would not be able to feed on the nectar.

5 Energy in biomass

5.1

1 Plants capture light energy and transfer it to chemical energy. They make food which is then eaten by animals. Plants start the process of energy transfer in living organisms.

5.2

1 Respiration in cells releases energy from food

5.3

1 Worms
2 Microorganisms (bacteria and fungi) which breakdown/digest waste materials from animals and plants or dead organisms.

5.4

1 Photosynthesis

5.5

1 Worms are detritus feeders and start the breakdown of the compost.
2 Smaller pieces have a larger surface area for the microorganisms to 'attack'. This will increase the rate of decomposition.

Answers to end of chapter questions

1 The mass of living material
2 Waste from living organisms containing carbon compounds (such as carbohydrates, fats and proteins)
3 Respiration and combustion (burning)
4 Reduce the number of stages. Carnivores have less energy available than herbivores who only eat plants.
5 Worms
6 A type of graph with arrow shapes which shows total energy taken in and how it is transferred.
7 The energy from respiration heats up the surroundings.
8 There are less stages in the food chain. Eating plants is the most efficient way of feeding the world population, but if we want meat less energy is wasted by eating herbivores.
9 The processes that remove materials from the environment are balanced by processes that return these materials. Materials such as carbon are constantly recycled.
10 There is undigested food in the faeces (cow dung), urea is lost in the urine, the calf transfers energy to move around, the calf produces methane which is lost to the atmosphere, the energy released in respiration is eventually wasted heating the surroundings.

6 Variation, reproduction and new technology

6.1

1 In the chromosomes
2 Genes control the development of characteristics (such as eye colour or thumb shape)

6.2

1 Asexual reproduction, because there is only one parent
2 Sexual reproduction, because the offspring has genes from both the mother and the father

6.3

1 The genes we inherit and environmental causes (such as diet)

6.4

1 Taking cuttings from mature plants is a quick and cheap way of cloning.
2 Animal embryos must be split into groups of cells and then each group is transplanted into a host 'mother'. There have to be enough hosts and some embryos may die during development. It also takes longer for the animals to develop.

6.5

1 An adult cell, such as a skin cell, and an egg cell

6.6

1 Enzymes are used to cut genes out of chromosomes

6.7

1 They will get a higher yield and therefore more money for their harvest.

Answers to end of chapter questions

1 The nucleus of gamete cells contains the genetic material which is passed from parent to offspring.
2 Identical twins are natural clones.
3 Clones have the same genetic material but during development the organism may be changed due to environmental factors, e.g. amount of light or nutrients.
4 The host animal is the one in which a transplanted embryo develops.
5 An electric shock is applied to the cell.
6 Offspring inherit genes from both parents. Different combinations of genes lead to the appearance of different physical characteristics.
7 A single embryo is formed which then splits into two in identical twins. In cloning the embryo is split into several groups of cells.
8 After sexual reproduction, a single embryo is produced. Before the cells specialise the embryo is split into several groups of cells. Each group is transplanted into a different host mother. The calves born are all genetically identical.
9 Embryo cloning top class animals is quicker and cheaper. Cattle only have one or two young per year. If prize animals are bred together the farmer can get large numbers of the prize calves by cloning the single embryo. Embryos can also be flown around the world to benefit other farmers.
10 A gene is cut from a chromosome of one organism using enzymes. The gene is then transferred to the chromosome of another organism. The gene then controls the development of a characteristic in the second organism.
11 Two of: Compounds such as insulin can be produced in large quantities. Antibodies can be produced to treat disease. Genetic disorders can be treated. Herbicide and insect-resistant crops can be produced. Food which lasts longer can be produced. [Other relevant answers are acceptable.]
12 A gene is transferred from another organism into the chromosome of the crop plant.

7 Evolution

7.1

1 About 3 billion years ago

7.2

1 Evolution by natural selection
2 Finches on the Galapagos Islands

7.3

1 Variation is due to differences in their genes.
2 If the environment changes the gene may control a characteristic which makes the organism better adapted to the conditions.

7.4

1 Animals, plants, microorganisms
2 They show the relationships between organisms.

Answers to end of chapter questions

1 The idea that organisms have developed from simple life forms and have changed (evolved) over time.
2 Lamarck suggested that characteristics which developed during the lifetime of the organism could be passed on. Darwin said that organisms with the best characteristics survived to breed and the offspring inherited the characteristic.
3 Scientists did not have enough evidence and they did not know about genes. Some people believed that God made all the animals and plants to look as they did.
4 Organisms compete for things such as food or light. If an organism is well adapted to its environment it will survive. Poorly adapted ones die before they breed.
5 If the offspring are produced by sexual reproduction, then the genes of both parents are inherited in different combinations when the gametes fuse.

6 Those that are best adapted or suited to their environment live long enough to breed. The weaker ones may die before they breed.
7 Organisms which are best adapted to the environment survive, breed and pass on their genes to the next generation.
8 Species are organisms which look very similar to each other and can interbreed to produce fertile offspring.
9 Three of: The climate may change – it could become hotter, colder, wetter or drier. A new predator may move into the area. A new disease may affect the population. A new competitor for the food supply may move into the area. There may be a loss of habitat such as nesting sites.
10 Evolutionary trees show the relationships between organisms and whether they had common ancestors.

Answers to examination-style questions

1 They have a larger surface area to volume ratio so lose heat quicker. *(3 marks)*
2 a Stem cells are removed from the embryo. *(1 mark)*
  b It involves sexual reproduction. *(1 mark)*
  c An embryo is formed. *(1 mark)*
3 a i **c** *(1 mark)*
  ii B *(1 mark)*
  iii **a** *(1 mark)*
  b 1/29 or 0.034 [allow 100/2900] *(1 mark)*
  c Enzymes *(1 mark)*
  work best at body temperature. *(1 mark)*
4 Marks awarded for this answer will be determined by the Quality of Written Communication (QWC) as well as the standard of the scientific response.

There is a clear and detailed description referring to the pin as a stimulus, the neurons in correct order and accurately named where identified, a synapse and the effector. The answer shows almost faultless spelling, punctuation and grammar. It is coherent and in an organised, logical sequence. It contains a range of appropriate or relevant specialist terms used accurately. *(5–6 marks)*
There is a description of most of the structures in a logical sequence and with most correctly identified. There are some errors in spelling, punctuation and grammar.
The answer has some structure and organisation. The use of specialist terms has been attempted, but not always accurately. *(3–4 marks)*
There is a brief description of a reflex action, which has little clarity and detail. The spelling, punctuation and grammar are very weak.
The answer is poorly organised with almost no specialist terms and/or their use demonstrating a general lack of understanding of their meaning. *(1–2 marks)*
No relevant content. *(0 marks)*

Examples of biological points made in the response:
- reference to pin as a stimulus
- receptor detects stimulus
- impulse passes along sensory neuron
- reaches CNS/spinal cord
- passes across synapse [only need to mention once]
- to relay neuron
- passes to motor neuron
- to effector
- muscle contracts
- pulls hand away from pin.

5 a Any two from: e.g.
- same volume of solution
[do not allow 'same size of container']
- left for same length of time
- same temperature
- same oxygen
- same pH
- same number of invertebrates/animals
[do not allow 'same number of species']
- same age/stage of invertebrates/animals *(2 marks)*

  b line of best fit/curve/point to point drawn going through 240–60 and 25 *(1 mark)*
  correct interpolation to *x*-axis *(1 mark)*
  [if no work on graph, allow 250]
  c i (C)
  50% killed at lowest/low copper concentration *(1 mark)*
  [ignore 'least survivors']
  ii any two from:
  involves counting
  easy to do
  invertebrates more sensitive
  needs less/no apparatus *(2 marks)*

C1 Answers

1 Fundamental ideas

1.1
1 Elements
2 An atom of hydrogen
3 A compound

1.2
1 Equal numbers of protons and electrons
2 13 protons, 13 electrons, 14 neutrons

1.3
1 Diagram: three concentric circles with dot or Al at centre, innermost circle with 2 electrons (dots or crosses), next with 8 electrons, outer circle with 3 electrons
2 Both have 5 electrons in highest energy level (outer shell).

1.4
1 Name of ionic compound, i.e. metal and non-metal, e.g. sodium chloride, magnesium oxide, etc.
2 Made from one calcium ion for every two chloride ions
3 It is made from three carbon atoms and eight hydrogen atoms.

1.5
1 Magnesium reacts with hydrochloric acid to produce magnesium chloride and hydrogen; one atom of magnesium reacts with 2 molecules of hydrochloric acid to give one magnesium ion and two chloride ions and one molecule of hydrogen.
2 a $H_2 + Cl_2 \rightarrow 2HCl$
  b $4Na + O_2 \rightarrow 2Na_2O$
  c $Na_2CO_3 + 2HCl \rightarrow 2NaCl + H_2O + CO_2$ [H]

Answers to end of chapter questions

1 Elements: Ca, H_2, Ne, O_2; Compounds: CH_4, HCl, MgO, SO_2
2 11 protons, 11 electrons, 12 neutrons
3 In order of atomic numbers (proton numbers)
4 Diagram: three concentric circles with a dot or S at centre, innermost circle with 2 electrons (dots or crosses), next circle with 8 electrons, outer circle with 6 electrons
5 Both have 3 (same number of) electrons in their highest energy level (outer shell).
6 CaO ionic, C_2H_6 covalent, H_2O covalent, KCl ionic, LiCl ionic, $MgCl_2$ ionic, NH_3 covalent, Na_2O ionic, PCl_3 covalent
7 Sodium atom loses an electron and becomes a sodium ion with a positive charge, chlorine atom gains an electron and becomes a chloride ion with a negative charge.
8 a lead nitrate + potassium iodide → potassium nitrate + lead iodide
  b two potassium atoms/ions, two nitrogen atoms, six oxygen atoms, one lead atom/ion, two iodine atoms/iodide ions
9 8.8 g
10 a $2Ca + O_2 \rightarrow 2CaO$
  b $2Na + 2H_2O \rightarrow 2NaOH + H_2$
  c $CH_4 + 2O_2 \rightarrow CO_2 + 2H_2O$ [H]

2 Rocks and building materials

2.1
1 As building blocks, to make calcium oxide, to make cement

2.2
1 Zinc oxide and carbon dioxide
2 magnesium carbonate + hydrochloric acid → magnesium chloride + carbon dioxide + water

2.3
1 calcium carbonate → calcium oxide + carbon dioxide
calcium oxide + water → calcium hydroxide
calcium hydroxide + carbon dioxide → calcium carbonate + water

2.4
1 Cement is made from limestone and clay, it is used to make mortar. Mortar is cement mixed with sand and water and is used to hold bricks and blocks together. Concrete is cement mixed with sand water and aggregate (stones or crushed rock) used to make blocks, beams, buildings and roads.

2.5
1 Advantages: More employment opportunities for local people, more customers and trade for local businesses, improved roads
Disadvantages: Dust and noise, more traffic, loss of habitats for wildlife

Answers to end of chapter questions

1 $CaCO_3$
2 By heating a mixture of limestone and clay in a kiln
3 Cement, sand, water, aggregate or crushed rock/stones
4 BreakBreaking down of a compound by heating
5 Calcium oxide and carbon dioxide
6 calcium oxide + water → calcium hydroxide
7 calcium carbonate is formed and is insoluble, calcium hydroxide + carbon dioxide → calcium carbonate + water
or $Ca(OH)_2 + CO_2 \rightarrow CaCO_3 + H_2O$
8 Acids react with calcium carbonate producing carbon dioxide and a salt. The salt dissolves in water and so the amount of limestone decreases or is worn away.
9 Calcium hydroxide reacts with acids, because calcium hydroxide is an alkali, and the reaction is neutralisation (the pH of the soil increases, which is better for growing crops).
10 $K_2CO_3 + 2HCl \rightarrow 2KCl + H_2O + CO_2$ [H]

3 Metals and their uses

3.1
1 Rock from which metal can be extracted economically
2 a Two metals from those below carbon in the reactivity series, e.g. zinc, iron, tin, lead, copper
  b Reduction

3.2

1 It is brittle.
2 They are harder, can be made with specific properties, can be made to resist corrosion.

3.3

1 It requires a lot of energy for high temperatures and electricity.
2 It is strong, resists corrosion, has a low density.

3.4

1 High-grade ores are limited or running out, to reduce environmental impacts.
2 Smelting, electrolysis, displacement

3.5

1 Strong, good conductors of heat and electricity, can be bent and hammered into shape
2 Good conductor of electricity, can be made into wires, can be bent into shape, resistant to corrosion
3 To make it harder

3.6

1 To save: the energy needed to extract it from its ore, resources, fossil fuels, land needed for mining and/or landfill, other specified environmental impact
2 Benefits: e.g. strong, not brittle, can be shaped, can be cut or joined or welded, cheaper than alternative metals. Drawbacks: e.g. needs protection from corrosion, heavy/dense, needs energy to extract/produce, extraction causes pollution.

Answers to end of chapter questions

1 Ore
2 It is very unreactive or very low in the reactivity series.
3 Strong, good conductors of heat and electricity, can be bent and hammered into shape.
4 Most pure metals are too soft for many uses, they need to be made harder by alloying (mixing with other elements).
5 Iron oxide is reduced by carbon when heated together. Iron oxide + carbon → iron + carbon dioxide
6 Low-carbon steel or mild steel, easily shaped; high-carbon steel, hard; stainless steel, resists corrosion
7 All steels contain iron and carbon, so are mixtures of a metal with at least one other element.
8 Three from: low density, resists corrosion, good conductor of heat and/or electricity, can be bent or hammered into shape.
9 Three from: Extraction needs several stages, uses a large amount of energy, uses a very reactive metal (for displacement), cannot be extracted using carbon
10 Three from: to save iron ore or reduce mining, to save energy or fossil fuels needed for extraction, to reduce waste going to land fill, to reduce imports of iron or iron ore
11 Phytomining and bioleaching. Phytomining uses plants to absorb copper compounds from the ground. The plants are burned and produce ash. This can be smelted to produce copper or reacted with acid to produce a solution that can be electrolysed or to which iron can be added to produce copper. Bioleaching uses bacteria to produce a solution of copper compounds that can be electrolysed or to which iron can be added to produce copper.
12 $2Fe_2O_3 + 3C \rightarrow 4Fe + 3CO_2$
$4Na + TiCl_4 \rightarrow Ti + 4NaCl$ [H]

4 Crude oil and fuels

4.1

1 Liquids with different boiling ranges separated from a mixture of liquids (crude oil)
2 It has the general formula C_nH_{2n+2}, it is a saturated compound, it has only single carbon–carbon bonds.
3 C_4H_{10}

4.2

1 Different hydrocarbons have different boiling points (so they condense at different levels).
2 Medium-high boiling point (about 250 °C), quite viscous/oily/thick liquid, not very flammable, burns with quite a smoky flame

4.3

1 ethane + oxygen → carbon dioxide + water
2 carbon monoxide, carbon, unburnt hydrocarbon, water
3 Acid rain

4.4

1 Particulates
2 Remove sulfur dioxide from waste gases after the fuel has been burned, remove sulfur from fuels before they are burned.

4.5

1 Biodiesel, ethanol
2 Advantage: no pollution or only product is water or can be made from water.
Disadvantage: difficult to store or production requires large amount of energy.

Answers to end of chapter questions

1 To make useful fuels/products
2 Carbon dioxide and water
3 Ignite/burn more easily, thin/runny liquids, burn with clean flame/little smoke
4 Two from: biodiesel, ethanol, hydrogen
5 Solid soot/carbon and unburnt fuel/hydrocarbons, produced by incomplete combustion
6 The fuel contains sulfur (compounds); these oxidise/burn to produce sulfur dioxide.
7 Poisonous gas carbon monoxide may be produced in limited supply of air.
8 The carbon was locked-up in fossil fuels; increases carbon dioxide in the atmosphere; carbon dioxide is a greenhouse gas; may cause global warming.
9 12 H joined to 5C, all single bonds, each C with four single bonds ($CH_3CH_2CH_2CH_2CH_3$). Four from: alkane, saturated, hydrocarbon, general formula C_nH_{2n+2}, has only single bonds, burns to produce carbon dioxide and water.
10 Crude oil vapour enters column, vapour rises, until boiling point of compound is reached, compound condenses (at that level), collected as liquid (from that level), high boiling fractions collected at bottom of column, low boiling fractions collected at top.
11 $C_2H_6O + 3O_2 \rightarrow 2CO_2 + 3H_2O$ [H]
12 $2H_2 + O_2 \rightarrow 2H_2O$, only product is water, no pollution, no carbon dioxide produced, can be made from water, electricity needed can be made using renewable energy source. [H]

5 Products from oils

5.1

1 One from: to make fuels that are more useful or for which there is more demand, large hydrocarbons do not burn easily or are less in demand. memorises
2 Three from: are unsaturated, have a double bond, have a different general formula, have fewer hydrogen atoms than the corresponding alkane, are more reactive, react with or decolourise bromine water.

5.2

1 From many small molecules or monomers that react or join together or polymerise to make a very large or very long molecule
2 Thousands or a very large number
3 Alkenes are more reactive or are unsaturated or have a double bond, alkanes are unreactive or saturated or do not have a double bond.

5.3

1 A type of smart polymer or a polymer that can change to its original shape when temperature or other conditions change.
2 Two medical uses: e.g. dental fillings, removable sticking plasters, wound dressings, stitches; and two non-medical uses: e.g. packaging, waterproof fabrics, containers, bottles, clothing, fibres for duvets, water-holding composts

5.4

1 The litter would be decomposed by microorganisms when in contact with soil, and so it would not remain in the environment.
2 It can be added to plastics made from non-biodegradable polymers so they break down into small pieces; it can be used to make biodegradable plastic.

5.5

1 sugar/glucose → ethanol + carbon dioxide
2 ethene + steam → ethanol

Answers to end of chapter questions

1 Two from: to make alkenes, to make alkanes with smaller molecules, to make fuels that are more useful or for which there is more demand, large hydrocarbons do not burn easily or are less in demand, to make polymers (from alkenes)
2 By heating a mixture of hydrocarbon vapours and steam to a very high temperature, by passing hydrocarbon vapours over a hot catalyst
3 Alkanes: C_5H_{12}, C_4H_{10}, C_6H_{14} Alkenes: C_3H_6, C_4H_8
4 A polymer has very large molecules made from many small molecules called monomers joined together by a polymerisation reaction.
5 Example of use of smart polymer, e.g. shape-memory polymer used for stitching wounds
6 Can be broken down by microorganisms
7 Three from e.g. use biodegradable polymers, recycle, use plastics with cornstarch mixed in, use light-sensitive polymers, collect litter/rubbish for proper disposal.
8 By fermentation of sugar with yeast, advantages: renewable source, room temperature, disadvantages: dilute solution of ethanol, needs to be distilled to make pure ethanol, slow, batch process;
by hydration of ethene with steam and a catalyst, advantages: pure ethanol produced, continuous process, fast, disadvantages: non-renewable source, high temperature needed
9 a $n\,\mathrm{C(CH_3)(H)}{=}\mathrm{C(H)(H)} \longrightarrow \left(\!-\mathrm{C(CH_3)(H)}-\mathrm{C(H)(H)}-\!\right)_n$ NB CH_3 can be shown as H—C(H)—H
b $C_2H_4 + H_2O \rightarrow CH_3CH_2OH$ (or C_2H_5OH) [H]
10 C_2H_4 [H]

6 Plant oils

6.1

1 (Crushing and) pressing and distillation (with water/steam)
2 They provide energy and nutrients.
3 Their molecules have carbon–carbon double bonds.

6.2
1 Cooks faster than in water, tastes better, improves the colour, better texture
2 Unsaturated oils are hydrogenated or reacted with hydrogen (at 60 °C with a nickel catalyst) so they become saturated and this increases their melting points so they are solids at room temperature. [H]

6.3
1 Opaque or not clear or cannot see through it, thick, coats solids
2 Substance that stops oil and water from separating. A substance with molecules that have a hydrophilic part and a hydrophobic part [H]

6.4
1 Benefits (one from): high in energy, contain nutrients, contain unsaturated fats, better for health Drawback: high in energy so easy to eat too much
2 Makes fats/oils less easily recognisable or food likely to have high fat content.

Answers to end of chapter questions
1 They provide a lot of energy.
2 Biofuel or biodiesel
3 Bromine water, turns from orange to colourless
4 Cook faster, taste better, better colour, better texture
5 Shake or stir vigorously or beat together (could also add an emulsifier).
6 Emulsifier, to prevent the oil and vinegar/water separating or to keep the emulsion stable
7 They are thicker than the oil and water they are made from, have better texture, appearance and ability to coat or stick to solids (for foods: taste better/smoother).
8 Some fats/saturated fats can cause health problems.
9 Either: crush the seeds, press the seeds, collect liquid, separate oil from water;
or: add seeds to water, boil and condense vapours/distill the mixture, collect liquids, separate oil from water
10 a React with hydrogen at 60 °C with a nickel catalyst
b To harden the oils, to make the oils saturated [H]
11 Emulsifier molecules have a hydrophilic or water-loving part (head) and a hydrophobic or water-hating part (tail). The hydrophobic part goes into oil droplets and the hydrophilic part stays at the surface keeping the droplets apart (dispersed) in the water. [H]

7 Our changing planet

7.1
1 Core (inner), mantle, crust

7.2
1 Convection currents caused by heating of the mantle by energy from radioactivity or decay of radioactive elements
2 We do not know enough about what is happening inside the Earth or we do not have good enough data or models to make accurate predictions.
3 He could not explain why the continents moved or they had their own/different/established ideas about the Earth.

7.3
1 Volcanoes
2 Algae and plants (photosynthesis)

7.4
1 There is insufficient evidence or there are lots of theories but no proof.
2 They contain all the elements needed to make amino acids, water (H_2O) contains hydrogen and oxygen, ammonia (NH_3) contains nitrogen and hydrogen, methane (CH_4) contains carbon and hydrogen, and hydrogen is hydrogen (H_2). [H]

7.5
1 In fossil fuels, in sedimentary rocks (including limestone)
2 78% nitrogen (almost 80%), and 21% oxygen (just over 20%)
3 It is a mixture of different substances that have different boiling points. [H]

7.6
1 Release, two from: burning, respiration, decay; remove: photosynthesis, dissolve in oceans/water
2 Burning fossil fuels

Answers to end of chapter questions
1 Core, mantle, crust, atmosphere
2 The resources are limited.
3 Three from: carbon dioxide, water vapour, nitrogen, ammonia, methane, hydrogen
4 Four from: nitrogen, oxygen, water vapour, carbon dioxide, argon, any other named noble gas
5 When the Earth cooled water vapour condensed.
6 They removed carbon dioxide and produced oxygen.
7 a Large pieces of the Earth's crust and upper mantle
b There are convection currents in the mantle caused by heating of the mantle by energy from radioactive decay of elements deep in the Earth.
c A few centimetres
d Earthquakes, volcanoes, mountains form.
8 a Natural processes maintain a balance, there is a cycle, carbon moves into and out of the atmosphere because of plants (out), animals (mainly in), oceans (in and out) and rocks (in and out).
b Burning fossil fuels (human activity)
9 He/scientists could not explain why the continents moved. It was not until the 1960s that new evidence was discovered.
10 There is little/insufficient/conflicting evidence and many possibilities but no proof.
11 a They used a mixture of water, ammonia, methane and hydrogen and a high voltage spark to simulate lightning. This produced amino acids/organic molecules, from which proteins are made. [H]
b A mixture of organic molecules/amino acids/molecules needed for life in water/oceans
12 a To separate the air into individual gases, to produce (liquid) nitrogen and oxygen (also argon), which have commercial uses or are raw materials. [H]
b Air is cooled until it becomes liquid, it is put into a fractionating column, nitrogen boils at the lowest temperature or is collected as a gas or is collected at the top of the column; oxygen remains as a liquid (with argon) or is collected at the bottom of the column.

Answers to examination-style questions

1 a 15 *(1 mark)*
b 15 *(1 mark)*
c 16 *(1 mark)*
d 5 *(1 mark)*
e 5 *(1 mark)*
f i phosphorus + chlorine → phosphorus chloride *(1 mark)*
ii 6 *(1 mark)*
iii covalent *(1 mark)*
2 a i calcium carbonate → calcium oxide + carbon dioxide *(1 mark)*
ii Thermal decomposition *(1 mark)*
b i Alkali(ne) *(1 mark)*
ii Forms calcium carbonate white solid/precipitate or insoluble *(2 marks)*
3 a i (Fossil) fuel *(1 mark)*
ii Causes acid rain or asthma or respiratory problems. *(1 mark)*
iii Electrolysis *(1 mark)*
b i To provide enzymes, to speed up reactions, to make copper sulfate or soluble copper compounds *(1 mark)*
ii iron + copper sulfate → iron sulfate + copper *(1 mark)*
iii Displacement *(1 mark)*
iv Two from: it is acidic or contains sulfuric acid, it contains iron salts/compounds, may contain other metal compounds, is harmful/toxic/damaging to plants/animals/humans *(2 marks)*
4 a high temperature *(1 mark)*
catalyst or steam *(1 mark)*
b Displayed formula for propene: three carbon atoms, with one single carbon–carbon bond and one double carbon–carbon bond six hydrogen atoms each with a single bond to a carbon atom so that carbon atoms all have a total of four bonds *(2 marks)*
c C_2H_4 *(1 mark)*
d Marks awarded for this answer will be determined by the Quality of Written Communication (QWC) as well as the standard of the scientific response.

There is a clear and detailed scientific description of the problems of plastic waste with The answer shows almost faultless spelling, punctuation and grammar. It is coherent and in an organised, logical sequence. It contains a range of appropriate and relevant specialist terms used accurately. *(5–6 marks)*
There is a scientific description of the problems of plastic waste. There are some errors in spelling, punctuation and grammar. The answer has some structure and organisation. The use of specialist terms has been attempted, but not always accurately. *(3–4 marks)*
There is a brief description of the problems of plastic waste. The spelling, punctuation and grammar are very weak. The answer is poorly organised with almost no specialist terms and/or their use demonstrating a general lack of understanding of their meaning. *(1–2 marks)*
No relevant content. *(0 marks)*

Examples of chemistry points made in the response:
Poly(propene) or poly(alkenes) or poly(ethene):
- are non-biodegradable
- cannot be broken down by microorganisms (in soil/environment)
- last for a very long time (hundreds or more years)
- large amounts used
- take up space in landfill/are bulky
- used as disposable packaging
- thrown away/become litter
- made from crude oil/use up finite resources
- difficult to identify and or separate from waste so recycling difficult
- incineration produces carbon dioxide (leading to global warming).

5 a Carbon dioxide (*1 mark*)
b Water vapour/methane/ammonia/nitrogen (not oxygen) (*1 mark*)
c Algae and plants (photosynthesis) (*1 mark*)
d There is insufficient evidence or no proof. (*1 mark*)
e Three named gases from nitrogen; **needed** [carbon dioxide; ammonia; water vapour or hydrogen that contain all four elements (C,N,H] and O) gains three marks. Three elements only or an incorrect gas (e.g. oxygen) gains two marks. Two elements only or one element missing and an incorrect gas gains one mark. **[H]** (*3 marks*)
f Nitrogen (with the lowest boiling point) comes out at the top. Argon from the middle Or oxygen and argon come out at the bottom (and need further distillation to separate them). **[H]** (*2 marks*)

P1 Answers

1 Energy transfer by heating

1.1
1 The higher the temperature of an object the greater the rate at which it emits infrared radiation.
2 A vacuum is a region that doesn't contain anything at all, even gas particles.

1.2
1 Houses in hot countries are often painted white because white is the worst absorber of infrared radiation.
2 The pipes on the back of a fridge are usually painted black because black surfaces are the best emitters of infrared radiation.

1.3
1 The particles in a liquid are in contact with each other but are not held in fixed positions like those in a solid.
2 The particles in a gas are much farther apart and move around much faster than those in a liquid.

1.4
1 The metal base of the saucepan is a good conductor so heat is conducted quickly to the food in the pan. The wooden handle is a poor conductor so it prevents someone picking up the saucepan getting burnt.
2 Air is a poor conductor so materials that trap air are good insulators.

1.5
1 Convection does not occur in solids because the particles are held in fixed positions and not able to flow.
2 A fluid becomes less dense when heated because it expands, so there is the same mass of material in a larger volume.

1.6
1 Decreasing the surface area of a liquid would decrease the rate of evaporation.
2 Decreasing the surface area would decrease the rate of condensation.

1.7
1 Painting an object dull black maximises the rate of energy transfer, because dull black surfaces are the best emitters of radiation.
2 Trapping air in small pockets minimises the rate of energy transfer because convection currents cannot be set up.

1.8
1 The energy needed is 2100 J.
2 The energy needed is 8400 J.

1.9
1 Fibreglass is a good insulator because it contains trapped air.
2 The pipes that contain the water in a solar heating panel are often painted black because black is the best absorber of radiation.

Answers to end of chapter questions
1 Dull black
2 All the particles are held together in fixed positions.
3 The most energetic molecules leave the liquid, so the average kinetic energy of the remaining molecules is reduced.
4 If the temperature difference is reduced, the rate of energy transfer decreases.
5 Conduction, convection and evaporation involve particles.
6 Energy from the Sun reaches the Earth as radiation that travels through space.
7 The colour of a surface has no effect on the rate of conduction.
8 Gases are poor conductors because the particles are far apart.
9 Metals are the best conductors because they contain free electrons.
10 Convection is the movement of energy through a fluid by movement of the fluid itself.
11 Cavity wall insulation traps the air in the cavity in pockets, so preventing convection currents from being set up.
12 The energy needed is 50 400 J.

2 Using energy

2.1
1 Elastic potential energy
2 From the food that you eat

2.2
1 Chemical to electrical to light and transfer by heating
2 Chemical energy in the fuel is transferred to the surroundings, which get warmer.

2.3
1 It is transferred to the surroundings which get warmer.
2 Because the law of conservation tells us that energy cannot be destroyed

2.4
1 The efficiency is 0.2 or 20%.
2 The efficiency increases.

Answers to end of chapter questions
1 Kinetic energy
2 Elastic potential energy
3 When an electric current flows
4 Electrical energy to kinetic energy and energy transferred by heating
5 Electrical energy to light and sound
6 Kinetic energy to gravitational potential energy to kinetic energy
7 Its efficiency decreases.
8 Efficiency of the motor is ¾ or 0.75 or 75%.
9 Because it is designed to transfer energy by heating, which is normally how appliances waste energy
10 So that wasted energy can be transferred easily to the surroundings making them warmer, rather than the television or computer
11 42 J
12 750 000 J

3 Electrical energy

3.1
1 Electrical energy to kinetic energy
2 A television/computer

3.2
1 12 000 W
2 400 W

3.3
1 2.25 kW h
2 2.16p

3.4
1 The removal or disposal of old equipment and environmental taxes
2 7.5 years

Answers to end of chapter questions
1 Electrical to energy heating bread
2 As light from the glowing filament
3 Heating the body of the kettle itself, and possibly sound
4 30 kW
5 A 2.2 kW hairdryer
6 Energy is measured in kilojoules.
7 100 W
8 1 kW h
9 The joule is too small to be useful in this situation.
10 40%
11 60p
12 11p **[H]**

4 Generating electricity

4.1
1 Coal, oil and gas
2 Nuclear fission

4.2
1 Gravitational potential energy
2 There are always two tides a day (tides depend on gravitational pull of the Sun and Moon), but on a calm day there may not be many waves (waves depend on winds, which are unreliable) [or equivalent answer].

4.3
1 Each solar cell only produces a small amount of electricity.
2 In many places in the world the hot rocks are too far below the surface to be used.

4.4
1 A large, flat area of high ground
2 A renewable energy source is produced as fast as it is used. A non-renewable energy source is one that is used at a much faster rate than it is produced.
3 Sulfur dioxide

4.5
1 Overhead cables are easier to repair and are cheaper.
2 A step-down transformer

4.6
1 The demand increases in winter because it gets colder so more electricity is used heating homes.
2 Gravitational potential energy

Answers to end of chapter questions
1 E.g. methane from waste, ethanol from fermented sugar cane, nutshells
2 The water must fall from a height to transfer gravitational potential energy to kinetic energy.

3 Energy can be obtained from falling water, waves and the tides.
4 A fossil fuel is a fuel that is obtained from long-dead biological materials: coal, oil or gas.
5 Heat in rocks deep below the Earth's surface
6 In portable devices that only require small amounts of electricity, such as watches and calculators. In sunny places that are not connected to a grid system, such as remote villages in hot countries.
7 A solar cell is a device that produces electricity directly from energy from the Sun.
8 A solar heating panel is a device that heats water using energy from the Sun.
9 Non-renewable energy resources are the most reliable.
10 They emit CO_2 that can cause global warming and SO_2 that can cause acid rain.
11 The pipes are usually painted black.
12 Geothermal energy is renewable, free and does not produce polluting gases.

5 Waves

5.1
1 They are pushed closer together.
2 Transverse, mechanical waves

5.2
1 10 m/s
2 Hertz, Hz

5.3
1 A line drawn perpendicular to a reflecting surface
2 The same size as the object

5.4
1 Because waves change speed when they cross a boundary
2 Because different wavelengths of light are refracted by different amounts

5.5
1 Because the wavelength of light is very short
2 All waves are diffracted.

5.6
1 20 Hz to 20 000 Hz (20 kHz)
2 An echo

5.7
1 The pitch decreases.
2 The waveforms are different.

Answers to end of chapter questions
1 The metre, m
2 A virtual, upright image, same size as the object
3 1.5 m behind the mirror
4 Violet
5 The reflection of a sound
6 The region in a longitudinal wave where the particles are further apart than in the rest position
7 Their speed changes
8 The spreading of a wave as it passes through a gap or around an obstacle
9 The air in the flute vibrates as you blow across the mouthpiece.
10 The frequency of the sound wave
11 3.3 m/s
12 20 Hz [H]

6 Electromagnetic waves

6.1
1 Hertz, Hz
2 Gamma rays

6.2
1 Radio waves

6.3
1 By applying an alternating voltage to an aerial

6.4
1 The observed wavelength increases.
2 The most distant ones
3 The furthest galaxies are moving the fastest so everything is expanding outwards.

6.5
1 The theory that the universe began with a massive explosion from a small initial point.
2 The wavelength increases.

Answers to end of chapter questions
1 Radio waves
2 Ultraviolet
3 1 000 000 Hz
4 Radio waves
5 Microwaves
6 By total internal reflection
7 The apparent change in wavelength and frequency of waves from a moving source
8 A very large collection of stars
9 It has been shifted towards the red end of the spectrum.
10 By observing the position of dark lines in the spectrum from the galaxy
11 It has become stretched out to microwave wavelengths.
12 The existence of cosmic microwave background radiation

Answers to examination-style questions

1 a Conduction (*1 mark*)
b The water at the bottom expands as it is heated and becomes less dense. This warmer water rise upwards and is replaced by cooler water at the bottom. This water is also heated and rises, setting up a convection current. (*4 marks*)
c $E = m \times c \times \theta$
$E = 1.2 \times 4200 \times 80$
$E = 403\,200$ J (*3 marks*)
d Some of the energy is wasted heating the body of the kettle. This energy spreads into the surroundings, making them warmer. (*3 marks*)

2 Marks awarded for this answer will be determined by the Quality of Written Communication (QWC) as well as the standard of the scientific response.

There is a clear and detailed description of how the kinetic theory explains the properties of solids, liquids and gases. The answer shows almost faultless spelling, punctuation and grammar. It is coherent and in an organised, logical sequence. It contains a range of appropriate or relevant specialist terms used accurately. (*5–6 marks*)
There is a description of how the kinetic theory explains the properties of solids, liquids and gases. There are some errors in spelling, punctuation and grammar. The answer has some structure and organisation. The use of specialist terms has been attempted, but not always accurately. (*3–4 marks*)
There is a brief description of how the kinetic theory explains the properties of solids, liquids and gases, which has little clarity and detail. The spelling, punctuation and grammar are very weak. The answer is poorly organised with almost no specialist terms and/or their use demonstrating a general lack of understanding of their meaning. (*1–2 marks*)
No relevant content. (*0 marks*)

Examples of physics points made in the response:
- particles in a solid are held next to each other in fixed positions
- they vibrate about these positions, so a solid has a fixed shape and volume
- in a liquid, particles are in contact with each other so liquid has a fixed volume
- the particles move about at random, so a liquid has no fixed shape and can flow
- particles in a gas are much farther apart than in a liquid and move much faster
- so gas has no fixed shape or volume.

3 a i Electrical to kinetic (*1 mark*)
ii Transferred to the surroundings, which become warmer (*1 mark*)
b i Useful energy transferred = 1000 – 300 = 700 J (*1 mark*)
ii Percentage efficiency
$= \frac{\text{useful energy out}}{\text{total energy in}} \times 100\%$
$= \frac{700}{1000} \times 100$
= 70% (*3 marks*)
c Energy = power × time or $E = p \times t$
Power = 800 W = 0.8 kW, time = $\frac{15}{60}$ = 0.25 hours
Energy = 0.8 × 0.25 = 0.2 kWh
Cost = 0.2 × 12 = 2.4p (*4 marks*)

4 a A non-renewable energy source (*1 mark*)
b The energy is used to heat water which becomes steam and turns a turbine that drives a generator. (*4 marks*)
c i Nuclear energy is reliable; only a small amount of fuel is needed to produce a large amount of energy. (*2 marks*)
ii A nuclear power station produces nuclear waste that is radioactive for a long time and must be stored or disposed of safely. Nuclear fuels are costly, but the energy from wind is free once the set-up cost has been paid. (*2 marks*)

5 a The back of the mirror is where reflection takes place. (*1 mark*)
b i A virtual image cannot be formed on a screen, because the rays of light that produce the image only appear to pass through it. (*2 marks*)
ii The image is: 4 cm tall, upright, 6 cm behind the back of the mirror. (*3 marks*)
c Real rays correct
Virtual rays correct
Image position correct (*3 marks*)

6 a The sound wave makes the particles of air vibrate.
The wave is longitudinal so the vibrations are perpendicular to the direction of travel of the wave.
The wave travels as a series of compressions and rarefactions. (*3 marks*)
b i Trace has same shape
Same frequency
Bigger amplitude (*3 marks*)
ii Trace has same shape
Higher frequency
Same amplitude (*3 marks*)

Glossary

A

Absorber A substance that takes in radiation.
Adaptation Special feature that makes an organism particularly well suited to the environment where it lives.
Adult cell cloning Process in which the nucleus of an adult cell of one animal is fused with an empty egg from another animal. The embryo which results is placed inside the uterus of a third animal to develop.
Agar The nutrient jelly on which many microorganisms are cultured.
Alkane Saturated hydrocarbon with the general formula C_nH2_{n+2}, for example methane, ethane and propane.
Alkene Unsaturated hydrocarbon which contains a carbon–carbon double bond. The general formula is C_nH_{2n}, for example ethene C_2H_4.
Alloy A mixture of metals (and sometimes non-metals). For example, brass is a mixture of copper and zinc.
Aluminium A low density, corrosion-resistant metal used in many alloys, including those used in the aircraft industry.
Amplitude The height of a wave crest or a wave trough of a transverse wave from the rest position.
Angle of incidence Angle between the incident ray and the normal.
Angle of reflection Angle between the reflected ray and the normal.
Antibiotic Drug that destroys bacteria inside the body without damaging human cells.
Asexual reproduction Reproduction that involves only one individual with no fusing of gametes to produce the offspring. The offspring are identical to the parent.
Atmosphere The relatively thin layer of gases that surround planet Earth.
Atom The smallest part of an element that can still be recognised as that element.
Atomic number The number of protons (which equals the number of electrons) in an atom. It is sometimes called the proton number.
Auxin A plant hormone that controls the responses of plants to light (phototropism) and to gravity (gravitropism).

B

Bacteria Single-celled microorganisms that can reproduce very rapidly. Many bacteria are useful, for example, gut bacteria and decomposing bacteria, but some cause disease.
Band Part of the radio and microwave spectrum used for communications.
Base load Constant amount of electricity generated by power stations.
Big Bang theory The theory that the universe was created in a massive explosion (the Big Bang) and that the universe has been expanding ever since.
Biodegradable Materials that can be broken down by microorganisms.
Biodiesel Fuel for cars made from plant oils.
Biofuel Fuel made from animal or plant products.
Bioleaching Process of extraction of metals from ores using microorganisms.
Biomass Biological material from living or recently living organisms.
Blast furnace The huge reaction vessels used in industry to extract iron from its ore.
Blue-shift Decrease in the wavelength of electromagnetic waves emitted by a star or galaxy due to its motion towards us. The faster the speed of the star or galaxy, the greater the blue-shift is.
Boundary Line along which two substances meet.

C

Calcium carbonate The main compound found in limestone. It is a white solid whose formula is $CaCO_3$.
Calcium hydroxide A white solid made by reacting calcium oxide with water. It is used as a cheap alkali in industry.
Calcium oxide A white solid made by heating limestone strongly, for example, in a lime kiln.
Carbon cycle The cycling of carbon through the living and non-living world.
Carbon monoxide A toxic gas whose formula is CO.
Carnivore Animal that eats other animals.
Cast iron The impure iron taken directly from a blast furnace.
Cement A building material made by heating limestone and clay.
Central nervous system (CNS) The central nervous system is made up of the brain and spinal cord where information is processed.
Charles Darwin The Victorian scientist who developed the theory of evolution by a process of natural selection.
Chemical energy Energy of an object due to chemical reactions in it.
Chromosome Thread-like structure carrying the genetic information found in the nucleus of a cell.
Clone Offspring produced by asexual reproduction that is identical to the parent organism.
Combustion The process of burning.
Competition The process by which living organisms compete with each other for limited resources such as food, light or reproductive partners.
Compost heap A site where garden rubbish and kitchen waste are decomposed by microorganisms.
Compound A substance made when two or more elements are chemically bonded together. For example, water (H_2O) is a compound made from hydrogen and oxygen.
Compression Squeezed together.
Concrete A building material made by mixing cement, sand and aggregate (crushed rock) with water.
Condensation Turning from vapour into liquid.
Conduction Transfer of energy from particle to particle in matter.
Conductor Material/object that conducts.
Conservation of energy Energy cannot be created or destroyed.
Contraceptive pill A pill containing female sex hormones which is used to prevent conception.
Convection Transfer of energy by the bulk movement of a heated fluid.
Convection current The circular motion of matter caused by heating in fluids.
Copper-rich ore Rock that contains a high proportion of a copper compound.
Core The centre of the Earth.
Cosmic microwave background radiation Electromagnetic radiation that has been travelling through space ever since it was created shortly after the Big Bang.
Cost effectiveness How much something gives value for money when purchase, running and other costs are taken into account.
Covalent bond The attraction between two atoms that share one or more pairs of electrons.
Cracking The reaction used in the oil industry to break down large hydrocarbons into smaller, more useful ones. This occurs when the hydrocarbon vapour is either passed over a hot catalyst or mixed with steam and heated to a high temperature.
Crust The outer solid layer of the Earth.
Culture medium A substance containing the nutrients needed for microorganisms to grow.

D

Decomposer Microorganism that breaks down waste products and dead bodies.
Denature Change the shape of an enzyme so that it can no longer speed up a reaction.
Depression A mental illness that involves feelings of great sadness that interfere with everyday life.
Detritus feeder See Decomposer.
Diffraction The spreading of waves when they pass through a gap or around the edges of an obstacle that has a similar size as the wavelength of the waves.
Displace When one element takes the place of another in a compound. For example, iron + copper sulfate → iron sulfate + copper.
Distillation Separation of a liquid from a mixture by evaporation followed by condensation.

Doppler effect The change of wavelength (and frequency) of the waves from a moving source due to the motion of the source towards or away from the observer.
Double bond A covalent bond made by the sharing of two pairs of electrons.
Double-blind trial A drug trial in which neither the patient nor the doctor knows if the patient is receiving the new drug or a placebo.
Drug A chemical which causes changes in the body. Medical drugs cure disease or relieve symptoms. Recreational drugs alter the state of your mind and/or body.

E

Echo Reflection of sound that can be heard.
Effector organ Muscle and gland that responds to impulses from the nervous system.
Efficiency Useful energy transferred by a device ÷ total energy supplied to the device.
Elastic potential energy Energy stored in an elastic object when work is done to change its shape.
Electrical appliance Machine powered by electricity.
Electrical energy Energy transferred by the movement of electrical charge.
Electromagnetic spectrum A set of radiations that have different wavelengths and frequencies but all travel at the same speed in a vacuum.
Electromagnetic wave Electric and magnetic disturbance that transfers energy from one place to another. The spectrum of electromagnetic waves, in order of increasing wavelength, is as follows: gamma and X-rays, ultraviolet radiation, visible light, infrared radiation, microwaves, radio waves.
Electron A tiny particle with a negative charge. Electrons orbit the nucleus in atoms or ions.
Electronic structure A set of numbers to show the arrangement of electrons in their shells (or energy levels), for example, the electronic structure of a potassium atom is 2, 8, 8, 1.
Element A substance made up of only one type of atom. An element cannot be broken down chemically into any simpler substance.
Emit Give out radiation.
Emitter A substance that gives out radiation.
Emulsifier A substance which helps keep immiscible liquids (for example, oil and water) mixed so that they do not separate out into layers.
Emulsion A mixture of liquids that do not dissolve in each other.
Energy level See Shell.
Energy transfer Movement of energy from one place to another or one form to another.
Enzyme Protein molecule that acts as a biological catalyst.
Epidemic When more cases of an infectious disease are recorded than would normally be expected.
Ethene An alkene with the formula C_2H_4.
Evaporation Turning from liquid into vapour.
Evolution The process of slow change in living organisms over long periods of time as those best adapted to survive breed successfully.
Evolutionary relationship Model of the relationships between organisms, often based on DNA evidence, which suggest how long ago they evolved away from each other and how closely related they are in evolutionary terms.
Evolutionary tree Model of the evolutionary relationships between different organisms based on their appearance, and increasingly, on DNA evidence.
Extremophile Organism which lives in environments that are very extreme, for example, very high or very low temperatures, high salt levels or high pressures.

F

Fermentation The reaction in which the enzymes in yeast turn glucose into ethanol and carbon dioxide.
Flammable Easily ignited and capable of burning rapidly.
Fluid A liquid or a gas.
Fossil fuel Fuel obtained from long-dead biological material.
Fraction Hydrocarbons with similar boiling points separated from crude oil.
Fractional distillation A way to separate liquids from a mixture of liquids by boiling off the substances at different temperatures, then condensing and collecting the liquids.
Free electron Electron that moves about freely inside a metal and is not held inside an atom.
Frequency The number of wave crests passing a fixed point every second.
FSH Follicle stimulating hormone, a female hormone that stimulates the eggs to mature in the ovaries, and the ovaries to produce hormones, including oestrogen.

G

Gamete Sex cell that has half the chromosome number of ordinary cells.
Gamma ray The highest energy wave in the electromagnetic spectrum.
Gas A state of matter.
Gene A short section of DNA carrying genetic information.
Generator A machine that produces a voltage.
Genetic engineering/modification A technique for changing the genetic information of a cell.
Geothermal energy Energy from hot underground rocks.
Global dimming The reflection of sunlight by tiny solid particles in the air.
Global warming The increasing of the average temperature of the Earth.
Gravitational potential energy Energy of an object due to its position in a gravitational field. Near the Earth's surface, change of GPE (in joules, J) = weight (in newtons, N) × vertical distance moved (in metres, m).
Gravitropism Response of a plant to the force of gravity controlled by auxin.
Group All the elements in each column (labelled 1 to 7 and 0) down the periodic table.

H

Hardening The process of reacting plant oils with hydrogen to raise their melting point. This is used to make spreadable margarine.
Herbivore Animal that feeds on plants.
Hydrocarbon A compound containing only hydrogen and carbon.
Hydrogenated oil Oil which has had hydrogen added to reduce the degree of saturation in the hardening process to make margarine.
Hydrophilic The water-loving part of an emulsifier molecule.
Hydrophobic The water-hating hydrocarbon part of an emulsifier molecule.

I

Immune system The body system which recognises and destroys foreign cells or proteins such as invading pathogens.
Immunisation Giving a vaccine that allows immunity to develop without exposure to the disease itself.
Impulse Electrical signal carried along the neurons.
Incomplete combustion When a fuel burns in insufficient oxygen, producing carbon monoxide as a toxic product.
Indicator species Lichens or insects that are particularly sensitive to pollution and so can be used to indicate changes in the environmental pollution levels.
Infectious disease Disease which can be passed from one individual to another.
Infrared radiation Electromagnetic waves between visible light and microwaves in the electromagnetic spectrum.
Inheritance of acquired characteristics Jean-Baptiste Lamarck's theory of how evolution took place.
Inherited Passed on from parents to their offspring through genes.
Input energy Energy supplied to a machine.
Insulator Material/object that is a poor conductor.
Internal environment The conditions inside the body.
Ionic bond The electrostatic force of attraction between positively and negatively charged ions.

J

Jean-Baptiste Lamarck French biologist who developed a theory of evolution based on the inheritance of acquired characteristics.
Joule (J) The unit of energy.

K

Kidney Organ which filters the blood and removes urea, excess salts and water.
Kilowatt (kW) 1000 watts.
Kilowatt-hour (kWh) Electrical energy supplied to a 1 kW electrical device in 1 hour.
Kinetic energy Energy of a moving object due to its motion; kinetic energy (in joules, J) = ½ × mass (in kilograms, kg) × $(speed)^2$ (in m^2/s^2).
Kingdom The highest group in the classification system, for example, animals, plants.

L

Limewater The common name for calcium hydroxide solution.
Liquid A state of matter.
Longitudinal wave Wave in which the vibrations are parallel to the direction of energy transfer.

M

Machine A device in which a force applied at a point produces another force at another point.
Malnourished The condition when the body does not get a balanced diet.
Mantle The layer of the Earth between its crust and its core.
Mass The quantity of matter in an object; a measure of the difficulty of changing the motion of an object (in kilograms, kg).
Mass number The number of protons plus neutrons in the nucleus of an atom.
Maximise Make as big as possible.
Mechanical wave Vibration that travels through a substance.
Menstrual cycle The reproductive cycle in women controlled by hormones.
Metabolic rate The rate at which the reactions of your body take place, particularly cellular respiration.
Microorganism Bacteria, viruses and other organisms that can only be seen using a microscope.
Microwave Part of the electromagnetic spectrum.
Minimise Make as small as possible.
Mixture When some elements or compounds are mixed together and intermingle but do not react together (i.e. no new substance is made). A mixture is *not* a pure substance.
Monomers Small reactive molecules that react together in repeating sequences to form a very large molecule (a polymer).
Mortar A building material used to bind bricks together. It is made by mixing cement and sand with water.
Motor neuron Neuron that carries impulses from the central nervous system to the effector organs.
MRSA Methicillin-resistant *Staphylococcus aureus*. An antibiotic-resistant bacterium.
Mutation A change in the genetic material of an organism.

N

National Grid The network of cables and transformers used to transfer electricity from power stations to consumers (i.e. homes, shops, offices, factories, etc.).
Natural classification system Classification system based on the similarities between different living organisms.
Natural selection The process by which evolution takes place. Organisms produce more offspring than the environment can support so only those which are most suited to their environment – the 'fittest' – will survive to breed and pass on their useful characteristics.
Nerve Bundle of hundreds or even thousands of neurons.
Nervous system See Central nervous system.
Neuron Basic cell of the nervous system which carries minute electrical impulses around the body.
Neutron A dense particle found in the nucleus of an atom. It is electrically neutral, carrying no charge.
Nitrogen oxides Gaseous pollutants given off from motor vehicles, a cause of acid rain.
Non-renewable Something that cannot be replaced once it is used up.
Normal Straight line through a surface or boundary perpendicular to the surface or boundary.
Nuclear fission The process in which certain nuclei (uranium-235 and plutonium-239) split into two fragments, releasing energy and two or three neutrons as a result.
Nucleus The very small and dense central part of an atom which contains protons and neutrons.

O

Obese Very overweight, with a BMI of over 30.
Oestrogen Female sex hormone which stimulates the lining of the womb to build up in preparation for a pregnancy.
Optical fibre Thin glass fibre used to send light signals along.
Oral contraceptive Hormone contraceptive that is taken by mouth.
Ore Rock which contains enough metal to make it economically worthwhile to extract the metal.
Organic waste Waste material from living organisms, for example, garden waste.
Oscillation Moving to and fro about a certain position along a line.
Ovary Female sex organ which contains the eggs and produces sex hormones during the menstrual cycle.
Overweight A person is overweight if their body carries excess fat and their BMI is between 25 and 30.
Ovipositor A pointed tube found in many female insects which is used to lay eggs.
Ovulation The release of a mature egg from the ovary in the middle of the menstrual cycle.
Oxidised A reaction where oxygen is added to a substance (or when electrons are lost from a substance).

P

Pancreas An organ that produces the hormone insulin and many digestive enzymes.
Pandemic When more cases of a disease are recorded than normal in a number of different countries.
Particulate Small solid particle given off from motor vehicles as a result of incomplete combustion of its fuel.
Pathogen Microorganism which causes disease.
Payback time Time taken for something to produce savings to match how much it cost.
Perpendicular At right angles.
Phototropism The response of a plant to light, controlled by auxin.
Phytomining The process of extraction of metals from ores using plants.
Pitch The pitch of a sound increases if the frequency of the sound waves increases.
Pituitary gland Small gland in the brain which produces a range of hormones controlling body functions.
Placebo A substance used in clinical trials which does not contain any drug at all.
Plane mirror A flat mirror.
Polymer A substance made from very large molecules made up of many repeating units, for example, poly(ethene).
Polymerisation The reaction of monomers to make a polymer.
Power The energy transformed or transferred per second. The unit of power is the watt (W).
Product A substance made as a result of a chemical reaction.
Progesterone Female sex hormone used in the contraceptive pill.
Propene An alkene with the formula C_3H_6.
Proton A tiny positive particle found inside the nucleus of an atom.
Pyramid of biomass A model of the mass of biological material in the organisms at each level of a food chain.

R

Radio wave Longest wavelength of the electromagnetic spectrum.
Rarefaction Stretched apart.
Reactant A substance we start with before a chemical reaction takes place.
Reactivity series A list of elements in order of their reactivity. The most reactive element is put at the top of the list.

Real image An image formed where light rays meet.
Receptor Special sensory cell that detects changes in the environment.
Red-shift Increase in the wavelength of electromagnetic waves emitted by a star or galaxy due to its motion away from us. The faster the speed of the star or galaxy, the greater the red-shift is.
Reduction A reaction in which oxygen is removed (or electrons are gained).
Reflector A surface that reflects radiation.
Reflex Rapid automatic response of the nervous system that does not involve conscious thought.
Reflex arc The sense organ, sensory neuron, relay neuron, motor neuron and effector organ which bring about a reflex action.
Refraction The change of direction of a light ray when it passes across a boundary between two transparent substances (including air).
Renewable energy Energy from sources that never run out including wind energy, wave energy, tidal energy, hydroelectricity, solar energy and geothermal energy.

S

Sankey diagram An energy transfer diagram.
Saturated hydrocarbon Describes a hydrocarbon that contains only single carbon-carbon bonds, they do not contain any C=C double bonds.
Secreting Releasing chemicals such as hormones or enzymes.
Sense organs Collection of special cells known as receptors which respond to changes in the surroundings (for example, eye, ear).
Sensory neuron Neuron which carries impulses from the sensory organs to the central nervous system.
Sewage treatment plant A site where human waste is broken down using
Sexual reproduction Reproduction that involves the joining (fusion) of male and female gametes, producing genetic variety in the offspring.
Shell (or energy level) An area in an atom, around its nucleus, where the electrons are found.
Smart polymer Polymers that change in response to changes in their environment.
Smelting Heating a metal ore in order to extract its metal.
Solar cell Electrical cell that produces a voltage when in sunlight; solar cells are usually connected together in solar cell panels.
Solar energy (light energy) Energy from the Sun or other light source.
Solar heating panel Sealed panel designed to use sunlight to heat water running through it.
Solar power tower Tower surrounded by mirrors that reflect sunlight onto a water tank at the top of the tower.
Solid A state of matter.
Sound A form of mechanical energy.
Species A group of organisms with many features in common which can breed successfully, producing fertile offspring.
Specific heat capacity Energy needed by 1 kg of the substance to raise its temperature by 1 °C.
Speed Distance moved ÷ time taken.
Stainless steel A chromium–nickel alloy of steel which does not rust.
Start-up time Time taken for a power station to produce electricity after it is switched on.
Statin Drug which lowers the blood cholesterol levels and improves the balance of HDLs
to LDL.
Steel An alloy of iron with small amounts of carbon or other metals, such as nickel and chromium, added.
Step-down transformer Used to step the voltage down, for example, from the grid voltage to the mains voltage used in homes and offices.
Step-up transformer Used to step the voltage up, for example, from a power station to the grid voltage.
Steroid Drug that is used illegally by some athletes to build muscles and improve performance.
Stimuli A change in the environment that is detected by sensory receptors.
Stomata Openings in the leaves of plants (particularly the underside) which allow gases to enter and leave the leaf. They are opened and closed by the guard cells.
Sulfur dioxide A toxic gas whose formula is SO_2. It causes acid rain.
Synapse The gap between neurons where the transmission of information is chemical rather than electrical.

T

Tectonic plates The huge slabs of rock that make up the Earth's crust and top part of its mantle.
Temperature The degree of hotness of a substance.
Temperature difference Difference in temperature between two points.
Territory An area where an animal lives and feeds, which it may mark out or defend against other animals.
Thalidomide A drug that caused deformities in the fetus when given to pregnant women to prevent morning sickness.
Thermal decomposition The breakdown of a compound by heat.
Tide Rise and fall of sea level because of the gravitational pull of the Moon and the Sun.
Tissue culture Using small groups of cells from a plant to make new plants.
Titanium A shiny, corrosion-resistant metal used to make alloys.
Transition metal These elements are from the central block of the periodic table. They have typical metallic properties and form coloured compounds.
Transverse wave Wave in which the vibrations are perpendicular to the direction of energy transfer.
Turbine A machine that uses steam or hot gas to turn a shaft.

U

Ultraviolet radiation Electromagnetic radiation just beyond the blue end of the visible spectrum.
Unsaturated hydrocarbon A hydrocarbon whose molecules contain at least one carbon–carbon double bond.
Unsaturated oil Plant oil whose molecules contain at least one carbon–carbon double bond.
Urea The chemical produced by the breakdown of amino acids in the liver which is removed by the kidneys.
Urine The liquid produced by the kidneys containing the metabolic waste product urea along with excess water and salts from the body.
Useful energy Energy transferred to where it is wanted in the form it is wanted.

V

Vaccination Introducing small quantities of dead or inactive pathogens into the body to stimulate the white blood cells to produce antibodies that destroy the pathogens. This makes the person immune to future infection.
Vaccine The dead or inactive pathogen material used in vaccination.
Vegetable oil Oil extracted from plants.
Virtual image An image formed where light rays appear to come from.
Virus Microorganism which takes over body cells and reproduces rapidly, causing disease.
Viscosity The resistance of a liquid to flowing or the 'thickness' or resistance of a liquid to pouring.
Visible light The part of the electromagnetic spectrum that can be detected by the human eye.

W

Wasted energy Energy that is not usefully transferred.
Watt (W) The unit of power.
Wave Disturbance in water.
Wavelength The distance from one wave crest to the next wave crest (along the waves).
Wave speed Speed of travel of a wave.
White blood cell Blood cell which is involved in the immune system of the body, engulfing bacteria, making antibodies and making antitoxins.
Withdrawal symptom The symptom experienced by a drug addict when they do not get the drug to which they are addicted.

X

X-ray High energy wave from the part of the electromagnetic spectrum between gamma rays and ultraviolet waves.